OVER
THE
INFLUENCE

JOANNA "JOJO" LEVESQUE

OVER THE INFLUENCE

A MEMOIR

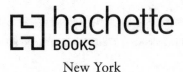

New York

Hachette Books
Hachette Book Group
1290 Avenue of the Americas
New York, NY 10104
HachetteBooks.com
Twitter.com/HachetteBooks
Instagram.com/HachetteBooks

First Edition: September 2024

Published by Hachette Books, an imprint of Hachette Book Group, Inc. The Hachette Books name and logo is a trademark of the Hachette Book Group.

The Hachette Speakers Bureau provides a wide range of authors for speaking events. To find out more, go to hachettespeakersbureau.com or email HachetteSpeakers@hbgusa.com.

Books by Hachette Books may be purchased in bulk for business, educational, or promotional use. For information, please contact your local bookseller or Hachette Book Group Special Markets Department at: special.markets@hbgusa.com.

The publisher is not responsible for websites (or their content) that are not owned by the publisher.

Print book interior design by Amnet ContentSource

Library of Congress Cataloging-in-Publication Data

Name: JoJo, 1990– author.
Title: Over the influence: a memoir / by Joanna "JoJo" Levesque.
Description: New York, NY: Hachette Books, 2024.
Identifiers: LCCN 2024019887 | ISBN 9780306833144 (hardcover) | ISBN 9780306833151 (trade paperback) | ISBN 9780306833168 (ebook)
Subjects: LCSH: JoJo, 1990– | LCGFT: Autobiographies.
Classification: LCC ML420.J737 A3 2024 | DDC 782.42164092 [B]—dc23/eng/20240430
LC record available at https://lccn.loc.gov/2024019887

ISBNs: 9780306833144 (hardcover); 9780306833168 (eBook)

Printed in the United States of America

LSC-C

Printing 1, 2024

Dedicated to:

Anyone who's ever been lost.

My beautiful, hilarious, incomparable family and friends.

*Everyone along this life journey who helped,
encouraged, challenged, been a mirror.*

Team JoJo.

*The people who hurt me and those I've hurt.
You have been my biggest teachers.*

The love of my life in canine form, Agapé.

CONTENTS

AUTHOR'S NOTE

Here's something they don't tell you when you start writing your memoir:

It's. Fucking. *Weird.*

Not so much the actual writing of it, although that's weird, too—trying to wrangle the thoughts out of your brain onto the blank paper (or Word document) in front of you. But the process of mining the deepest, darkest crevices of your experience—and letting *everything* come up to the surface for air—is a little mortifying. Nothing really prepares you for what it feels like to exercise your demons out of your body and look at them in black and white. This process has been a lot about humility and accountability as much as anything.

As someone who broke into the music industry as a preteen, I know there will be people who immediately write me—and this book—off as the musings of a child star grown up. We naturally look for ways to simplify someone's life into a digestible bite and try to figure out where to put the "blame" for the bad stuff, but that's just not how I see it. In my story, there are no victims and no villains—just messed-up people (myself very much included) in a messed-up industry in a world that keeps turning while we flail around, grasping onto things and people that resemble sta-bility, even in the eye of our own personal shitstorm. And there's redemption. And hope. And the opportunity to dust off your life and take the reins.

Now feels like the best possible time to release the shame, embarrassment, and fear of rejection that I absorbed over the years and wore like a second skin.

The experiences I'm sharing across these pages are all true. I've changed some names and identifying details to protect the privacy of others who I don't fuck with anymore or whose stories are not mine to tell. Other folks I kept their names in, because it is what it is. *shrug* This part was the biggest piece I wrestled with when I decided I wanted to share my life story: the wanting to do right by the other people in (or no longer in) it, while still being transparent. Earnestly desiring to paint human beings with dimension, texture, and color kept me awake and staring at the ceiling or busying myself with various procrastination tactics over the past year and some change. But, since humans are designed to share their stories, I wanted to see what I could really remember of mine when I took the time to try. To the best of my memory, I included snippets from real conversations—if not with the exact words, then at least in a way that captures the underly-ing feelings and meanings behind them.

Thank you for choosing to spend your time with me like this. It means more than you'll ever know.

Love,
Jo

INTRO

THE ONLY LITTLE GIRL IN A.A.

God, grant me the serenity to accept the things I cannot change,
the courage to change the things I can,
and the wisdom to know the difference.

SOME PEOPLE LEARN THE SERENITY PRAYER THROUGH TALK THERAPY OR WHILE READING self-help books. But as someone who was born and raised inside the smoky, fluorescent-lit halls of Alcoholics Anonymous, I honestly can't remember a time when I *didn't* know the prayer word for word. It's always been echoing around—to me, within me, from me, now tattooed in black and green around my right wrist. Somehow nostalgic and aspirational at the same time.

It's not just that I spent a lot of time in A.A. meetings as a kid. My parents *met* in A.A.—(romantic, I know)—so I literally wouldn't *exist* if it wasn't for that program. Do I feel a little guilty telling you that? You know, 'cause the whole point of A.A. is that it's "Anonymous"? Yes. But I'm no stranger to guilt, and I know now, as I've always known, that addiction isn't just any old part of my story; it's the foundation that everything else in my life was built upon.

I get frustrated when people reduce addiction to one substance or another.

It's *deeper* than that.

In a TEDx Talk, Dr. Gabor Maté describes it like this: "The Buddhists have this idea of the hungry ghosts. The hungry ghosts are creatures with large empty bellies and small, scrawny necks and tiny little mouths, so they can never get enough, they can never fill this emptiness on the inside. And we are all hungry ghosts in this society, we all have this emptiness, and so many of us are trying to fill that emptiness from the outside, and the addiction is all about trying to fill that emptiness from the outside." Sure, that could be drugs and alcohol, but it could also be with other things, too, like consumerism, sex, food—the list goes on. The problem is that none of these things address the real root of this emptiness, and so we can *never* fill ourselves up from the outside, no matter how hard we try. Before we know it, we end up in these self-destructive loops that we can't escape, self-destructive loops that can consume us from the inside or run us right into the ground.

Like my parents (and plenty of other relatives on *both* sides of the family tree), I spent a great deal of my time on Earth trying to figure out how to fill this predisposed emptiness. It started with external validation. There was just nothing more thrilling than impressing the adults around me, nailing an audition for a show or talent competition, or hearing the roar of applause from a big audience. Then, after I landed a record deal at twelve, the stakes got higher and the highs hit harder. But no matter how "successful"

I got, no matter how many songs hit the charts or movies performed well at the box office, my ghosts just got hungrier and hungrier. When my career stalled and it felt like everything I'd been working toward from childhood was going up in smoke, I turned elsewhere—to alcohol, drugs, sex, love, food, self-loathing.

It was.

Never.

Enough.

I spent years looking for an answer, listening to everyone around me—family members, friends, frenemies, lovers, collaborators, religious leaders, record execs, managers. Many of them had conflicting opinions about what I should say or do. How I should behave. Who I should hang out with. Which songs I should sing.

Tell me what I need to do to feel good again.

Self-doubt sauntered in, and I second-guessed everything, silencing myself in order to follow the advice of people who were older and swore they knew what was best for me.

It turned out they didn't have the answers either.

This book is not me wrapping up my thirty-three years in a bow and saying, "Hey, you! I have it all figured out now! Come join my cult!" I'm not here to sell you anything and I'm far from an enlightened guru, but I've certainly learned and grown a lot in ways I didn't expect. The year 2024 marks the twentieth anniversary of my first album—the beginning of my career as a recording artist. It's been the ride of a lifetime. But in the past few years, I've realized how little even the closest people to me actually know my real story. I had so many feelings I didn't know what to do with or how to process, so I locked them away and denied their existence. At a certain point in my twenties, I stopped letting people in. I froze and thought it was my job to protect, defend, and project a certain image. It only created more distance and less connection.

But the idea of letting it *all* out—A.A. meeting–style—sounded like freedom. Amid all the self-doubt and questioning, my story *is* worth sharing. And here's what I know: I've never been good at playing the game, but I'm great at telling the truth. It's time to stop letting anyone or anything else write the narrative for me.

This is *my* story.

In my *own* words.

Let's fucking do this.

OVER
THE
INFLUENCE

CHAPTER 1

PRECOCIOUS

DAD SAID HE NOTICED MOM FROM THE SECOND SHE WALKED INTO THE VFW (VETERANS OF Foreign Wars) building in Keene, New Hampshire, where his A.A. group held their meetings. It was the summer of 1989, and Mom was "the new girl" who also happened to have a rockin' bod and pretty face. She'd had a catastrophic start to her life—when she was three, her entire family was in a car crash and she lost her mom, baby sister, and older brother right before her eyes. Though her dad, other brother, and she survived, they never fully healed from the trauma. How could anyone? All three of them eventually learned to cope by drinking to numb the lingering pain and guilt—but you couldn't tell all that from looking at her. She was nine years younger than Dad and appeared out of his league at first, but he played the long game, building up a friendship and getting to know her. Slowly but surely, he won her over.

By the time my parents connected, Dad had already been in and out of rehab more than a couple times. Unlike her, he was into narcotics, not alcohol. (I actually never saw him so much as pick up a beer more than a couple of times in my whole life.) But instead of going to N.A. (Narcotics Anonymous), he preferred the community of A.A. since it was a "better crowd," as he said. He'd get a few months or even several years under his belt and then fall off the wagon. But he always returned, and by his midthirties, he had so much experience with the Twelve Steps that he started sponsoring people.

Despite their differences, they had a lot in common. Both were gifted singers who even made some money performing, but they each had to take up other jobs to support themselves. They also had secondary addictions and did not discriminate when it came to distracting themselves from the discomfort of being in their own skin. Food, love, and substances would all jockey for first prize.

Mom initially didn't want to start dating again until she had a year of sobriety under her belt, but Dad was hard to resist. She ended up having her very first "sober sex" with him ten months later—and got pregnant the first time they hooked up.

Shit got real *really* fast. Dad thought it was too early in their relationship—and recovery—for a child. Apparently, he tried to convince her to go to the clinic, but Mom thought that going through with having this baby would give her the purpose and direction she needed in her life. So they moved into a teeny apartment and tried to make it work—even when it really didn't. On good nights, they'd make up dances around the kitchen, laughing hysterically, feeding each other and harmonizing to James Taylor. But on bad nights, Mom's depression and distrust seeped into every inch of their small space, and Dad's pent-up rage would eventually burst through, especially whenever she accused him of falling off the wagon.

She had good reason to believe he was using again. He'd even *admitted it* out loud at a meeting, right in front of her, even though later that night when she brought it up again, he denied he'd ever said it. Dad could talk his way out of a paper bag.

Some nights, their arguments would even get physical. Mom eventually got scared enough that she could potentially lose the growing baby inside of her to get on a housing list for abused women. But like clockwork, things would get good again. He'd love on her extra hard, beg for forgiveness, promise to change, they'd fall back in love, and things would be amazing until they weren't. Mom had been in all types of up-and-down relationship dynamics before. It wasn't her first—or worst.

The difference was that now she was about to have a whole other life to think about. If she couldn't make the best decisions for herself, she'd have to do it for her daughter.

Mom's commitment to sobriety only intensified after I was born on December 20, 1990. She spent a lot of time in those A.A. meetings in my early years, and she took me right along with her.

Some of my first memories are from those mothball-smelling church basements and drafty meeting rooms. I'm a toddler, swinging my little legs and fidgeting on a folding chair in the corner, the harsh lighting buzzing overhead. This was where toothless bar brawlers with thick Boston accents hardened by life sat next to community college students who were court-mandated to be there. Whether they were first-timers or five-thousandth-timers, they'd share the grittiest details of their addictions, and I'd sit there, wide-eyed, taking it all in.

Surrounded by the stench of stale cigarettes and burnt coffee, I'd occasionally bump into old men with mean, leathery faces and women with puckered, overlined lips from sucking extra hard on cigarettes. There was always at least one person in the group who looked scary as fuck. My eyes would dart to the door as soon as I noticed the knob start turning. Most of the time, I'd hear a set of battered work boots stomping out snow across a tattered welcome mat just outside the door, and it would just be an Irish dude with a name like Sully or O'Shaughnessy, but honestly, you just never knew who might walk in at any moment. Most of the people in those meetings tried to treat me with kid gloves, but it didn't stop me from getting the gist: being an addict is gross and not fun and no matter what happened when I grew up, I *never* wanted to wind up back there as one of them.

I don't remember other kids being around, but I do remember sticking my Magic Marker'd hands into the Dunkin' Donuts donut hole box and seeing how many individual half-and-half creamers I could drink before I got a tummy ache. I was focused on keeping myself entertained more than anything, but I knew these meetings were important to Mom. I'd pick my eyes up from my dinosaur coloring book and observe her shedding lots of tears, wondering why she cried so much. Outside of work and church, the only people she really hung out with were the rough-and-tumble folks from these meetings. When other kids from school said their parents were going to a meeting, I realized they didn't mean *this* kind of meeting.

I understand now that my parents were just trying to get out of a pattern that they'd both found themselves in for all of their adult lives. And the religious framework of "the program" told them that the only way they'd be able to do that was by surrendering, admitting, and claiming their powerlessness. If it sounds a little weird that I was listening to the darkest confessions of addicted adults at such a young age, I'd have to agree. Kids are sponges and I can only imagine exactly what I heard and saw. But it felt normal back then. The energy in there could go from solemn to nurturing and hopeful to chaotic all within an hour, and yet it was still one of the only places I saw Mom really let down her guard.

Other than those meeting rooms, I don't really have one particular image of a "childhood home" that immediately comes up for me. Home was wherever Mom and I happened to be—as long as we were together. I was happiest when she was reading library books to me, or while I watched her singing Christmas carols with her troop all dressed up in a bonnet and Victorian garb, or any time I found myself sitting in the passenger seat of her red Ford Festiva, singing along to Kiss 108 FM, watching the ground fly by beneath us through the hole in the floor.

Mom and Dad broke up and got back together a couple of times, so we ended up moving around a bit. My favorite spot was when we all lived together in a cute little house in Nashua, New Hampshire. It was perfect to me, with a front *and* a backyard. I had a little hamster named Arnick, and we had little baby ducks outside, too, in a corral. There were also geese at a nearby pond, and we'd go together as a family to feed them little bits of bread. Things were good. Low-key, it looked like a lower-middle-class dream. For me, the memories *are* like a dream. The house came alive with music and singing, Dad playing either guitar or harmonica, while Mom tinkered away on the electric piano. Even when things went awry, like the time the house got infested with termites, there was always a fun upside, like the fact that we got to stay with Nana and Papa (Dad's parents) down the street and swim in their pool every day.

To me, Mom was the most beautiful person in the whole world, with a thick mane of golden-blonde hair that fell to her waist and a signature swatch of bangs resting just above her eyebrows. She had a dancer's frame, with long lean muscles. But I always felt her fidgeting around, buzzing with tension, never quite at peace in her own body. I couldn't put my finger on it at the time, but now I can recognize and empathize with the deep sadness within her, one that she tried to contain as much as she could. She kept a gorgeous crystal bluebird of happiness on the kitchen windowsill, telling me that "it keeps the darkness out and lets the light in." But that didn't stop her from needing to walk miles in the state forest every day, vigorously swinging her arms, sweat dripping down her face, her hands clenched tightly into fists. She knew being active was good for her mental as well as physical health, but no matter how much she moved, it was like she couldn't outrun the negativity in her brain. She was always moving. People would compliment her all the time, but she'd always brush it off, saying that she'd gained five pounds, or that she was eating too much junk food, or that she used to look better. But she looked perfect to me.

And that VOICE. Mom truly had a gift from God: a strong, clear, angelic soprano range that moved any and everybody who heard her sing, from the barstools at night gigs (where she'd order club soda with a lime) to the pews at St. Mary's. She was humble about it, but I think I understood that deep down, she knew how good she was. She was always the first pick for any solo at church if she was available; no one else ever came close to measuring up. I'd crawl up into the church loft, right next to the organ, and listen to her voice as it sailed up to the heavens. If there wasn't anyone else around—or if the organist was one of the friendlier ones—I'd even sit up on the seat and let my feet dangle over the pedals, running my fingers lightly along the various knobs and keys, pretending I was playing right along with her. And when she wasn't singing, she made sure music filled our home at all times, everything from Michael Jackson and Whitney Houston to Joni Mitchell and Carly Simon, from "Amazing Grace" and "They'll Know We Are Christians By Our Love" to *Guys and Dolls* and *The Phantom of the Opera*. To this day, I know a lot of my eclectic tastes in music can be traced back to the variety of songs she introduced me to back then.

I adored Mom, but *Dad* was larger than life to me. He had a kind smile and a handsome face that kept him looking younger than his years. Plump at best, morbidly obese at worst, his weight was evenly distributed throughout his six-foot-tall frame, and it was easy to spot him from a distance because of the thick, shiny black hair on his head and the perfectly trimmed mustache under his nose. Dad's physicality was outsized only by his infectious smile and an undeniably charismatic presence that could light up any room. When he walked through the door after a day of work as a headhunter (weird-ass name for "job recruiter"), I threw my arms around him and held on for dear life. He was my personal teddy bear, with big bear hugs and huge paws that he'd let me punch and cheer me on like I was a prize-winning boxer. When he was in a good mood, he made me feel so safe and calm. When he wasn't, it felt like the rug had been pulled out from under me, and I wondered if I had done something to make him change. I loved nothing more than curling up into his lap and watching TV with him, even if he'd usually fall asleep and start snoring five minutes in.

Mom said it "scared the shit out of her" how naturally singing came to her little girl (at around two) and how self-possessed I was. Of all the things I inherited from my parents, a passion for music was the one that came through the strongest. She said she didn't know where I got it. But I do. It was allllll from them. Just like I'd tried to mimic Mom's sounds, I'd do the same with Dad. Singing was another one of our languages. It was so common for us to be vocalizing all day long—at home, in public, it didn't matter. There was no shame, just the freedom in finding something that felt good in our bodies and seemed to bring smiles to people's faces. He was the soulful one who could growl, scat, and sing the blues, whereas Mom was more about her sheet music and hitting the notes on the page. Dad also loved taking long drives to clear his mind and would let me ride shotgun sometimes, blasting his favorite tunes and encouraging me to sing along. I *loved* experimenting with different sounds, seeing what my voice could do.

But honestly—it wasn't all roses. Over the years, Dad's weight and a knee injury he'd picked up at work took a toll on him, and he relied on more and more support from his former job and the government. There were even whispers from certain family members that he'd injured himself just so he could collect disability payments and have a legit reason to stay on pain meds. But only Dad could tell you that for sure.

Even as a young kid, I could feel the inconsistencies of my parents' individual moods and their energy toward each other. I'd be confused and wanting to understand what was happening and how I could help because I wanted us to stay together as a family. I'd get told everything was fine—but I somehow knew it wasn't true. There was such a stark difference between what they told me and how things felt. Whenever they'd get in a fight, I'd tuck myself into this one part of my room and sing into the corner, focusing on my dioramas and dinosaur figurines, positioning my body so that the sound of my own humming bounced back to me and almost drowned out their arguing. But inevitably, Dad would storm out of the house and pull out of the driveway, and I'd chase after him, crying and wailing until my throat hurt. I usually blamed Mom for upsetting him, for making him leave.

Even though Dad was my hero, Mom was my rock—the one who was always there, the one who never left, the one who did everything she needed to make ends meet. She worked as a nanny during the day and came home every night exhausted but smiling through it for me, making us stir-fry or grilled cheeses with potato chips and grapes and a pickle on the side. By the time I was five, she and Dad decided to split ways for good, and, swallowing her pride, she moved us back to Foxborough to live with her dad.

Looking back now, I know it must've been *really* hard for her to make that decision. She and my grandfather, Tom, didn't have the greatest father-daughter relationship. Ever since that car crash that took the lives of his wife, oldest son, and newborn daughter, my grandfather became a hardened man. After they got home from the hospital, he never talked about it again; instead, he carried his grief with him wherever he went, walking around that working-class town filled with rage and resentment, drinking away his pain. After a couple years of cold and chaos, he remarried a woman with her own children, bringing Mom into a Brady Bunch–type family. Mom and her brother, Brian, suddenly had two new brothers: Mark and Scott. Then, Tom and his new wife, Constance, had one more kid, Connie. Now a pre-teen, Mom felt swept under the rug. Like she'd been replaced by a cuter, sweeter, less damaged daughter.

Like me, Mom's passion for music got her through some of the hardest times in her childhood. She's always been an amazing singer, with one of those voices that fills up a whole room with its resonance. Her biological mother, Sonja, had been a gifted singer and pianist, too. After high school, Mom even earned a partial scholarship to Syracuse University for musical theater. Unfortunately, toward the end of her freshman year, she got mono and strep, missed a lot of classes, got discouraged, and ended up spending more time in bars than in classrooms.

Cutting her losses and licking her wounds, Mom moved back in with her dad and stepmom. By that point, both my grandfather and Mom were using alcohol to numb the pain that had never really gone away, and Mom felt like she wasn't wanted there. It didn't help that her dad was prone to bursts of anger, *especially* when he was drinking. It wasn't long before she moved in with a boyfriend, picked up a waitressing gig, started singing in rock bands, and doubled down on her drinking. For the next few years, she kept repeating this self-destructive pattern over and over again, with different boys, across different New England towns—all until she ended up in Vermont, starting her first recovery program.

Since then, she had come *far*. She was several years sober. She had a steady job. And she was raising me pretty much all on her own. For her to part ways with Dad and move us back in with her dad, back to the same town that had caused her so much heartache—that was a sacrifice she made for *me*. For *us*. And though I might not have appreciated it back then, I look back now and realize that beneath all that pain was a woman who loved me more than *anything*—and was willing to do whatever it took to keep a roof over our heads.

Back in the mid- to-late 1990s, Foxborough (or Foxboro—dealer's choice, according to the US postal service) was one of those little Massachusetts suburbs with a Friendly's ice cream place, a YMCA, and a decent high school football team—all twenty-nine miles south of Boston, where "the accent" was still strong. The town wasn't diverse; it was mostly the descendants of a lot of English, Irish, and Italian families who'd lived there for generations. There were fewer than fifteen thousand full-time residents, so the streets easily become bloated and swarming with cars on game days when the Patriots played at Gillette Stadium off Route 1.

Other than that, it was a pretty classic small-town burb. Kids could safely ride their bikes up and down Central Street and pass the Booth Playground, and the only off-putting thing they'd see was an abandoned mental hospital (patients had been left to "figure it out for themselves" after the state cut mental health funding in the 1970s). It was also a town rooted in small businesses. Besides the Cumberland Farms convenience store and a Dairy Queen, Foxborough wasn't really a "chain store" kind of place. More like, everyone knew everyone, and store owners always knew their customers and just what their order was. *"Linda'll have the steak & cheese, toasted—no olives. Steve'll have his White Russian with extra Stoli, light ice."* There was also a popular pub called the Ancient Marinere, a favorite of my grandfather's, which was within walking distance of his home (though sometimes, he'd get too drunk to make the walk back).

I was an only child, and I *hated* it. It just didn't seem fair since all the other kids seemingly had built-in friends in their siblings. But I got to fill up my day with lots of activities, like bike riding, fishing with my Aunt Connie and Uncle Dale, checking out books from the Boyden Library, and doing art projects (think: popsicle sticks, sequins, puffy paints, googly eyes galore). Mom fully nurtured my free spirit and let me explore literally anything I was curious about. One thing I was really into from a young age was dinosaurs. (Yet another future tattoo seed planted.) I *loved* pretending like I was riding on the back of a triceratops or a T. rex or even a pterodactyl, high above the ground, watching everyone and everything below us turn into specks of dust. And that was just the start of it. I was full of enthusiasm and interests. I was definitely "a lot." But Mom, to her credit, never made me feel like I was ever too much. Having no brothers or sisters, I concluded, was actually awesome because I got Mom all to myself—after she was done helping raise other people's kids, anyways.

Even though Mom always encouraged me to march to the beat of my own drum, the families she nannied for could sometimes get a little worried about the influence I had on their kids. One time, I brought back a book on Wicca from Salem and couldn't wait to show it to them. Around the time of my first Holy Communion (I would've been seven or so), I was casting little spells in this Jewish family's coat closet. Needless to say, the parents had a sit-down discussion with Mom the next day. So much for starting my first coven.

Keep in mind, too, that these folks had homes so big, we could fit our room in the back of Grandad's house into them—several times over. I didn't really think about how we lived a bit differently from most people in Foxborough until I went over to someone else's house. There was one frenemy in particular from school, and I remember she lived in what looked like a gray-carpeted *palace*, with endless nooks and crannies for hide-and-seek, a trampoline, a fridge filled with pepperoni Lunchables, cabinets stuffed with Gushers and Dunkaroos, an aboveground pool, and a pontoon boat parked on the lake out back. I was never quite sure whether this girl liked me or not. I wasn't sure I liked her either. But she wanted to sing, and I was always singing, and I wanted name-brand snacks, and she had a cabinet full of them, so I'd say the "friendship" had mutual benefits for both of us.

More than hanging with kids my age, though, I wanted to hang with my favorite family members, who I knew *actually* liked me. Mom's half-sister, my Aunt Connie, and her husband, Uncle Dale, lived only a bike ride's distance away. Think of a fast-paced nonstop energy like Robin Williams but with the thickest Boston accent you've ever heard—to the point that it sometimes sounds like another language: that's my Uncle Dale. Anytime he sat behind the desk at his office, he would incessantly tap his foot and shake with excitability—always moving, always on the edge of saying something crazy. You'd think he was on coke or speed, but it was just extreme ADHD that ensured he had more than enough energy to keep up with me. I'd be chillin' on a yacht in the South of France by now if I could bottle up his frenetic, positive spark and sell it in pill form. His wife Connie was a beautiful, warm, hardworking real estate agent, as well as a home chef and baker. "Martha," Dale called her because of her prowess in the kitchen. People often said I looked more like Connie than Mom because of our big cheeks and the way they squished our eyes down smaller when we smiled. The word *townie* doesn't always have the best connotation attached to it, but in the best sense of the word, my aunt and uncle fit the bill. They were Mass-born and never left, had a tight-knit group of close friends since high school, more often than not had a beer in their hands or a vodka soda roadie in the cup holder, and they'd give you the shirts off their backs, no question, if you asked.

Connie and Dale were second parents to me, and I was always super grateful to have them in my life. Dale made elaborate forts in the middle of their living room, brought home yummy pizza, took me to get my nails done, and challenged me to games at the local arcade for hours. They never missed a school recital or holiday concert. It was blindingly obvious how crazy I was about performing, and next to Mom and Dad, I knew they were my biggest fans. I'd fixate on remembering everything about one album—like MJ's *Bad* or the soundtrack from *The Bodyguard*—for weeks straight, and they'd let me try out all my new songs and dances for them, using their respective offices or the living room of their apartment as my stage. And whenever Connie visited the beauty salon in town, Head II Toes, she let me tag along with her and sing for the ladies there, many of them her friends. I'd walk in, grab a Werther's candy from the dish at the receptionist's desk, and just smirk to myself, knowing I was soon about to blow their hair back with what I could do with my voice. If there were new women in there, I couldn't *wait* to see their reactions—the expressions on their faces when I opened my mouth. I'd ask people if they had a song that they wanted to hear next time, and I'd come back having learned it.

Everyone called me "precocious"—I thought it was an amazing sounding word—and I was more than willing to use whatever it meant to my advantage. At some point, I think Connie might have suggested that I should ask the ladies at the salon for a dollar or two after these little performances. Before you knew it, I was belting in the middle of the room as acrylic nails got filed down, asking these grown-ass women to open up their pocketbooks and give me a tip. Sometimes they'd ask me to sign autographs. Then I'd get dropped off back at Mom's with a hard-earned eight bucks in my jacket pocket, proud as hell. I guess you could call those my first gigs.

In the center of Foxborough, just off the roundabout, lies the Orpheum Theatre, where local productions of popular plays and musicals have been put on for years. Mom believed I had something special and took me to audition for the six-year-old character in *The Who's Tommy: The Musical*, which Mom explained was a really cool rock show that the Orpheum was putting on. I didn't care at *all* that the character was supposed to be a boy. Throw a bowl-cut wig on me and I was in.

I had more confidence in my skills than most adults, but nerves still swirled around in my belly as I walked out on that desolate stage, looking out at the red velvet theater chairs filled only by the three casting people who would decide my fate. It felt like the beginning of something. Mom was watching from behind the lobby window, and I could feel her up there with me, cheering me on. I knew she thought I was the most talented kid in New England, and that meant a lot because *nothing* impressed her— she just didn't think many things or people were great. But. If she thought I was good enough, then I was good enough. The part was *mine*.

The pianist ushered me in, and without a drop of hesitation, I belted out the first few words of "On My Own" from *Les Misérables*: "On my own, pretending he's beside me." And then I lost myself in the lyrics, the feelings, the *music*.

As soon as I finished, the director chuckled and said, "Quite the powerful voice and quite the song choice for such a tiny little girl!" Mom had helped me prepare the *Les Mis* song, which was more relevant for a theater audition than, say, "Get On Up" or "River Deep, Mountain High." He then gave me a chorus from a song in *Tommy* to learn quickly and asked me to act out a few lines with different emotions. I walked out of that audition and into the lobby with my head held high. The bug had officially bitten me.

I think I got that role! They said I was amazing! I'm going to be really famous one day . . . I remember thinking to myself as Mom and I walked back to Grandad's house. I was excited to tell him the great news of my first step toward stardom, but he could be moody, so I tried not to take it too personally when he feigned enthusiasm and grumbled something like "Good for you" before going back to his beer and the news.

At that point, I was floating on air; not even a grumpy old man could get me down. I'd never felt better in my *life* than I had on that stage, basking in the applause, standing tall and powerful in front of an audience of one or one thousand, knowing I could do something they couldn't. The sheer audacity to believe I belonged up there, at my age—I knew people were impressed by it. And I *loved* feeling impressive.

When they called to say I got the part, Mom first told me that I didn't. Then, not able to keep up the charade for long, she laughed and said, "I'm just kidding, Jo, YOU GOT IT!!! You're going to be so amazing!!!" I started jumping and shrieking and running around the house.

Even though this early greenlight into the theater was encouraging, Mom made sure to keep my musical horizons open. Going to see live music around Massachusetts and New Hampshire was a regular weekend deal for us. She'd sung in several rock bands throughout her twenties and seemed to have a knack for finding places to hear people jam. Somewhere near the Cape, she discovered a band called Big Daddy and the Accelerators. The front man, Darwin, all six foot five of him, was an African American and Native American artist who rocked a massive cowboy hat, turquoise and bone jewelry, leather vests, and custom boots. I was in awe of him. Mustached with skin the color of earth, he sang the *hell* out of the blues and had a captivating stage presence that far outshone the venues he was playing. Above everything else, he radiated an electric positivity that made me want him to acknowledge my existence. I knew I couldn't leave that show without him hearing me sing. It probably sounds strange for a six-year-old to be so self-possessed, but there I was, instinctively aware that soul and blues music connected to something deep within me.

After the show, Mom told him that I was a singer and asked if I could sing something for the band. The next thing I knew, "Old Time Rock and Roll"—a song they had just covered in their set—growled out of me as I snarled my lip like Elvis and shimmied around on the linoleum tile floor. Big Daddy was tickled.

"Wow!!!" He stepped back with his hands on his hips, taking in my little frame, freshly cut bangs (like Mom's), multicolored scarf tied as a headband, plaid crinkle top with spaghetti straps, jeans, and my favorite sparkly purple jellies. "Where in the world did you get that big voice? HA! You are really something!! And what do you know about *soul*, lil' mama?" He had me sing again for his lady and some other people he knew. "I just really can't believe my ears and eyes. Tell me, Joanna—what do you want to be when you grow up?"

"Well, obviously, I want to be a famous singer!" The people around us laughed, but I was undeterred. I felt like it was the most obvious thing in the world.

"Can I sing with you sometime?" I asked him. I honestly had no thoughts or agenda beyond "I would love to be up there and you seem really nice." And from that day on, he let me sing with his band whenever Mom could get us to one of their gigs. He always gave me a star's introduction as if I were Chaka Khan or something. The band even let me sit in with them when they performed on local broadcast TV. This was my first taste of what it felt like to be on the other side of the camera, where I knew in my heart that I belonged.

CHAPTER 2

TEACHER'S PET

EVEN THOUGH I LOVED LEARNING, SCHOOL WAS A DOUBLE-EDGED SWORD. YES, IT WAS A PLACE where I could feed my insatiable curiosity and learn about the world around me, but it was also a place where I was forced to deal with other kids, kids I didn't like because they didn't like me. I honestly don't know which came first.

Every time I walked the long hallway of Vincent M. Igo Elementary to my second-grade class, I felt like I couldn't wait to get into my seat and get to work. Better yet, I couldn't wait to be *working*, just like grownups did in the real world. Even from an early age, I never felt like I'd learn everything I needed to learn inside the walls of a classroom. I genuinely loved and looked forward to art, history, English, and music class, but besides that— socializing, making friends, seeing what new backpack or Sailor Moon binder Schuyler or Solveig had—I truly couldn't have cared less. I could never keep up with all the latest trends, and it seemed like I was always saying or liking the wrong thing. I would have much rather stayed at home with adults listening to *real* music—not the boy bands and other stuff the kids my age listened to. It all made me feel so "other."

Luckily, I wasn't totally alone. I had a best friend who felt different in her own way. For a few years, we did *everything* together, including taking karate and discovering how good it felt to hump pillows. She knew my darkest secrets and deepest dreams, and she wanted to be a singer and actress too—just like me. That's why it hurt so much when she eventually cliqued up with some other girls and turned making fun of me into a sport. I don't know exactly how or when things turned, but before I knew it, a group of kids started an "I Hate Joanna" club. I was so confused about what exactly I had done to warrant that. I made it a point to be kind to everyone, and I tried to stay out of people's way. I was embarrassed to tell Mom and Connie and Dale I had lost the *one* friend I thought I could count on.

My eccentric, attention-loving, afraid-of-getting-in-trouble little self fell into the role of a teacher's pet too easily. Before I even hit double digits, I just wished I could just hang out with Mrs. Haney or Mrs. Horton instead of the other kids. I just didn't quite fit in with girls my own age, who seemingly had not a care in the world and shopped at stores like Limited Too and resembled Disney Princesses. My vibe? I was a sensitive little ragamuffin, rockin' a mix of Kmart and hand-me-downs and styling it into my own thing. Mom encouraged me to wear the wildest colors and put my outfits together however I wanted. She used the word *funky* a lot to describe her own style choices, and it trickled down to me. A typical outfit for me might have looked like this: a black-and-white jacket that reminded me of *101 Dalmatians*, a sheer purple top with an orange camisole underneath, some trippy jeans, and the coolest light-up sneakers I'd ever seen from Payless.

There were no rules. I just dressed however I felt. Sometimes, I felt like a witch. Sometimes, I felt like Mick Jagger.

Naturally, being such a free spirit and generally not quite fitting in with my peers made me a prime target for bullying. I couldn't even tell you specifically what these other kids bullied me about. But most days, I felt like I didn't know where I could sit at lunch. Walking home from school, I wished I could disappear into the bushes, singing my comfort songs to myself, as kids whizzed past me on the bus, heckling and yelling mean things. There were even a few girls and boys who tried to stuff me inside lockers—and succeeded a couple times. They'd whisper to each other behind an open hand to an ear and then look at me and laugh, making the circle they were standing in in the hallway tighter, stonewalling me from their conversations. When the "I Hate Joanna" club swelled up to more than a handful of members, I'd had *enough*. Knowing that I could curl up deep into my imagination and daydream of becoming a rich and untouchable performer, leaving this stupid small town behind—that was pretty much the fuel that sprung me out of bed in the morning.

Even as a little kid, I was full of curious and creative energy. For as long as I could remember, adults told me I was an artist, and I felt like they could see into my soul: performing and writing came so easily to me, all at once. I tried to keep the music under my breath, but it would always come out gushing like water from a tap, and before I knew it, I'd be on top of the jungle gym at recess, belting at the top of my lungs for everyone to hear. Some kids watched in open-mouthed wonder, while others just rolled their eyes. But I cared more about letting out the feelings bubbling inside of me than I cared about what they thought. I had something I was *really* good at. Math might be impossible, but I always knew if I could just make it to recess, where I could sing outside and let the wind carry my voice higher and higher, I'd be okay.

That jungle gym was my castle and the sand my moat, and if Whitney was the Queen of the Night, I was Princess of the

Playground. Flying high, letting my legs flail beneath me on a rickety swing, I could close my eyes and feel the energy of the crowd in Gillette Stadium, imagining myself up there on an illuminated stage, mic in hand. Strong and in control. I'd be commanding the attention of thousands in a tight outfit, athletic and energetic just like Shania Twain, riding the high of an adoring crowd and the mastery of the gifts I'd been given. I wanted to inhabit that world *so bad*, nothing else mattered. I was constantly buzzing with the possibilities.

Not all adults thought all this creative energy was a good thing, though. My doctor told Mom that he thought I should be medicated, probably for some kind of autism or ADHD. But Mom was convinced that I was a genius and had me take some online test to prove it.

"Just under Einstein!" she squealed after we got my results back. "Jo, you are *brilliant*." Well, boom. There you have it. I tried to remind myself of this whenever someone made me feel small. Plus, I knew in my gut I wouldn't be in Foxborough forever. Whenever Mom and I went into the city to see music, I was surrounded by people from all walks of life, people who had better places to go and more things to do. I knew I belonged *there* instead of back in Foxborough, but I still toed the line between craving acceptance from everyone around me and yet not wanting to be like anyone else.

The bullying got both better and worse after I was on national TV for the first time. Bill Cosby rebooted *Kids Say the Darndest Things* in the midnineties, showcasing a brand-new crop of precocious kids to the world (the original show ran from 1959 to 1967). There was a big advertisement in the back of the *Boston Globe* calling for talented kids to audition at Faneuil Hall, a mall right by the Freedom Trail where they were taping their Boston special. The minute I saw it, I begged Mom to take me to audition. There were few things she hated more than driving—especially in the city—but she took me in, regardless.

When I got there, I let myself loose on the casting team: singing; dancing along to Michael Jackson; doing impersonations of Cher, Elvis, and Prince; telling them I would "switch stations" anytime they pressed an invisible button.

Want to see me do anything else? I'll try that, too!

Along with a handful of other kids from around the area, I got called back to be on the show. Mom and Dad both came into the city to support me from the audience, sitting right next to each other and looking the part of a perfect couple even though they had broken up by then. More than that, Mom was dating somebody else, and she and Dad were barely on speaking terms. But it meant the world to me that they were both there for me, together, and I was so happy that my cheeks were sore from smiling.

While I was up there waiting for my turn to talk with Mr. Cosby, I counted the people in front of me and realized that the audience at the Orpheum for *The Who's Tommy* had been bigger. But somehow the intimacy of this space and knowing that these cameras were going to broadcast me into the homes of millions of people made my nerves dance even harder. Now, sitting underneath the bright lights of Faneuil Hall, I could barely see the assortment of faces and expressions in the audience—but I knew my parents were there, and even if I flopped and couldn't get a single note out, they loved and believed in me.

"Nerves are natural, Jo. It's a good thing! I always feel like I'm going to throw up before I sing," Mom reminded me. She'd trimmed my bangs the night before and done my hair in the pretty half-up half-down style that I loved on her. A lady backstage put some powder on my nose and tasty cherry Chap-Stick on my lips.

Even though there was a lump in my throat and a sudden throbbing in my chest, I felt it wasn't more than I could handle. I thought about how Dad had whispered to me earlier that I was a star, and he was so proud of me. I held on to that with everything I had while I watched Mr. Cosby talking to the two other kids up onstage with me. No matter how much time he spent with them, my mind became fixated on making sure I left him and that audience thinking I was special. The nerves bubbled up as I watched the time ticking down on the teleprompter, kicking my legs under the lime-green chair.

Was he ever going to come over to me?

Would they run out of time before I could even talk to him?

What if I don't get the chance to show everyone how good I am?

Finally, Mr. Cosby made his way across the stage toward me. It was *my* time to shine. I laid the personality on thick and played into it when he mentioned something about Dad and Mom that obviously wasn't true, like something about them sharing a bed. If you knew us in real life, you'd know they weren't together. But nobody in the audience knew that, and I quickly realized in moments like this, the truth wasn't important. I leaned into the joke. My parents laughed and so did everyone else.

Whenever I saw Mr. Cosby or the audience reacting favorably to a certain aspect I showed, I did even *more* of it. More growling, more volume, more sass. Just like in my audition, I transformed into a human radio, and he'd change the station. People always had a big reaction to me having so many different types of songs at the ready to drop on a dime. I pushed through the nerves and held nothing back, high-volume vibratos rocketing past missing teeth and tumbling through my lips. I let 'em have it. I wasn't going to let a single second go to waste.

By the time my moment was over, it felt like it hadn't even begun. Suddenly, I was backstage, in the middle of a hug sandwich with my parents and everyone was smiling and congratulating me. It all happened so fast, but the live taping ended up being a huge hit, and the producers told us even Mr. Cosby was very impressed. I was missing a front tooth and kept excitedly pressing my tongue through it. Afterward, we went to eat at Pizzeria Uno to celebrate, and everything felt so strangely awesome. I didn't want to ask too much of God, knowing He had the literal world on His plate, but there was still a part of me that hoped that maybe if I was special enough and did a good enough job, He could somehow bring my parents back together.

A few months later, after the show had aired and everyone in my hometown had seen and either loved or hated me for it, we heard from the show producers again when they invited us to Hollywood, California, to film another episode. I was told I was "Mrs. Cosby's favorite." *Hell yeah.*

Back at school, the lunch monitors who oversaw our break would sometimes ask me to sing in front of a captive (but not necessarily *captivated*) audience of students. All this adult validation of my voice made me feel so powerful—especially since the other kids had always made fun of me for it. Every time they smiled or cheered me on, an additional surge of energy and enthusiasm coursed through me—as if I could handle even a drop more without short-circuiting.

Whenever I was sitting at a table by myself, or they could tell I'd had a hard day with bullies, the lunch monitors would invite me to come up and sing for them. When they gave me that knowing "wink and nod" to come on up and do my thing, I felt like the sound Dad's Mac desktop computer made when it was turned on. "DUNNNNNNNNNNN!" It no longer mattered that I was eating by myself or that none of the other kids liked me. Shaking internally with nerves, I'd decide what I was going to sing as I walked over from wherever I was sitting to the front of the lunchroom. Would I give 'em a lil' "On Broadway" by George Benson? "Chain of Fools" by Aretha? I'd sing something the adults knew and the kids didn't care about at all. But it didn't matter; these lunch monitors would make these asshole second graders listen to me sing some decades-old song, and for those three minutes, you couldn't tell me *nothin'*.

Between the monitors, guidance counselors, some of the teachers, and the nurses, I had an army of adults at school who I could run to whenever my sensitive soul could no longer take the isolation or ridicule from my peers. And run to them I did. Over time, I adapted the skill of making myself believe I was sick so that I could be sent home. The key here was truly believing that I wasn't feeling well so I could convince Mom that I needed her to leave work and come get me. The power of my mind. She always believed me.

When I was at home winning the war against going to school, I got to watch my favorite daytime talk shows—the ones with those talent segments that were popular in the 1990s. A few times a year, these hosts—people like Oprah, Ricki Lake, Maury Povich (before all that "you-are-not-the-father" stuff), Rosie O'Donnell—would highlight talented kids from around the country. I knew I just *had* to be one of those kids. After Aunt Connie got a camcorder, she offered to film me singing in her apartment. Mom would then make VHS copies and send them to the addresses spelled out at the end of each show.

The Oprah Winfrey Show was the pinnacle as far as these kinds of television shows went. And why shouldn't we aim high? I never got the sense that there was anything I couldn't do.

Especially after my first taste of performing live and being on television. Within a week of sending out these tapes, Mom heard back from a couple of the shows' producers. Before long, we were on a bus ride to NYC, gearing up for a performance on *The Rosie O'Donnell Show* and shortly after that, *Maury*. Then someone from Oprah's office in Chicago asked if they could play my tape during one of their "amazing home movies" episodes.

Why, yes—yes, you can.

And I hope everyone at my fucking school sees it and poops their pants.

How Mom kept food on the table during this time is a miracle. Thankfully, the church she worked for, St. Mary's, was understanding and flexible while she took me up and down the East Coast for auditions; they probably understood because she'd been singing for them for so long. Nannying was the steadier gig for her during these years but Mom still primarily considered herself to be a singer while we pursued my fledgling dream of becoming a star.

New York City was exactly the kind of stimulation I craved. Times Square was a thrilling dreamscape: with every imaginable color blasting into my eyes, mixing with endless sounds, scents, and textures everywhere I turned. I, too, was a neon light, burning bright and requiring your attention. I believed wholeheartedly in the lyrics to that Frank Sinatra song, the one that says: "If I can make it there, I'll make it anywhere . . ." And the way George Benson described it? I legitimately thought there was glitter in the pavement beneath our feet.

Sometimes, Mom and I would take the four-hour bus ride one way for an audition and then get right back on and travel four hours back. But when she had extra money, we stayed at the Days Inn, walking distance from Grand Central Station. I thought the "crazy people" on the streets were both scary and funny.

They said the wildest shit that made no sense—"I'd be like Eric Clapton on yo ass!"—and sometimes tried to follow us, but Mom would grip my hand tighter and dip into a McDonald's to get them off our scent. When I wasn't recording for one of the shows, I was sometimes singing my heart out on a street corner, right underneath a glowing marquee after a play let out. I'd purposely wear a big hat so I could put it out busker-style and catch a dollar or two from the people who formed a crowd around me and cheered me on. Mom didn't so much as encourage this behavior as she made sure there were no perverts lingering and supported me doing what I wanted to do. She said she felt like she needed to help me achieve my dreams. We were an unstoppable team.

When I performed on *The Rosie O'Donnell Show*, I noticed that feeling creeping up on me again. The nerves. The excitement. The high of the clapping and wooing from the audience after my performance. I felt like a *celebrity* when I got to sit in the interview chair and chat with Rosie for a few minutes. Adults were always asking me questions and seemed to care about my responses.

Coming back to Foxborough after so much attention and excitement was a buzzkill, but one good thing came of it: I crossed paths with a fellow ball of energy while we lined up to get popsicles at the Booth Playground Summer Camp. Her real name was Charlena, but she went by Nene. I had noticed her being really good at jump rope from afar, so I was excited when she came up to talk to me. She was beautiful, curious, and confident—the girl didn't have a shy bone in her body. Nene was a grade above me (which seemed like a decade back then) and she wasn't the most popular kid, but a lot of people seemed to like her and *nobody* messed with her. And for some reason, she took a liking to me. I thought she might have seen me on TV, but she hadn't; she just struck up a conversation with a solo stranger one day by the playground.

For the first time in a long time, I had a real friend again. We'd stay on the phone talking for hours about our dreams, boys we had crushes on, how our moms were annoying and their boyfriends sucked, how she was going to be the next Oprah and I was going to be the next Celine Dion. We had sleepovers and rode bikes and collected coins from my couch cushions to get ice creams at Friendly's. She cornrowed my hair, patiently taught me how to do it myself, and then let me practice on her. We spent hours on the sidewalk trying to do a dance called "the tick," where we'd shake our hips within an inch of our lives, singing "Awwww break it down with the tick. Awwww break it down with the boom boom tick ta tick ta boom tick." We had some things in common; we were both raised by single moms and neither of us had name-brand clothes. But we shared what we had; for her, that meant two cool older sisters, cable, and Jamaican food at her apartment, and for me, that meant razor scooters, a massive CD collection, and art supplies. She's been my ride-or-die best friend and sister ever since.

Meanwhile, Mom was feeling lonely. She hated not having a man in her life. The newest one was fifteen years older than her, and they got married less than a year after meeting, which came as a real shock to our family. Mostly because of how outspoken she was about how she didn't actually like him and that she was only with him because she didn't want to lose his friendship or be alone. He had a last name that for some reason made me think of the word *armpit* every time I heard it, and he smeared ChapStick all over his face in lieu of moisturizer. I guess he loved having a greasy-ass face. Whenever he'd put his oily mustache close to my mother, it made my stomach churn. I felt like he had this weird seventies porn star sexuality about him. He would grab and touch Mom, and they would tongue kiss right in front of me, and the whole thing just made me *so* icked out.

As much as I disliked him, he offered us more financial stability than we'd had in—maybe ever. We moved into a bigger duplex in Foxborough, one with both an upstairs and a downstairs level as well as a front and backyard. I even had my own room for the first time. But the house felt haunted, and I never was totally comfortable sleeping there by myself. I had chronic nightmares and so did Mom. Mine were about mummies coming up from the tombs in Egypt, rising from the dead and swimming across oceans just to wrap me up and suffocate me.

The fact that my beautiful, wonderful, talented mom—a woman whose bed I had always shared up until that point—was now sleeping next to this greasy-faced man made me really mad. As often as she possibly could, without getting into a fight with her new husband, she crept out of their bed and slept with me instead, for both our sakes. Not only did I love getting to snuggle with Mom, but I took pleasure in trying to drive a wedge between them.

I wanted him *gone*, and I did everything I could to show him how much I hated him. To be fair, he didn't do anything to try to make things better. Mom and I were both deathly afraid of bugs, and one time, he thought it would be funny to chase us around the house and outside with the biggest stink bug I'd ever seen. Bloodcurdling screams and tears poured out of Mom and me as we fled to the safety of her red Ford Festiva and frantically locked the door. It was apparent to me that he took pleasure in inflicting this torment on us, which was a little weird. Fortunately, their marriage barely lasted two years.

Life in Foxborough started to feel more and more intolerable. After getting tastes of the big city, I was constantly restless, like there was an hourglass filled with sand inside of me and there was only so long I could stay in this town. I told Mom I was gonna die if I was there any longer. I knew what to say to bring the drama.

By that point, Mom had taken a job as a house cleaner to have more flexibility so she could cart me around to auditions. I was even starting to book a few gigs: an indie movie, a Hood milk commercial, a voice-over role. But when we moved to the bottom of an old duplex on Central Street, I became acutely aware of how stressed she was about money. I hated seeing her work so hard only to barely get by. I wanted to help take care of us. I had this deep sense that things might get better for us only if *I* made them better.

In the new place, there was enough room for me to have a bed in the living room, but I still slept in her bed, where we clung tightly to each other at night. I liked being the big spoon. Sometimes, I could feel her crying next to me, and I would assure her that everything was going to be okay. Now in her thirties, Mom was raising me on less than $10,000 a year and just wanted someone to acknowledge that she was doing a damn great job at it. 'Cuz she was. We had everything we needed and, most of all, each other. But I couldn't quiet the nagging feeling in my gut that a massive change in our lives was just around the corner if only I could be "discovered" by the right person who would make me a star.

She believed it, too.

CHAPTER 3

THE BIRTH OF JOJO

IT WASN'T ALL A STRUGGLE FEST, THOUGH; THERE WAS LOTS OF BRIGHTNESS. WHEN I WAS eight years old, promoting my latest television appearance (yes, I hear how wild that sounds), I did a little phone-in interview on Kiss 108 FM, the biggest pop station in New England, and was gifted tickets to go to their summer concert. It was my first time going to a big concert, and I was *PUMPED!* Mom and I put together a funky outfit for me to wear: a tiny, blue-plaid, spaghetti-strap crinkle shirt that expanded to fit when I put it on, jeans with stripes on the side that matched the colors in the shirt, and Mom's pink, black, and purple scarf that I tied in my hair just behind my bangs. The bright yellow Band-Aid covering a bee sting on my arm added even more color to the mix, and I took some Elmer's glue and stuck a rhinestone outside of one of my eyes.

One of the most exciting acts of the Kiss Concert 1999 lineup was Britney Spears. A few months earlier, when I'd been playing the role of Mustardseed in *A Midsummer Night's Dream*, one of the cooler older fairies had played Britney's debut single, ". . . Baby, One More Time" on the boombox in the fairy dressing room. Although it wasn't the kind of thing I typically listened to, I actually loved how fresh and soulful yet sticky it felt to me. The song made me want to move. It had a pulse through it that made me really *feel* something.

Around the same time, Nene and I had become huge fans of Christina Aguilera's sparkly outfits, confidence, and massive voice. But this was back in the late 1990s and early 2000s when women in music—pop music most of all—were brutally pitted against one another, and all their fans were expected to follow suit. There was a Claymation show on MTV called *Celebrity Deathmatch* where clay versions of artists and actors would literally battle it out to the bloody, bitter end. It was intentionally gruesome and utterly ridiculous, but that's what fandoms felt like back then. You were either Team Britney or Team Christina, and whichever choice you made said something about who you were. But I didn't like those rules. Britney was an amazing performer and I respected her, even though I was normally pretty judgmental about lip-synching, and there were rumors going around then that she was doing that at her shows. For whatever reason, I honestly didn't care.

On June 5, 1999, at the Tweeter Center Amphitheater in Mansfield, MA, I found my eight-year-old self face-to-face with Brit Brit in all her teen queen glory. An excited stranger in her twenties ran up to me and Mom in the audience, saying she knew who we were from seeing me on TV. Her name was Nicole, and she said I was super talented and wondered why I wasn't going backstage to meet some of the acts. Apparently, my talent afforded me entry into places like this.

Nicole was basically my first PR person without actually being one. With her leading the charge, we made our way up to the first line of backstage defense, and Nicole introduced me as someone they *had* to hear. I sang a song for the first guard, a local security guy hired to make sure overzealous fans couldn't find their way backstage to "disturb the talent." Then he called out to the next guy farther into the backstage area to come check me out, and that got Mom, Nicole, and me backstage. Then I sang for *another* guard who oversaw the dressing room area, and he introduced us to Big Rob, Britney's ubiquitous security guard that I'd seen behind the scenes with her on MTV's *Making the Video*. I sang for Rob—he dug it—and he essentially peeled back the velvet rope to Britney's bare-bones dressing room, where she was a self-illumined object of focus at the center of her dancers.

I was in awe of being that up close to her after seeing her performing onstage earlier, and I geeked out when I spotted her iconic head-mic on a small table in there. At seventeen, she was in a totally different age group than me, and to my eight-year-old self she seemed savvy and wise. Maybe it's a Sagittarius thing. She was sweet and curious as to who this little girl with a missing tooth and a Boston accent dressed like a hippie rocker was in her dressing room. I asked if I could sing for her, and she patiently gave me the floor, so I sang "Respect" by Aretha Franklin. She put her hands up to her cheeks and dropped her mouth.

"Oh my *Goddddd* . . . !" she drawled in that Louisiana twang I had heard so much of on MTV. Then there was all this commotion around me. The dancers took pictures and asked me to sing again, this time filming it with the latest tech: a handheld camcorder. Her whole team made their way into the dressing room and just kept cheering me on. A few got close to Mom and asked her questions in hushed tones; others just stood back and ogled.

I was so proud of myself. These performers in their cargo pants and tube tops were so *cool*, and my talent had softened their energy toward me, so much so that I now felt accepted and welcomed. Like we were kin. Britney said out loud to the room that she was about to start a production company of her own and maybe we could do something together someday. It all felt positive, but I had no idea what any of it actually meant. I'm not sure if Mom did either.

Months later, just before my ninth birthday, we received a contract from the offices of Britney's attorney, Larry Rudolph, outlining a deal that would make me her first signing. I was eager to get going, but Mom took time to process it and think about what it would really mean to let her child—who hadn't even hit double digits yet—start making an album. She respectfully declined, and I was convinced that she was actively ruining my life.

"What if this is my one and only shot? And you just literally threw it away!!!!!!"

"It's not, Joanna. What's meant to be WILL be. You're just way too young right now. You'll be eighteen before you know it, and then you can do what you want."

I was brooding and heartbroken for months. I held it over her head and told her I questioned if she really believed in me. But underneath all that resentment, I knew she did, and I'd just have to keep fighting to show her I was ready for the big leagues.

After doing a few TV appearances, commercials, and theater bookings, I started to earn a little money. I even got my SAG/AFTRA card, which meant that even though I'd have to pay dues, I could also reap the benefits of being someone who worked in film and television, like good health insurance and prenegotiated minimum rates that I would have to receive for my work as a union member.

Less than two years after my TV debut with Mr. Cosby, the show brought Mom and Dad back together when they flew all three of us out to California for me to film another episode of *Kids Say the Darndest Things*. I hoped it would be the moment when my parents finally rekindled the flame between them, but instead, the energy throughout the trip felt like Mom versus Dad. It was clear that I had to choose a side, and I knew the only choice was Mom. It felt like I was always being tested. Which hotel room did I want to stay in? Did I want to go take a hike with Mom or stay in and watch a movie with Dad? I missed Dad and wanted to spend as much time as I could with him since I didn't get to see him that often. Having to choose *sucked*, but I innately knew Mom would be inconsolable if I wasn't completely loyal to her. Still, I could feel Dad's sadness at my distance.

Los Angeles had a different energy than New York City. It's hard to pinpoint exactly, but (as someone who's pretty much a Los Angeleno now) for lack of better words, there's this glimmering veil of absolute horseshit that covers the industry-oriented parts of LA. A lie-to-your-face fakeness. Of course, I'm overgeneralizing, but in NY people won't just say or do anything to make you like them; you gotta actively be about something for real to make it there. Be it the industry or the smog, there seems to be an air of desperation that exists in Hollywood that doesn't exist in the same way in Manhattan. All that said, it's also where the sausage is made and that sausage is TV shows. After being out there for *Kids Say*, Mom and I decided that we should go back out for "pilot season" since the next logical step in my career was for me to act on a scripted show, like Amanda Bynes (*All That* and *The Amanda Show*) or Hilary Duff (*Lizzie McGuire*). I was comically confident I could make it work; I felt like I could do what they did *in my sleep* if only I could get out there and show the casting directors all I was capable of doing.

I never doubted that Mom thought I had talent, but now she had started to tell me—on at *least* a biweekly basis—that I was getting "too big for my britches." That I was getting too excited about myself and I shouldn't forget where I came from. That she "would always be that pin to pop the inflating balloon of [my] ego." She obviously wanted me to stay humble and not turn into a conceited prepubescent monster, but it's like every time we rolled out of Foxborough, it became all the more obvious that I wouldn't ever fit in or be happy there. How could I stay in a town where my peers didn't even try to understand me? When we started going to these auditions, I finally met other kids who liked the things I did. Maybe I *wasn't* so strange or different after all.

Both of my parents encouraged me to keep on being myself, insisting that the mean kids at school were jealous that I had talent and already knew what I wanted to do with my life.

"Some people never figure that stuff out their whole lives!" Dad kept telling me. He had this fun "fuck 'em all" attitude toward "those little a-holes." I got to see Dad a few days a month, almost every other weekend. I'd tell him about how bad it was at school, and he would jokingly threaten to "drive down to The Igo and give 'em all a piece of my mind." This was particularly funny because Dad had the friendliest smile and could win over almost anyone with his disarming personality; he was like a slightly older Jack Black with a mustache. But it wasn't just talk; I knew he could quickly snap into a serious expression and cut anyone down to size with his words, if need be. When his energy shifted, he could truly suck the air out of a room. He would have—verbally or otherwise—beat up any bully (or their dad) for me in the blink of an eye, and that made me feel really proud.

When Dad was good, he was my hero. But when he wasn't good, it could be dangerous. Every once in a while, when he would come pick me up for the weekend, he was visibly out of it. Of course, it would've been understandable for him to be tired after the ride; it's about a ninety-minute drive from Nashua down to Foxborough. But from what I heard Mom and other family members talking about, it wasn't the drive that made him so run-down; it was the pills. He got carried away sometimes. I never knew how he might be when he showed up—but I still always wanted to go with him whenever I got the chance, no matter the condition he might've been in.

One winter day, we were driving back up to New Hampshire and he dozed off at the wheel. In the past, he'd fallen asleep for moments here and there, but he always snapped out of it just in time for it to be okay. We'd even laugh about it, and I'd joke that he needed to pick up a larger Dunkin' iced coffee on the ride down. But this time, I felt the car start doing something I had never felt a car do before—and suddenly, we were hydroplaning across five lanes of traffic on the highway.

Dad sobered up in an instant, and we both screamed at the top of our lungs. Everything felt like it was in slow motion, and yet life flashed before my eyes. He reached out his big paw over my little hand and told me in his most sincere and strong voice, "I LOVE YOU, JOANNA! IT'S GONNA BE OKAY!" As the other cars on I-95 miraculously veered out of our way, we eventually found ourselves on the other side of the highway, not too far down, on a snow-covered embankment. We looked at each other in astonishment. He hugged me and told me to "breathe, breathe, breathe" as I started hyperventilating in shock. We should not have been okay—but somehow, we were. He comforted me, and we stayed on the side of the highway for quite some time before turning on the engine and driving back out there again. People pulled over to check on us in the meantime. We thanked God.

That incident aside, my car rides with Dad were among my favorite moments with him. We'd roll down the windows and blast whatever CD he had been jamming out to most recently. He loved the Beatles, the Tubes, Chicago. "Take it eeeeeeeeaaaaas-syyy . . ." he'd wail into traffic in a smooth, rich tone. I could usually hear the smile in his voice whether he was speaking or singing. He showed me how singing into the wind produced a different sound than singing down to the floor. And when I turned my head toward him, it created another, slightly different result. I loved our weekend experiments in acoustics. We'd also listen to talk radio and hear people's takes on current events. He'd tell me the most harrowing and dramatic tales from A.A. meetings and ask me to tell him about my dreams and what songs I had become obsessed with since we saw each other last. When I had his full attention like that, I felt like I was on top of the world.

I was constantly singing with both my parents, both in and out of a car, trying to sound cool like Dad or emulate the operatic melodies Mom would practice. When I turned eleven, Mom's biological grandmother passed away and left a sum of money that would have taken Mom years to make on her own. By then, Mom's red Ford Festiva with the hole in the floor was nothing if not an accident waiting to happen, so we walked into a Toyota dealership and Mom let me pick out the model and color of her new ride. A Toyota Echo: seafoam blue, baby. It reminded me of the Santa Monica ocean that we'd dipped our toes in, dreaming of what could be if we moved there. It felt like the Echo was just the start of good things to come.

After getting a recommendation through one of her housecleaning clients, Mom met Eddie, an old rocker who had converted a church into a full-on home studio right in the center of Foxborough. She'd been looking for someone to record a demo of me singing and was willing to pay him to help us. I don't know if he ended up charging anything, but he brought in some of his musician friends to create the live tracks for me to sing over. He taught me all about how to sing into a studio mic and what a pop filter/popper-stopper was (basically, it's a mesh windscreen inserted in front of a mic that serves to reduce popping sounds, or "plosives," on *p*'s, *b*'s, and sometimes *t*'s and *k*'s). He also showed me that it's helpful while recording to take one headphone off when adding vocals one on top of the other because you can hear both what you're singing AND what you're stacking onto.

In less than a week, we were in possession of the first recordings of my voice: a CD full of soulful covers like "Superstition," "See-Saw," and "Shakey Ground" (little did I know all these titles would foreshadow the next twenty or so years of my life—ha!). My freckled face and blue eyes gleaming through my bangs were on the front of a CD cover that someone Mom had worked for had made for us. Mom gave them out to her friends at church and left them on the coffee tables of the houses she cleaned. We even brought them along with us to the WaterFire festival in Providence that took place every weekend over the summer, where I'd also randomly take my hat off, put it on the ground, and sing for passersby on the streets.

Ever since hitting my double digits, I'd been laying it on *thick* to Mom about moving away from Foxborough. She'd come back and say we could move a town or two over, but deep down, she knew that wasn't what I had in mind.

"We have this demo. Now what do we *do*, Ma?" I pushed her, knowing she wanted me to be happy, and promising that I'd take care of her—of *us*—when I became rich and famous.

She laughed and said she didn't need or want me to do that.

"Okay, but I want to! Just believe in me, Ma! Come onnnnnn. You *know* I'm good. Why can't we take a chance? I can do this!

Don't you think? It's the only thing I want in the world! If something doesn't happen in a year, I'll never ask you for anything again. I swear!!"

It was *so obvious* to me that California was the next step. After wearing her down over the course of a year, she reluctantly agreed and we headed west. My brain was fizzing with excitement over being powerful enough to create this kind of change in our lives. If you ask Mom about the move now, she'll likely tell you that she *never* wanted to go to Los Angeles. She'll say that she was at a great place in her life back then and she was just starting to get settled in Foxborough, but I wouldn't let up—that I swayed her and she just didn't know how to stand up to me, let alone anyone else. I believe her. But as a grown-up now, this bothers me. I don't want to invalidate her feelings, but I also don't think it's fair to put that much responsibility on, or power into the hands of, an eleven-year-old.

On a phone call with her great-aunt and uncle, Mom learned that one of her cousins had moved out to La Habra, California, about forty-five minutes from LA. When we first decided to move out there, Mom had expected that we would just live in a cheap motel for a while, but then this cousin got in touch with her and said we could live with him as long as we needed. It felt like a gift from above. With a stack of my black-and-white headshots and résumés, no industry connections, and the leftover money Mom had just gotten from her grandmother, Connie and Dale helped Mom pack up her brand-new car and put it on a big truck, and the two of us boarded a flight for the West Coast. I honestly couldn't believe all my pleading actually worked *THIS* well. I was even more powerful than I'd previously calculated.

As soon as we got settled, Mom enrolled me in the public elementary school in La Habra so I could finish up the rest of fifth grade. When I hoisted myself onto the school bus the first day and looked back at her waving and smiling reassuringly from the street, that familiar anxiety crept in. I wished with every bone in my body that I could just stay home and read books with Mom. But I'd wanted this. *I* was the one who begged to move out here. So I turned up the corners of my mouth to a smile and tried to be as unscared and friendly as possible toward the unfamiliar faces on the bus. Unfortunately, my new classmates were just about as welcoming as the kids back in Foxborough had been. The entire classroom erupted in laughter when I asked the home-room teacher: "Excuse me, where's the bubbla?" in my thick accent. My cheeks flaming, I scurried away to quench my thirst at the drinking fountain as my tears mixed in with the water streaming out of the tap.

Within just those first few days, the kids quickly zeroed in on what to tease me about. My accent. My chunkiness. My "rat face." My caterpillar eyebrows. My freckles. My voice, and the way I was always singing under my breath in the hallways. Being a teacher's pet. Not having the right lunch. They could probably tell that I cared a *lot*. I was fresh meat to them—and it was all fair game.

I tried to act like this new wave of bullying didn't affect me and like I had transcended it. I didn't want Mom to think the move had been in vain. But the truth was that I was dying inside. I started to feel like I would never ever belong *anywhere*. I never knew where I could sit or who I could sit with. It felt like all of my peers were whispering about me behind my back. Moving across the country and having the same shitty experience with kids my age seemed to prove that the problem wasn't anyone or anywhere else: it was me. I longed for someone to tell me how I should be, what I should do so that I could just stop being on the receiving end of all this hate. I was willing to do anything short of changing who I was—if that makes any sense. In the meantime, I counted down the days until I landed my dream role and found an escape route out of that hellhole.

Before I knew it, it was officially the 2003 pilot season. From January to April every year, the first pilot episodes of new TV shows were greenlit and cast, shot, edited, and presented to networks, and a select few of those would then be chosen to film a whole season of episodes. Hopeful actors from all over the country and the world flocked to LA for the chance to land a recurring role in one of these shows. I went out on a *lot* of auditions. I was cute and quirky and special—just like every other kid in line. Still, unlike the majority of these other kids, I somehow managed to book my first job in a Nickelodeon show called *Ned's Declassified School Survival Guide.* I was going to play the role of Lisa Zemo, a nerdy, unpopular student who was destined to one day take off her glasses and become cool (remember: this was the early 2000s, just post–*She's All That*, and all a girl on screen had to do to become beautiful was take off her outdated specs and throw in some contacts).

On the one hand, getting the part made me feel like I was good enough to land a role, but the casting also ended up further reinforcing the insecurities I had about being weird and not fitting in. I had initially auditioned for the main girl role—Ned's best friend, Moze—but the part had gone to a prettier, older girl named Lindsey Shaw. I didn't even question it; I just innately understood that she must have been better than me.

Still, I loved being on set, learning and working alongside adults. There were a number of us kids on set—it was a Nickelodeon show, after all. (And, by the way, maybe something was protecting me—maybe I dodged a bullet. I've seen the doc and listened to the podcasts and OH MY GOD.) We all had to clock in a minimum number of school hours with appointed on-set teachers. They'd even outfitted a room with desks, supplies, a computer, and a whiteboard so we could finish our schoolwork. I wasn't a big fan of this setup; I honestly hated that I had to do anything that would take me away from working.

We shot the pilot episode over the span of a few days and then went on with our lives. During pilot season, anything goes, and you have to try your hardest not to get too attached. You just never know if the network will pick up a show or not. No matter *how* good you think the pilot is or how connected you feel to it, there are a TON of factors that go into something getting green-lit, let alone becoming successful. And so I went back to public school and kept auditioning, while Mom cleaned more houses.

Around the same time, a VHS tape Mom had sent out of my singing landed me on *America's Most Talented Kids*, which was hosted by *Saved by the Bell* alum Mario Lopez. On set, some kids were dressed up like full-blown popstars or pageant winners. Meanwhile, I wore Mom's clothing—a long, sparkly skirt and shiny gold top, tucked in at the waist—which looked hilarious on my eleven-year-old body. I went out there and served vocal growls, auburn curls, and dramatic hand gestures to implore the audience to rock with me.

Moments after I performed a schmaltzy "Chain of Fools" (my go-to song that I'd pull out for competitions and performances), the lights suddenly felt hot over my head and my hands started sweating, fingers curled into tight fists like that Arthur meme. The audience was staring at me as we all waited to hear the results. Next to me onstage stood a very tall girl who was around my age and had just played a phenomenally impressive concerto on her violin. I couldn't get over how calm she seemed when I felt like I was on fire. When it came to this show, I expected to win and go to the next round. I *had* to. Period. I just couldn't live with people at school being able to call me a "loser" and knowing they were literally correct.

When Mario announced the violinist's name as the winner and the crowd roared with approval, my heart stopped beating in my chest. A fiery wave of embarrassment rose up within me as her big, beautiful—complete—family beamed with pride from the audience. I couldn't look at Mom just yet; I knew I would lose it the second we made eye contact. So I tightened up and made sure not to fall apart in front of the cameras, smiling and clapping and congratulating this towering girl, even though inside, I couldn't help but feel that her victory meant I was no longer that special.

Backstage, Mom ran up to me, keys jingling from her belt loop, wrapping me up in her arms and holding me while I sobbed, draining my tears into her soft leather jacket. She told me that it was just a drop in the bucket and had no bearing on how phenomenal I was. We somberly walked back into the hallway holding area where all the other kid competitors and their varying degrees of stage parents were. We were surrounded by families celebrating or sobbing, throwing confetti or tantrums. Mom probably knew I needed a place to cry privately, so she ushered me over to a comfortable spot where I could fully mourn my short-lived career.

In the midst of all this chaos was a sharply dressed man a little older than Mom. After we got settled, he beelined over to us and introduced himself as James Womack, the brother or cousin or something of Bobby Womack, an R&B singer whose name I recognized but wasn't super familiar with. He said that me losing was going to be a blessing in disguise.

"Those people don't know real *talent*, real *soul*," he reassured me. Thankfully, James said that *he* did. He wanted to take me and Mom around to introduce us to some people that could help us. There were stars in his eyes. He looked at me like I were a diamond in the rough—as if, with just a bit of his guidance, I could be shined up and turned into what I knew deep down I was always meant to be: a *superstar*. Someone who never needed to go back to her small town or feel embarrassed ever again.

As soon as we agreed to get onboard, James immediately started calling all the people in his social network about me. He even called up people he didn't know super well but thought might be the right fit for my voice, age, situation.

Looking back, my heart breaks a little bit when I think about how naive Mom and I both were. I was only in sixth grade. Mom had *no* experience with doing business. We just loved music in a very earnest way. Although by now she had read *Everything You Need to Know About the Music Business* over several bus rides back and forth to auditions in NYC, the industry was about to prove so much more complicated than the pages of any book could possibly convey.

Now we were on the other side of the country, the entertainment capital of the world. Mom and I only had each other, but we were partners. That's fully how I felt. Up until then, it had just been me and her against the world, almost like we were a single unit, our hearts connected by an invisible string so that we could feel what the other felt without even saying anything. We both believed something like this could happen, and now, *finally*, there was someone else who really recognized my talent, who knew this business and wanted to take us under his wings. We decided that we agreed with James—the *America's Most* loss *was* somehow meant to be since there was so much more waiting for me on the other side. This perspective shift took me from the brink of prepubescent depression to flying high on adulation and optimism within the span of an hour.

James wasted no time setting up meetings and showing Mom what he could do as a manager, but Mom was adamant that no one would ever look out for my best interests in the same way she would. So she took on the role of my manager, not necessarily because she wanted to, she said, but because it was simply the only way it could work with me being so young. She oscillated between accepting that performing was what I wanted to do more than anything and threatening to take me out of the business and make me wait until I was eighteen and could pursue a career for myself. Whenever she got scared or didn't like the way I talked back to her, this was her go-to warning. Mom always seemed stressed out, but I truly thought that with James in the middle, guiding us, some of the pressure would be taken off her, especially since he had far more experience in this world than we did.

It was immediately on and poppin'. An invisible door had somehow been swung open for us and a path cleared. James hustled up meetings with some important people, just like he'd promised; we met with a handful of record execs, and even the owners of the Sacramento Kings, the Maloofs. Every single time, I walked confidently into whatever situation was in front of me and performed. It didn't matter who it was or what they had or where we were—they were going to *feel* my presence. By the age of twelve, I had watched more than enough *VH1 Divas* performances to know how to turn on the star power and impress an audience. And I was determined to make this work.

The first time I met record producer Vincent Herbert was at a random office space that acted as a makeshift studio. He had a massive, Questlove-style afro and a robust frame that flopped around underneath an XXXL white T-shirt, baggy jeans, blindingly white sneakers (I had learned from Nelly's iconic song that they were Air Force 1s and keeping them "crispy" while stomping around in them was really fucking important). After James introduced us, he encouraged me to "go ahead and do your thing, Joanna . . ." So, on cue as always, I performed my heart out.

Vince had initially looked at me with subtle suspicion when we first walked in, but all that changed after I opened my mouth. Suddenly, his eyes were filled with warmth and intrigue. I treated that room like it was the world's stage, sliding and growling all over Stevie Wonder's "Superstition," showing off my adolescent attempt at runs, doing whatever I could to prove that I was unintimidated. When I finished my audition song, the room was silent and I felt like an alien that was being examined in a sterile lab facility. Then he ran into the hallway, joyfully proclaiming to the walls how great I was; a couple minutes later came back in with more people for me to sing for.

After another round of positive feedback, he put on a beat that rattled out of the speakers, the one he'd been messing around with when we first walked in. It was SO loud and very much the coolest thing I had ever heard. It hit *hard* with aggressive drums and these slinky synth stabs and a "pocket" that made Vince and James and the other people in the room all lose their minds and make faces like they were smelling something yucky. I didn't know music like they did, but I knew this beat FELT good. It had real energy and I could show off on it.

When Vince asked me if I liked it, I didn't hesitate for a second. Even though my childhood was mostly spent listening to Motown, MJ, show tunes, and rock 'n' roll, whatever *this* was spoke to me somewhere deep in my soul.

"Yeah, it's cool," I replied nonchalantly, leaning back in my little East Coast attitude. I could tell we were playing a game with each other, but deep down, I felt excited that he would even consider letting me sing on this beat. Vince smirked and asked if I'd ever tried writing a song.

I chuckled. "Duh, I've been writing since I was five."

"Okay, okay . . . but have you ever freestyled?" he challenged.

"Oh, I do that all the time." And I guess I did . . . on those long car rides with Dad. But who the hell did I think I was? *THAT. GIRL.*

That first day, in under an hour, we wrote a song called "Yes or No." The engineer had the beat looped so we could keep adding more to it. "Waiting for you to call, don't change the situation at all. I know that you got a girl . . . you say you still want me in ya world . . ." The lyrics were basically about some boy who was giving me the runaround at school, saying he liked me, but I wasn't quite sure. So in this song, I was asking: "Do you really like me? YES OR NO?" We laid down some vocal takes, and then the engineer "comped it together"—like magic. Up to this point, I had only ever sung full takes all the way through and didn't know that this was how the professionals did things. I learned at least half a dozen new studio terminologies and gobbled them up with a spoon. I knew I was learning from someone who *really* knew what they were doing, and I was eager to learn as much as he was willing to teach me.

Vince had come up under Rodney "Darkchild" Jerkins's tutelage through the New Jersey music scene and had experienced some success a few years prior with Destiny's Child, working on their first single "No, No, No Part 1." He had also contributed to the reworking of an Isley Brothers song for Aaliyah called "At Your Best (You Are Love)." He had a baby face, and when he nodded his head along to the music he BLASTED at full volume, he'd get so lost in the moment—so relaxed and present—that his tongue jutted forward, his mouth went limp, and his eyes closed, all melting into the song. His speaking voice was raspy, thin, and kind of high-pitched, almost as if he had a piece of food stuck in his windpipe; he spoke softly, with a lisp. He was goofy and effervescent and really kind. It was like having another kid in the room—but one who thought I was cool and awesome. We connected instantly.

Time literally flew by that day, and now, nothing else in the *world* was more important to me than creating with him and being accepted and celebrated by him. At first, I was afraid Mom might change her mind and say I couldn't make more music with Vince, that I was too young, or that we needed to move back to Massachusetts so I could focus on school. But miraculously, she liked him, too. And more than anything, she liked seeing how happy the music we made during that session made me.

We just clicked. Apparently, he was thirty-three when we met (at the time, he told us he was twenty-three, shaving a good decade off his age), but he acted like he was only a few years older than me, so I never questioned it. And the way he told stories was *thrilling.* He transmitted this palpable energy, whether he was speaking about the early tragic loss of both his parents, or how he came to work in the music industry, or his dreams for what we could do together in this "game." Honestly, I had never met anyone quite like Vince.

Vince was also the one to ask me if anyone ever called me "JoJo," which, I don't know . . . maybe *some* family members did *sometimes*? But it was mostly "Jo." Or "Boo Boo" from Dad. Anyways, he thought it would be "a dope name for me."

"But what about K-Ci and Jojo?" I asked. I liked that song "Aaaaaallllll My Liiiieeeeeiiiiifeeee" and started singing it. He assured me that it didn't matter and everyone would know the difference. So just like that, Joanna became JoJo. According to Mom, he didn't really ask her what she thought about it. And even though she wasn't super comfortable or happy with me going by a name that wasn't my own, she pushed that feeling down and got on the ride.

Now Barry Hankerson wanted to meet me. Mom and I hadn't heard of him before, but we obviously googled him and found out that he was Aaliyah's uncle. Nene had been *obsessed* with her. Just two years prior, I had walked into Nene's bedroom to find her under the covers, completely distraught at the news of the plane crash that had cut Aaliyah's life short at the young age of twenty-two. We always got so excited whenever her "Are You That Somebody" video came on Nickelodeon, and we loved watching her performance on *All That*. She was untouchably cool and out-of-this-world gorgeous, with an angelic voice beamed straight down from heaven.

Barry had started his label, Blackground Records, after taking his niece around to every record label, only to be turned down time and time again. Before that, he was a Black Panther and Gladys Knight's husband and manager (and even a costar in a bizarre 1970s action flick called *Pipe Dreams*), and he'd also managed R. Kelly and been involved in a number of various business ventures. He made something from nothing. Before we went to meet him in person, Vince gave us a bit of this backstory, and Mom and I were both so inspired and excited by the independent spirit he represented. He was a man who made things *happen*— and it felt like he could make them happen for us, too.

On the day of the meeting, a driver picked us up from Mom's cousin's place in La Habra in a nice town car. The driver was dressed in a fancy suit and flashed us a friendly smile that revealed a mouth of metallic teeth. As we drove over to Barry's, the three of us chatted about the differences between Boston, LA, and

Detroit, where he was from. He also talked a lot about how amazing Barry was and how much we'd love him, all while we drove up to the golden gates of one of the biggest homes I'd ever seen in my life. The driver let the voice on the other side of the intercom know that we had arrived, and the gate pushed back to let us in.

Gazing at the marble floors and tall ceilings, Mom and I made our way through the beautifully appointed mansion until we saw the man in the flesh. Barry was just finishing a phone call, and we had obviously caught him on the tail end of wrapping up something important. The whole scene felt like something out of a movie to me. He had an understated yet elegant physicality, a gentle but commanding presence. He spoke like a man who had seen everything and had the wisdom of several thousand years. Basically, it was giving Confucius. I instantly wanted him to teach me how to be powerful and transcendent like he was.

I sang my tried-and-true rendition of "Chain of Fools," checking off my list of impressive performance points to drive home (conviction, eye contact, runs, range) while simultaneously letting myself get lost in the lyrics. By the end, he didn't react in a way that I could read right away. There was no applause, no smile. The room was pregnant with silence. He remained quiet and staring for some time before saying anything. Inside, I felt like I was going to cry, but I knew it would be very weird if I did. The last thing I wanted him or Mom to think was that I was just a child who couldn't handle their feelings. Barry had been around some of the most amazing talents of all time, and I buzzed with anticipation, each second dragging me further and further down into an anxious spiral.

Who was I to think I could walk in here and make an impression on this man?

I blew it.

He took a long, deep breath and looked down, slowly wringing his hands. Then, softly, and with some wetness in his eyes, he said, "I just saw Babygirl over your shoulder going, 'Uncle Barry . . . she's the one.'" *Woah*. After a second of confusion, I quickly understood that he was referring to Aaliyah.

This was different from any meeting I had ever been in.

This was *beyond*.

Barry unfurled a warmth and wisdom unlike anything I'd ever experienced. He said he knew how vulnerable we were—how people out here were wolves—but he was going to treat us like family and show us the ropes of the industry. How to protect ourselves and keep our souls while navigating it all. He even told Mom that he'd take her under his wing so she could manage me without James if she wanted to. We had come to the meeting without James because Vince was the one who'd made the connection. Besides, Barry asked, "Why cut up the pie more than it needs to be, right?"

First things first, James was out and Mom was in. Barry told us he would set us up with our own place to live, and I could get started working on an album ASAP. WTF! This man was so generous and confident and cool. And he believed in me enough to put his money up. Whereas other executives we'd met with wanted me to wait a couple more years to develop as an artist before making an album, Barry was ready for me to start yesterday. I couldn't believe it. This was music to my impatient ears. Even as a preteen, I felt such a strong sense of urgency, like my career, my *life* depended on this forward motion. Barry and Vince had a specific vision for me, and this seemed like the most incredible opportunity. Even better than the Britney situation we'd passed up.

"We can't let this slip away!" I gripped on to Mom's arm on the armrest for dear life as I begged her on the car ride home.

"What if this is my last shot like this? Ma, isn't this what we came to LA for?"

Other meetings paled in comparison. There were certainly no ghostly apparitions of posthumous pop stars. Over the next couple months, we continued to meet with labels and had pleasant encounters with a handful of other executives in their corner offices. The gold and platinum plaques lining the walls seemed to be there just to signify to us that they had done big things before and could do them again. Every time I showed up and sang, people seemed like they were really into my talent but were apprehensive about getting into business with someone so young, especially one who was being managed by their completely inexperienced mother.

Vincent and Barry, on the other hand, had officially joined forces, and the full-court press was *on*. They promised us that Barry would stake his whole career and company on my success. They also warned us that if I were to sign directly to a major label, I'd end up getting lost in the shuffle, and wouldn't receive the care and development like I would at their boutique label.

All this time while we were still meeting with rival record execs, Vince was staying in touch with me (and Momma D, as he called Mom) and making sure to never let us stray too far out of his orbit. He could see I was a music/music history junkie obsessed with absorbing as much greatness as possible, so he was constantly showering me with old and new CDs to dive into. We'd dissect our favorites the next time we saw each other. This was the only homework I actually cared about now. I was expanding my musical palette and there wasn't a single moment in the day where I wasn't listening to or thinking about music. He took us around to various producers and writers, assembling his dream team for what would be my first album. At his strong suggestion, we soon stopped taking meetings with other labels, and a contract was drafted for me to sign to his production company, which was called Da Family ("because you guys are my family now. It's all about us, lil' sis. You're all that matters to me.") Da Family was a joint venture with Blackground, one that would then be distributed through Universal Records, per their agreement.

This was the moment I had been waiting for, but I definitely didn't realize at the time just how fucking terrifying it must've been for Mom. She was out there, still reeling from her childhood wounds, without a husband or partner to back her up, trying to maintain sobriety, parenting this child people were calling a prodigy, and being thrown into an entirely new city and industry far from anything she had ever known. We spoke about it recently with the luxury of hindsight, and she admitted that back then, she just pretended to know what people were talking about when it came to industry terms, deals, contracts—even if she had no clue. She thought it would protect us if she acted like she knew what was going on. But it got worse the further along we went, each new opportunity and nuance snowballing her into a storm of unknowing and overwhelm. Looking back, she wishes that she'd stopped long enough to ask someone to just slow down and explain things to her, but she was so afraid of looking stupid or feeling embarrassed. I *really* get that—the discomfort of being a beginner and wanting to resist it at all costs. But that resistance also meant that we were catapulted into a world that was completely foreign to us, essentially feeding ourselves to the wolves we'd been warned about.

Mom may not have known a lot about the industry at the time, but she was no fool. She retained a lawyer that was recommended by the author of *Everything You Need to Know About the Music Industry*. She had cold-called him, explained our situation in detail, and asked if he would represent me. Although he declined, he recommended another entertainment lawyer named

Dina Lapolt. She negotiated the contract with Da Family/Black-ground/Universal and walked us through the process where a court-appointed person would act as my "guardian ad litem." Dina explained that the deal would be ratified by the state of New York and that said guardian would stake their name on confirming that the contents of the agreement were fair and that I was being looked after and treated as a child should be. Meanwhile, she'd be there to guide us and tell us whether this was a good deal or not, as Mom had virtually no experience as to what a good deal might look like. Dina assured us that this was the best-case scenario for someone like me.

Before I knew it, I was signing on the dotted line, my little twelve-year-old trying-to-be-perfect cursive: "Joanna Noelle Levesque pka JoJo." Mom signed her name underneath mine. As we walked out of the office, the sun setting on life-as-we-knew-it, we literally skipped hand in hand down Sunset Blvd., singing the New Radicals' "You Get What You Give" at the top of our lungs: "You've got the music in you . . . don't give up, you've got a reason to live . . . can't forget, we only get what we give!"

CHAPTER 4

MEDIA TRAINING

FOR THE SECOND TIME IN TEN MONTHS, WE MOVED BACK ACROSS THE COUNTRY TO Edgewater, New Jersey, right along the Hudson River and across from New York City. Mom did question why we had to move so far again, especially when Blackground had offices in both New York and California. Our family in Massachusetts joked that we were getting shipped off to "the armpit of America." But I was optimistic and down for a change.

It felt like I was learning something new about a different culture or religion or lifestyle every day. For example, I don't think I had ever been around a Muslim person until Barry. He always had the Fruit of Islam (the security wing of the Nation of Islam) present in the studio and sometimes guarding me or driving a car he'd send over to take us to the studio (if, for some reason, we didn't take the ferry). These men were impeccably dressed and had an air of untouchable sophistication—respectful and deeply professional. "The Nation" was a big part of Barry's life, as we quickly discovered. He was close friends with Minister Louis

Farrakhan and would apparently host NOI meetings at his home or in the Blackground offices. After watching videos of Mr. Farrakhan, I could see the resemblance between him and Barry, not only in their physicality but in the way they both spoke with undeniable charisma and unwavering conviction.

I didn't even know there could be so many discussions surrounding race, but now it was constant. Blackground was a Black-owned, Black-operated record company, and I thought that was awesome. It was inspiring how Barry had defied the odds, and I loved that I now had an opportunity to be a part of his legacy. When I was younger, I used to say if I couldn't be a singer then I wanted to be a civil rights attorney. Aligning with the underdog and standing up for equality just felt right. He impressed upon us time and time again how special it was that I was white but was still able to sing the way I sang. He brought up the idea of the "Great White Hope" that we'd seen throughout music history, and he told me I was walking in the footsteps of performers like Elvis and Justin Timberlake. Barry also said that it was a fine line I had to walk—knowing that I'm clearly white but "sing Black." It was a dose of cognitive dissonance as he encouraged me to not feel too bad about embracing the privileges that came with that. Like Mom, I pretended to understand, but obviously I couldn't. Mind you, this was at a time when most liberal white folks claimed they didn't or couldn't "see" race, so all these frank conversations about history and race and my place within it all, while a bit confusing, were quite an education. I took to it like the teacher's pet that I was.

While Barry focused on what I represented, Vince seemed more obsessed with making sure I looked fresh. It was the height of the 2000s, which meant colorful Juicy Couture sweatsuits with Swarovski crystals on the butt and a new pair of blindingly white AF1s every week. He threw them straight in the trash after they started to get marked up or creased even a little bit. Mom was appalled at the wastefulness. She shook her head and wore the disturbance on her face at the sheer thought of throwing away perfectly good sneakers when there were so many people who needed shoes to wear. But I was in *awe*. To be able to do that must mean you don't worry about money, which must mean you're successful. Vince also hooked me up with a stylist and a choreographer, and Universal got me a media trainer. After school, Mom and I would make our way into the city on the ferry and walk a few miles to the Universal Building, where we'd take the elevator up to the top floor and I'd go into a small office and learn how to conduct myself, how to make people like me. This was perfect because I had been trying to figure that one out since first grade.

The media trainer was tasked with teaching me how to sound charming in sound bites and anticipate how I might deal with certain questions so that I wouldn't accidentally offend anyone. Essentially, I was learning how to sell a product (myself!) to the widest possible audience. She would always call out whenever I was fidgety or tapping my foot, or using *likes* and *ums* and veering off topic. She explained that what I was actually listening to or inspired by back then wasn't mainstream or well-known enough for me to be relatable. Inspired by the conversations I was having at Blackground, I'd been reading *The Autobiography of Malcolm X* and getting even deeper into my favorite album, *Voodoo* by D'Angelo. The teen magazines, she warned, wouldn't "get it"—nor would they print it. And the goal was to make me the most easily acceptable version of myself. Not changing who I was, she stressed, just polishing it up for the world to see and connect with. So we spent a lot of time coming up with more on-trend and digestible answers. I had learned years before that, in entertainment, the truth doesn't always matter. It never quite sat right in my system, and was fully against what Mom had taught me, but I took to this training naturally, and it wasn't long before I felt like I was passing fake interview tests with flying colors. I wanted to excel, always. To understand and be good at what people I liked set before me. For them to find me exceptional and beyond my years.

After killing it at media training, we'd head over to the studio and I'd learn whatever song Vince and his crew had been working on for me that day. Mom told me she was uncomfortable with the subject matter of some songs, but I didn't care. Looking back on the lyrics of "Breezy" now . . . yeah, we had *no idea* what was going on there:

That's big pimpin', but you wouldn't listen,
He's mine, not yours, better fall back.
I get shoppin' sprees off the heezy.
I get dough to blow, please believe me.
You don't want the one on one take it easy.
You're just the jump-off. I'm his breezy."

I mean, today, I could translate this into Victorian English, but at the time, it read like a foreign language. Sure, Dad had once taken me shopping at Limited Too after getting a big check from a workplace injury settlement, but I didn't think it was "off the heezy." Regardless, I was not about to let Mom embarrass me in front of Vince or get in the way of this flow. I rolled my eyes in the way only a twelve-year-old can and begged her to chill. Even though the vernacular I was singing was mostly unfamiliar to me, Vince held my hand as he showed me the lay of this new landscape.

Sometimes I wondered if it mattered that the lyrics of songs like "Homeboy" (*"My homie since knee-high, we came up on the southside where ya had to beat the streetlights home. We got into some street fights but the next day we'd be right back at it . . ."*)

didn't resemble my real life in the slightest. Sure, I had grown up poor but not on the "Southside," and I *definitely* had never been in a street fight. But then again, whenever I sang other people's songs like "Shaky Ground" or "The House that Jack Built," I hadn't known the same pain they sang about either—I just channeled my own feelings into the song. Mom had her reservations about this disconnect, but I just didn't want the train to stop.

Instead, I wrote my own songs and put my actual twelve-year-old thoughts onto the page. Like, "Keep on Keepin' On." I'd gotten a CD of beats from a producer I was working with and played my favorite track nonstop on a Walkman disc player as I paced around our apartment complex. I wanted to encourage other kids who had felt like me. Bullied, not having a whole lot, feeling like too much and not enough.

"You got to keep on keepin on . . . you got to keep your head up high you got to work with what you've got, and someday you will fly."

Within a couple hours of singing out melodies and writing down poetry into one of my school notebooks, I had a song. I ran inside to sing it to Mom. She held me and cried. She really believed in me as a songwriter. So, she fought for that song to be a contender for the album. But I soon started to understand that what was most expected of me from the label was to focus on the bigger picture they had in mind.

I was going to public school in Bergen County, NJ, and recording at night and on the weekends at Sony Studios in Hell's Kitchen on Fifty-Fourth and Tenth. Sure, I came in once again as "the new girl," but now, I was the new girl *with a record deal.* That meant something to at least *some* of the kids there. There were also a lot of music industry people living in that area and commuting into the city. One boy was Mario Winans's stepson;

another was Gerald Levert's son, LeMicah. The first would end up being my boyfriend for a few weeks, and the second would end up being one of my best friends for life.

Now, in sixth grade, I was often the racial minority in the room and yet fully comfortable stepping into spaces where I was the "token." After growing up in Foxborough, a town as white as snow, I was now living in the melting pot of the world, experiencing Cuban and Puerto Rican food for the first time, recording my first album right next to the hip-hop music that would take over the radio. I'd be in the studio, and in the next room would be G-Unit or Dipset (aka the Diplomats). All the kids in my school were *GASSED*. In some ways, I was relieved that I wasn't getting bullied anymore, but I also felt a little resentful and developed another level of distance from my peers, assuming the only reason they liked me was because of my new connections. Other kids aside, it felt impossible to stay focused on schoolwork, and Mom didn't like that I was putting less and less effort into it. But the way I saw it? I was already living my *dream*. What the hell did I need school for? I was *in* a career already. Wasn't that what people went to school to get?

During the summer break after I graduated elementary school, Mom and I were flown back to LA to work with some producers out there. One of the sessions was with two Danish hitmakers named Soulshock and Karlin, who Barry felt had a song for me. These were the same guys who'd made R&B classics for Toni Braxton, Monica, and my ultimate vocal goddess, Whitney Houston—so I was more than happy to meet with them.

The song Barry wanted me to cut was called "Leave (Get Out)." After listening to the demo, I didn't get it. Neither did Mom. The song sounded a bit formulaic and low-key, void of the edgier sound we'd been making in New York. How would this song even fit on the album, which was fully centered around R&B and hip-hop? I asked Vince what he thought, and he said he really liked it and knew I could kill it. Both he and Barry seemed like they really wanted to hear me on it, so I decided they knew best, bottled up my opinion, and went in there to record it.

While I got settled in the sound booth, fitting the headphones' velvet covers over my ears, Karlin came out from the other side of the studio glass to adjust my mic. He smelled like cigarettes and pepperoni and spoke shortly to me with his thick accent; it's possible he was not particularly enthused that some random preteen was going to be cutting this song that he felt had hit potential. We started with the chorus and then worked our way backward to the verses and bridge. These producers in LA had a particular way of cutting vocals that was different from the ways I'd worked in the past. They would have me sing the song down once or twice, and then sing it in pieces, and then sing line by line over and over and over again. Then they would take the best lines or words or syllables and Frankenstein it all together in whatever way they deemed best for the song. It was kind of irritating to be in the studio singing for up to ten hours at a time working on a single track—was this normal?—but I quickly adapted and accepted it as the way things were done in the big leagues.

Though I initially wasn't too hot on the song, it started to grow on me the more I sang it. It had energy and angst, which I appreciated and somehow resonated with, even though the subject matter was much more suited for someone who had actually been in a relationship before. But I'd never wanted to be young, anyways. We spent the day getting my delivery right: pop-y and punchy. Memorable. I also learned how to use what they called "vocal fry" at the beginning of words for added effect.

After working together for a while, it seemed like the Scandinavian had softened a little and was starting to like what he heard.

He ran back into the booth to show me his ideas for the finishing touches.

"So I want you to try screaming these words in between the lines in the chorus . . . like:

"Get out (LEAVE!!!!) right now.
It's the end of you and me.
It's too late (NOW!!!!)
And I can't wait for you to be gone.
'Cause I know about her (LOSER!!!!!!!!)
And I wonder (WHY????????) how I bought all the lies.
You said that you would treat me right,
But you were just a waste of time (WASTE OF TIME!!!!!)"

I couldn't help giggling because his accent was funny and I loved how excited he was. It felt wrong yelling like that—Mom had always warned me not to yell because I could ruin my voice—but it felt kinda fun to freak out and play a different character. After we finished recording for the day, Mom and I left the studio, not giving it a second thought.

That trip, we were staying at Le Montrose Hotel off Sunset Blvd., which was within walking distance of the spot where I had just signed my first recording contract. It was also close to the *Hustler* building. Every day, Mom and I would cover our faces and pretend not to look at the strap-ons and ball gags in the window as we walked by on our way to get Diet Snapples and sandwiches down the street. It wasn't the first time we'd avoided the topic of sex around each other. There was a time when she worked the front desk at a video store back in Massachusetts, and I'd go there after school, only to wade my way through the dirty movie section with all the posters and freaky covers whenever I needed to use the bathroom. I'd also noticed Dad's stash of frisky magazines that he kept hidden in a closet in his apartment. Safe to say, from early on, I was aware of and curious about sex—and it seemed increasingly unavoidable.

Around this time, Vincent was taking us around to a bunch of studios scattered throughout the sprawling city: Larrabee on Doheny, the Edmonds building on Cahuenga, and a couple home studios tucked in the Valley. One of my favorite studios to work out of was the Edmonds building because that's where The Underdogs were. The Underdogs were a production and songwriting collective that included Harvey Mason Jr., Damon Thomas, Eric Dawkins, and Antonio Dixon, and they also had up-and-coming songwriters like James Fauntleroy as a part of their constantly rotating and expanding mix of creatives. There was a gym in one of their studio rooms, and they would often work out there, eat there, party there, and make music there. It was basically a one-stop shop once you walked out onto the fourth floor of that building.

Back in the early 2000s, The Underdogs had been having a lot of success with B2K and Tyrese, and I couldn't *believe* that I would get to work on tracks they'd created for me. After I sang a couple covers, freestyled over a beat with Vincent, and generally proved myself worthy to them, they played us a song that they had just finished that they thought I would sound great on.

"Never Say Goodbye" was a gorgeous, heartfelt ballad about falling in love for the first time. It was so tender and soulful yet simultaneously very sweet. I loved it right away and couldn't wait to show off on it. But over the next week or so of working there, The Underdogs patiently taught me how to create a compelling vocal performance that built up over the course of the track, one that didn't give away every single trick I had right off the bat.

They told me to focus on tone and intention, and they gave me different ways of phrasing things than I was used to. This methodology was all very intentional and deliberate, and it ultimately helped to create a certain feeling that would better support the lyrics and melody.

To start off a recording, Eric would lay down a reference of how he thought a particular section should be delivered and then I would go into the booth to replicate it in my own way. I could memorize a song in a matter of minutes and figure out what kind of harmonies would work best with it pretty naturally. But training my brain to hear some of the harmonic landscapes these guys had in store for me took me to a whole other level. I hadn't had more than a handful of random vocal lessons here and there, nor did I play an instrument proficiently. Until then, my lack of formal training had been a source of pride for me, like I didn't need those things to be "good enough." But now, surrounded by men I considered to be musical geniuses, I wished that I had stuck with piano and could understand more of the musical shorthand language they spoke.

Being in that studio was a master class in music production and vocal technique. The next song we did was the more up-tempo Caribbean music–inspired track called "Baby, It's You." We talked about who might be a good rap feature on it, and I blurted out: "Oh my God, BOW WOW!" before turning bright red when all the guys around me erupted in good-natured laughter. He was my and Nene's shared crush at the time, but she'd graciously given me her blessing to "go for it" if I ever met him in person. I had daydreams of us falling in love and being on the cover of *Teen People* magazine as the new "it couple." It didn't matter that he was sixteen and I was only twelve. Not to me!

There were so many talented people coming in and out of the studio, I felt like I was in a dream. I got to meet Tank, my labelmate at Blackground, who seemed larger than life with his tattooed arms, big personality, and even bigger talent. It felt like everybody at the studio really loved each other and that making music could be the most fun thing on the planet. These people took me under their wing like a little sister and were super respectful of "Momma D." It really felt like we were one big family, with Vince as my favorite big brother and ultimate protector.

That LA trip ended up being a big success and yielded a lot of songs that Blackground and Universal were excited about. While on the West Coast, I also did my first big photo shoot. Barry thought it'd be cool for me to be featured on an electronic scooter. Apparently, I had places to be. Even though I felt a little stupid trying to look tough on this metallic scooter, he had done such iconic things with Aaliyah that I trusted he'd make me look good, so I rolled with it.

The photographer also wanted me to hold dogs on a leash *while* riding the scooter. One of my Nana's beloved Dobermans had bit me in the face when I was five, but thankfully, I was *almost* over my intense fear of dogs when this photo shoot came around. The ones the photographer had me holding on a leash were velvety Shar-Peis, dogs that seemed much more roly-poly and simple than vicious. I couldn't help but wonder if they had me shooting with this breed because they thought *I* looked like a Shar-Pei. These were the things that started to cross my mind. There was a reason for *everything* with Barry. An agenda or meaning behind every single word, detail, outfit, person at the office or on set.

When I went over to look at some of the shots of myself on the camera monitor, I saw an alien looking back at me. Oh my GOD. Was my forehead really *that* big? My nose *that* crooked and wide? My lips *that* small? I had never really seen myself like this before. It was like a twisted exaggeration of what the mirror reflected.

And if people were seeing what I saw, why were they lying and saying I looked great? Mom was always deflecting compliments, shrugging them off and saying she wasn't as beautiful as the women she would be competing with for single men in big cities like NY and LA. So if by her standards *she* wasn't even pretty or skinny enough for a man's affection, then how could I ever be attractive enough that boys would want to put a poster of me in their locker or above their bed? She always told me when she thought I looked nice, and she'd stress that talent was the most important gift to bring to the table. But I was realizing more and more how often people said one thing out loud and thought another inside—myself included. I was reluctant to share any of these thoughts too loudly, but in that moment, these photographs seemed to confirm my fears that I would never look the part.

The spiral was quick and rapturous. I went back to our hotel room and climbed into the bathroom sink, my bare feet flat against the empty basin, looking in the mirror, and started digging into my skin with Mom's tweezers. Anxiety expanding with every breath, I couldn't stop picking and squeezing the bumps on my skin until I bled, working all the undesirableness out of my pores.

CHAPTER 5

"LEAVE (GET OUT)"

IN EARLY SPRING OF 2003, NICKELODEON HAD COME BACK AROUND AND TOLD US THAT *Ned's Declassified School Survival Guide* had been picked up. They were excited to hear that I'd been working on an album and apparently wanted to expand my character—maybe even have her sing on the show. Initially, Mom and I were scheduled to meet with them by ourselves, but Barry said he thought it would be best if he were there, too, so we could all be on the same page, especially since music could potentially be involved (and anything involving my recorded singing voice now legally belonged to Barry). When it came time for the meeting, Barry sauntered into the boardroom with no fewer than half a dozen of his associates we hadn't met before (I can't remember if that included the Fruit of Islam or not), and they all sat around the table with sunglasses on and serious expressions. Mom barely got a word in, as Barry totally took over, warning Nickelodeon that he wasn't going to let his artist be taken advantage of and that *he* would let them know what our terms were.

Mom was frozen in her seat. She knew Barry had far more experience than she did in the entertainment world, but I think she was embarrassed about the way he undermined her in front of these Nickelodeon folks who she'd been dealing with the past couple years. After the meeting, we stood outside while Barry convinced us that being a part of that show, for what they were offering me and what the time commitment would actually be—well, it just wouldn't make sense. I trusted that Barry knew what he was talking about. That this wasn't right for me, and he wasn't about to let some big corporation get over on us. So we walked away.

Back in New Jersey, there were talks of putting out a first single. We started spending more than half the week at Universal, meeting with different departments and playing them music as we made it. Vince was an expert at creating hype, blasting my music in a conference room so loud that it would seep through the walls and into corridors, where people would ask, "Who is THAT?" Then they'd peek in to see little me, bopping my head, eyes closed like Vince, swimming in my Celtics throwback jersey dress and AF 1s. Vince made sure that whenever we walked in there, we looked cool, trendy, and on-brand—that our presence was felt every time we stepped into a room. And my new publicist, Phylicia. She was just as hungry and new to the industry as I was. We both had things to prove. She worked tirelessly to come up with a plan to highlight my strengths and capitalize on my potential, marketing me as Universal's new teen icon with a fresh voice and an even fresher persona, one that could straddle the line between R&B and pop.

I remember coming home from school one afternoon, dropping my backpack by the door, and Mom telling me the label wanted to go with "Leave (Get Out)" as my first single. I'd completely forgotten about the song after I recorded it, and honestly the choice felt totally out of left field. I had gotten comfortable inhabiting this whole world of R&B and to me, this song was on some Disney Channel shit. I was confused as to what they were trying to do here.

I cried. Then Mom cried, too. She didn't like the song at all and thought it might jeopardize people ever taking me seriously. We called Vincent and Barry on speakerphone and pushed back, asking, "What about 'Baby, It's You'? Everybody *loves* that one, and it always gets an amazing reaction! Who actually *LIKES* 'Leave (Get Out)'?" Barry explained that taking a more urban-leaning song to radio for my first single would be too hard, but with "Leave," we could hit multiple radio formats and *then* follow up with "Baby, It's You." Vince sold us on trusting the process, that this was the right introduction "into the marketplace." Mom thought we should stand strong and fight for the songs we really loved. I could tell she was rattled when I was so quick to cave in. Pissed off. But I didn't want to go against Vince and Barry, so I took their side. "Joanna, what the hell? United we stand divided we fall," she said after she had told me how angry she was that I hadn't acted like we were a team. Sure, I wallowed in internal turmoil and confusion for a few weeks, but since I had absolutely no reference for any of this shit, I decided my feeling discomfort wasn't as important as trusting my new musical family—who'd had success in this very arena several times before—to guide my career in the right direction.

After months and months of Blackground and all the departments at Universal working together behind the scenes, "Leave" seemingly flew up to the top of the Top 40 & Rhythm charts. Little did I know then that when they first sent out my song to the radio stations, they hadn't included a picture of me on the front of the disc (probably because they wanted listeners to assume whatever they wanted about my age or my race without it being a hindrance or a barrier).

But if they'd had any reservations about sending out those discs, the execs had zero when it came time to send me out to visit and perform for what felt like every pop and rhythm radio station in America. Flanked by a rep from Universal, Mom, Eli (an indie rep that Barry had brought onboard), and a marketing person for Blackground, I sang live in sterile radio offices: a little verse/chorus snippet of "Leave" at the pop stations and then my cover of SWV's "Weak" at the more "urban"-leaning stations. We must have hit at least fifteen different cities around the country in only three weeks, with the goal of getting them to add the record to their rotations. First, it would be programmed to play at an undesirable time slot when their audience wasn't most active, and then it might be positioned against another new song in a "battle of the bops" type of thing. After getting good feedback, it would be moved up to prime time—mornings and afternoons—before, hopefully, being played all throughout the damn day. Nonstop. Ad nauseum. *This* was how hits were made.

Phylicia got me appearances on *Total Request Live* (TRL), and my stylist, Crystyle, immediately started working on custom looks for me to wear. She'd cut up Celtics jerseys or dress me up in a pink denim jumpsuit adorned with patches, and there were cute nods to my New England roots. Now, whenever I went on TV shows or had live appearances, I got my hair and makeup done by professionals. I'd catch myself in the mirror, and I didn't see a thirteen-year-old girl anymore; I saw an eighteen-year-old pop-star. And that's *exactly* what I hoped other people would see, too.

Behind the scenes, when photographers, interviewers, or other artists asked how old I was, I'd respond coyly, "Well, how old do you *think* I am?" People usually guessed sixteen or seventeen, and I was more than happy to send mixed messages. Being perceived as a grown-up meant I could be peers with the people I already preferred being around: adults. I had felt inconvenienced by my youth for so long, looking up at the adult world I wanted to be a part of. And now, here I was.

People were starting to pay attention and compliment me on my talent and original music, and yet whenever I went to shoots or industry events, I felt just as ostracized as when I was in elementary school. Once again, it seemed like no one wanted to sit with me. Everyone for the most part was polite and kind, but what seventeen- to twenty-one-year-old *wants* to hang out with a thirteen-year-old? It doesn't really matter how mature that thirteen-year-old is—or thinks herself to be. She's still thirteen.

I remember when *Teen People* invited me to be in an editorial where I shot with another new artist, eighteen-year-old Ciara. She was tall and slim and stunning. Her song "Goodies" was burning up the charts and ushering in a whole new style of music they were calling "Crunk 'n' B." Standing next to her on set as the lights got brighter and the photographer yelled out how great we both looked, I felt stumpy and stupid and infantile. Every time the camera flashed, she was *serving*. Honestly, all I could do was try to keep smiling with my hand on my hip, changing my angles up every now and then to give the photographer as many options as possible—and make it through the day without crying.

Simultaneously, I felt higher than I'd ever felt in my whole existence. I couldn't get enough. Performing live was an exhilarating, out-of-body experience, and singing my own new music felt different than churning out the soul/blues/rock 'n' roll covers I would perform accompanied by a karaoke track. Now I had dancers and staging and little moves I was doing in addition to my vocal stylings. Rehearsals at gritty industrial studios in New York City with Laurianne Gibson, my choreographer, were often punctuated by her emphatic yelling and kooky catchphrases like "*Yasssssssss* kitten, drink the *miiiiiiiilk!*" I was no dancer, but she made me feel like I was "a muthafuckin superstar" and taught me how to perform into the mirror, evoking my "eye of the tiger," using the entire length and depth of the room, playing on my strength of making eye contact, being intentional with every movement.

Hours upon hours, day after day, I would rehearse with a dance troop called the Amount Boyz, who Laurianne had hired to back me up onstage. They were all in their late teens and early twenties, yet they were just a few inches taller than me, so it looked like a good fit. I had little crushes on two of them, but they obviously paid me no mind whatsoever other than being friendly and professional.

See, I had not been kissed yet and I was *desperate* to change that. New York City offered such a wide assortment of cute boys to be crazy about. They were everywhere. Playing basketball in the parks. On bicycles whizzing past me. On the ferry Mom and I took from Edgewater every day. They were always in motion, glistening and unavailable. And I was thirteen, with hormones flying into high gear.

When it came time to shoot my first music video—for "Leave (Get Out)"—Mom, Vince, and the whole Blackground/Universal crew all accompanied me to LA. It was so exciting; custom looks were being tailored perfectly to my measurements, hair and makeup choices were being discussed, young adults who looked like teenagers were being cast to play my friends and love interest. I even got to be on the choosing side for casting, which felt like my own version of payback for all the times I was on the "pick me!" end of a commercial or musical theater audition. We saw dozens of candidates in person and reviewed even more headshots, and from there, we put together a cute group of girls to play my squad. I hoped they would genuinely like me.

Picking out a boy to interact with had me *so* giddy. A gaggle of Aaron Carter lookalikes walked in and out of the stark audition room, and it wasn't that I wasn't attracted to them, it's just that none of them rang true for me. I wanted to cast someone who looked like Lil' Bow Wow but got clear resistance from my team, who wasn't sure how the audience would react. Let's say 2004 was . . . different from today. Having people who looked different from me was important because it reflected my reality, though. So I pushed back, and eventually, they agreed to me casting this cute, sweet, young Latino guy.

The high school we'd be shooting at loomed intimidatingly on top of a hill, revealing itself slowly as we drove up early in the morning. Even though I was only in middle school at the time, the vision that director Erik White went with for the music video boosted me up to high school, bolstered by bright colors and quick edits. I shimmied and interacted with the camera as if it was the boy who had "gone behind my back and called my friend," just like the lyrics said. Every ounce of attitude I had, I channeled into that shoot. But in reality, I felt those new-girl-on-the-first-day-of-school nerves again, even though I *knew* that all the people I saw scattered on the lawn, in movie trailers, and being transported from base camp in buses were there for me.

Most of all, I remember the lights, the blinding brightness of the lights on set—some tall as streetlamps and strong as the sun—and being told to stare directly into them because it looked cool on camera and made my eye color pop. I did anything and everything they asked; there was nothing I wouldn't do and no amount of takes that were too many. Comfort was secondary, as I'd figured out years prior. It takes pain and perseverance to be a star.

The most bizarre thing about being the star on set this time around was that people wouldn't stop asking me what I wanted. "Are you okay? Do you need a water? A straw? A snack? Do you want this chair to sit down on? Do you want me to stand here and hold this portable fan on your face and spritz you with water while you take a moment to breathe?" This was the flip side of popstar discomfort: never having to do the little things yourself. It felt kind of weird and fake to have all these people fawning over me, literally running to take care of my every desire, telling me how incredible I was. I won't lie; I didn't *hate* it. But Mom was visibly uncomfortable and recoiling.

Even though I wanted the other people on set to like me, I also really wanted to make sure Mom was okay, that she still loved me and thought everything was going well. She seemed upset a lot in those days; I felt a growing confusion and tension radiating off her, and she could shift from warm and present to closed off in a matter of seconds. I didn't know how to take it. Whenever her mood dropped, I instinctively thought that it was my fault and I must've done something to prompt this change, and I would ruminate on ways that I could bring back the version of Mom that was so loving, amazing, and playful.

Mom wasn't the biggest worry on my mind at the shoot, though. It was taking too long for me to get boobs. I was impatient. My first music video was about to immortalize me in time forever, and my flat chest was yet *another* thing that revealed my true age to the world without me even saying a word. In my stylist's kit, she had these things she called "chicken cutlets," which could be adhered to the chest to create more oomph. I convinced her to let me stuff my bra with them and quickly went from being a virtual pancake in my initial red-and-white leotard and jean combo to all-out busty by the final look in my "Boys Stink" tank top and skirt.

During the whole shoot, Barry sat low in a director's chair, watching every take through dark sunglasses, giving his opinion to Erik while giving me a thumbs-up, flashing a big smile, and then going back to having seemingly serious discussions. I was so curious about what the men were talking about. Did they still feel I was worth all the time and money they were spending on me? Obviously, I had no idea about budgets at the time. But there was no *way* this video was cheap. Videos cost money to make, right?

As anxious as I felt, Vincent and Laurianne were the ultimate cheerleaders. LG, as Vince called her, pulled me aside after the second-to-last take of a performance setup and gave me the pep talk of a lifetime. She doubled down on what she saw in me: the eye of the tiger, a superstar quality that was truly rare. She was absolutely beaming with belief in me, and I wanted nothing more than to keep making her proud. By the end of the sixteen-hour shoot, I had no concept of how this video would turn out, what an edit would do to the setups we shot, or if I was even pulling off looking like a cool high schooler. I was excited and running on pure adrenaline, but deep down, I felt a bit like an imposter. Because I was.

When I performed "Leave" on *TRL* for the first time, I thought about all the kids from Foxborough and La Habra who would be glued to their TVs watching me. *GAGGED.* "Damn it, I really should've been nicer to her . . ." I imagined them thinking. Well, eat your fucking hearts out, assholes. I'm looking down from Times Square, waving at my *fans* who have come from far and wide, holding up signs bearing my new moniker, screaming at the top of their lungs trying to get me to look in their direction. And what were all those girls back home doing now? Sucking dick in the back of a beat-up Ford Focus in the St. Mary's parking lot? I heard all kinds of rumors about the kids who'd made my life hell back in Massachusetts, and it was SO satisfying to think of the distance between where they were and where I was in that moment.

Not long after premiering the video and performing on *TRL*, I became somewhat of a staple at that studio. People were loving this damn song, and it was steadily rising in the *Total Request*

Live's Top 10 every day. I genuinely enjoyed interacting with my new fans—many of them older, prettier, more stylish than me. Sometimes I couldn't believe how embracing of me they were. They thought *I* was cool?! It was a nonstop avalanche of validation, burying my self-consciousness from all angles.

I still felt like the "other," but at least this version of me was kinda famous.

CHAPTER 6

HIGHER & HIGHER

IN THE LATE SPRING OF 2004, AN OPPORTUNITY CAME THROUGH FOR ME TO OPEN FOR THE one and only USHER on the European leg of his Truth Tour, which followed up on the success of his fourth studio album, *Confessions*. This record was taking the world by storm, with hits like "Yeah!" and "Burn" rocketing up the charts, and news of a messy cheating scandal was adding even more heat to his fire in the media. Usher had started out super young like me, but he'd reinvented and sustained himself, and now, he was at the very top of his game.

I'm still not sure who exactly reached out to whom when it came to me getting the chance to join that tour. Barry was so deep in and invested by this point that I honestly believe he would've paid whatever was needed to ensure I was an international success. "By any means necessary," he'd smile and say, quoting Malcolm X, one of his heroes. I had never felt anything but neutral about the color of my skin, but through Barry and my proximity to the Nation of Islam I was now starting to discern that for some people, my whiteness reminded them of injustice and oppression. Of colonialism and inhumanity. I felt a deep sense of guilt. Wait, so *is* this okay for me to be doing? Barry and Vince assured me it was. As a white girl who performed what could be called both pop and R&B, the opportunity to open for a hugely successful, genre-crossing chart topping and iconic artist made me feel incredibly lucky. Validated. Embraced. "Invited to the cookout," as Vince said.

This leg of the tour overlapped with the end of my school year and finally allowed me to achieve my ultimate dream: dropping out of school for work. *Kinda.* Mom had begged the principal and superintendent to let me stay enrolled at Leonia Middle School, but they had a very strict policy about no student being out of the classroom for more than a certain number of days each year. She seemed heartbroken; I was on cloud nine. It was suggested to her that a traveling teacher named Stephanie could come on the road with us and teach me all the subjects I would've been learning in regular school through a private distance learning program called Laurel Springs. Mom agreed to this compromise. She would mail off my schoolwork to be graded to a PO box in Ojai, California, and I could still transfer the credits back to a regular school if need be after the tour ended. Most importantly, I would still be on track to graduate high school with a diploma and able to go to college if I wanted.

So my traveling teacher Stephanie met us at the airport one day, looking like she could've been Marilyn Manson's next ex-girlfriend. She had long, jet-black hair with bangs that fell just above her long eyelashes, full lips, and a slim, curvy body that she loved showing off in rock 'n' roll T-shirts and low-rise pants. She was single and you could *tell*, just by looking at her. She absolutely loved attention, particularly from men. This woman was a *trip*. Mom quickly regretted introducing her to me as I latched onto this new character like a newborn on a nipple.

Our first few stops on the tour were in Germany. For the opening act, it was just me, a DJ, and four Amount Boyz dancers onstage. At the time, "Leave" was just starting to get some traction outside of America—it wasn't nearly the success overseas that it was in the States—so I was a tiny stranger to most of the people in that audience. And these crowds were *massive*. These were by far the biggest stages I'd ever performed on, even though I had just a bitty sliver of the stage, sectioned off by a black curtain, in comparison to the space and spectacle of Usher's set.

As new as I was, it felt natural for me to go out there and be blinded by the lights, only able to see a few faces staring up at me from the audience. I decided it was better that way. I always tried my hardest to make and keep eye contact with the people I saw, like Laurianne had taught me. To "pafooorrrrrrrmmmmmmm" no matter what, to fake it until I made it—even and especially when things went wrong. It was my superpower to be able to push through no matter what. Whenever I couldn't hear myself (which I often couldn't), or sounded flat, or tripped onstage, I internally yelled at myself to keep going. To feel the fear and channel it. To never let "them" get into my head and win. Night after night, I'd perform a handful of songs, attempt to work the crowd, and then watch the headliner as I ate as many European snacks as I could carry from backstage.

Before I headed out on tour, Vincent had advised me that I should always watch other artists, especially those who were more successful than me and had more years under their belts, to see what I could learn from them. Usher seemed to know every aspect of his songs inside and out. It seemed like even tracks from the new album were embedded in his bone marrow. He would accent beats in the track or additions from the band with his dance moves that I didn't notice at first. The cleanliness of the lines he made with his arms, the isolation of different parts of his body from his neck side to side to his torso, pelvis, feet—he was in full control. He'd kick his mic stand to the floor, and it would defy gravity, springing back up to meet him again like it, too, was a fan who couldn't get enough. He let the sweat drip off his face in buckets, but it wasn't gross—it was *awesome*. No matter how hard he was working, he'd always play it cooler than cool. And he had his own version of MJ's famous moonwalk, one I tried so many times but could never quite figure out. I always had the best seats in the venue, right at the front of house where his sound engineers mixed or on the side of the stage where the crew was. Every night was another two-hour master class in how to own the stage as a true superstar.

After we went through a few cities, I got pushier about meeting Usher in person. After all, I still hadn't even talked to the man yet! Just like on the music video set, I realized by that point that I could say things I wanted and then someone would somehow magically make them happen. After the crew got the hint, they arranged for me to slip into one of his meet-and-greets and spend a few minutes with him.

When I finally met him, he was incandescent. A superstar in all his glory. I was spellbound. The man spoke like he sang, melodically and perfectly. I could barely form words, but I'm pretty sure the only ones that found their way out of my mouth were nonsensical. Here I was, officially out of my depth. Not only was this a massive music superstar that I idolized; he was also really, really, *really* hot—and this combination was just too much for my thirteen-year-old heart to handle. I never saw him again on that tour except for on the stage. But I knew that he started out really young as well, and during our short interaction I felt like perhaps he—more than most—knew what I might be going through.

The next night, we performed in France, and I got booed and had drinks thrown at me and my dancers for the first (and hopefully last) time. Talk about a high to low. Just like when I had lost on that talent show a year and a half earlier, again I felt like my short-lived career was over. The adults on my team comforted me and tried to put things in perspective: the audience was drunk as hell, they'd come out to see Usher, the show was running behind, and they were just being rude and impatient dickheads. We laughed and I sniffed back my snot and tears as I put on a faux French accent and made self-deprecating jokes. But I was still mortified thinking about how my dancers and team probably felt bad for me.

The next night, I was scared to hit the stage, but my team had given me so much love and a big pep talk. We figured it probably wasn't going to be any worse than it already had been—and we were right. It ended up being just another reminder that "only those with seriously thick skin make it in this business," and if I wanted to make my career last, I had to learn how to grin and bear it.

In addition to getting a master class in performing from Usher, I also took advantage of the unique opportunities my new schooling setup provided. One of the cool things about being tutored on the road was that Stephanie was able to tailor some of my history and literature lessons to where we would be on tour. So, for example, while we were in Germany, we dove deep into learning about the Holocaust.

On a rare day off, we visited a memorial and a museum. Stephanie had me write a paper about what we saw. As I looked out the window from the tour bus, I watched the countryside fly by, overwhelmed by what had happened in this part of the world. Could it happen again? And how lucky was I to be free? To be alive in this time. Safe. Doing this thing. I felt undeserving. And I knew I needed to stay grateful. I'd sit up at the front of the bus with the driver and, history nerd that I was (am), ask him to tell me about what it was like for his parents' and their parents' generations. To be in Germany and be performing for all these humans packed tightly into an arena—body to body, coming together to sing and dance—was such a privilege. Because only several decades prior, people had been forced body to body into venues to meet unimaginably tragic ends.

In the hotel room that night, Mom was the big spoon. It was like being exposed to such a raw, unimaginable part of history had reawakened the most vulnerable parts of ourselves—and the weight of how much had changed in the past year had finally started to press down on us. There was so much out there she could no longer protect me from, or even explain, now that we were experiencing so many new things out in the world. It had been just the two of us for so long and now, faced with so much uncertainty and intensity all at once, I could feel her starting to pull back from everyone else around us.

Mom was on edge for the rest of the tour. While in Europe, she had started really doubling down on her already skeptical approach toward other people, especially those who Barry had started to surround us with. She simply didn't know how close they were with him or if they could really be trusted. After a few too many nights without sleep, Mom broke down on the bus in front of a woman from the label that she trusted a least a little bit, tearfully voicing her concerns about things like how everything in this industry was influencing me and the way Barry conducted business. She'd even started hearing rumors that he was dangerous to be affiliated with. Mom was deeply afraid that this was all going to wind up being too much, too soon for me.

After letting her unload, the woman posed a question to Mom. "Diana, do you think this is what's right for *you*? For you to feel like you're being ousted from the position of parent in your own child's life?"

Around the same time, another person on the bus had started talking to Mom separately about the gossip and unsavory business dealings going on at Blackground. Mom was confidentially advised that we get as far away from the company as we could and as soon as possible, warned that we were on a sinking ship. Mom grew paranoid and terrified. I think this might have been where she started drinking again. Nothing crazy, just some wine with dinner. When in Europe, do as the Europeans do, type shit. Over time, the volume of this "wine with dinner" slowly increased, but I encouraged it, hoping the alcohol might lighten her up a little.

After my run on Usher's tour finished, Mom and I headed over to London to do some promo for "Leave" and the eventual album. Jomo, the VP of Blackground and Barry's son, called to let us know that my first single had hit number 1 on the Top 40 chart in America. It was official; at just thirteen, I was the youngest solo artist *ever* to have a number 1 on that chart. Mom and I celebrated the best way we knew how: we ate an entire pizza together in our hotel room. She was excited and happy for me, but also really tried to not make too big of a deal out of it or add to the big head she said I was getting.

She kept saying she felt like she was losing me. And—she wasn't wrong. I felt like she wanted to keep me stuck in her orbit, when all I wanted was to ride the rocket ship we were on out into the vast unknown. I was hooked on the feeling of success, and it seemed like Mom was only wanting to hold me down.

Though I was over the moon about seeing the name "JoJo" next to the number 1 spot, I don't think I really understood at the time what that actually meant. It felt even more surreal because I hadn't been in America for months, and yet all this forward motion and momentum had been happening while I was across the pond. Still, I knew that I'd just entered a new realm. I was now officially a part of an elite club of successful, chart-topping artists who had come before me—before I'd even gotten my period. I'd reached a pinnacle in my career, one that most musicians would never reach in their *lifetime*. You couldn't tell me *shit*.

Riding high on the wave of this news, we headed back home to capitalize on the moment: it was time to shoot a video for the next single, "Baby, It's You," and finally release my debut album. Once "Leave" went number 1, it was easier to get Bow Wow (he had recently dropped the "Lil") to jump on the remix for "Baby, It's You." I had never stopped telling people at my labels how much I wanted him on that track! And somehow, once again, my desires came to fruition. Given time, persistence, and a nice paycheck, he finally delivered a verse that I thought was perfect to take the song to the next level and maybe even expand my audience from MTV to BET as well. For me, getting accepted by the hosts and viewers of *106 & Park* would be even more important and meaningful than *TRL*.

I felt the treadmill underneath my feet picking up and moving faster. Every day, there was a new schedule of interviews and obligations. Designers who wanted me to wear their clothing or attend their fashion show next season. I was living all the stuff I saw on TV. Sometimes I would pretend I was filming an episode of MTV's *Diary*: "You think you know . . . but you have no idea . . ." I lapped up all the drama and excitement like a kitten with milk. There were always so many people around me now: an ex–White House personnel bodyguard when I was in NYC, more folks from the labels, people trying to get me to take pictures with their products, my publicist nearby to tell them no, new producers Vince wanted me to meet, random folks who wanted to get a closer glimpse of the whole thing. It was all so much and yet I couldn't get enough. How could we expand this further, get more, go higher?

In late June 2004, the *JOJO* album debuted at number 4 on the Billboard 200 Album Chart. Universal had very low expectations for sales, which made Barry furious. He said he thought we could have debuted even higher had they done what he said and ordered more copies to stock on shelves. Back then, a label had to predict and order the number of physical CDs to ship to stores—but they didn't want to order a big number of units only to have them sitting on counters not getting bought. I didn't let that stay in my mind for long though. I had a release party at Planet Hollywood in Times Square after a *TRL* appearance where all my fans walked over with me, and it felt like I'd finally made it. The record eventually went platinum. I'm pretty sure the labels were happy about it—it had already gone much farther than they anticipated, and they couldn't ignore what was happening in real time. I didn't have much spare time to worry; I was busy performing on a mall tour all around the country, where kids would show up in droves no matter what city or town we were in. Meanwhile, the second single, "Baby, It's You," had dropped and the video we shot at Magic Mountain in Southern California turned out really cute, but it wasn't quite hitting the same level of success as "Leave (Get Out)." Some wrote it off as me not following the same formula as the song's predecessor, saying that fans were only going to want more of the same from me.

Still, people seemed to really like the album. I was being praised for my voice and the fact that I wrote or cowrote a handful of tracks. While "Leave" was still soaring across the mainstream radio waves, the "urban" community, as it was (offensively) referred to back then, seemed to appreciate my cover of SWV's "Weak." I think folks could feel how much I respected and revered Black culture. A highlight for me was when I got to go into the studio and record a duet with Cheryl "Coko" Gamble—lead singer of SWV—with her signature voice and iconic long nails. She showed me such warmth and love, and it was so fun to get to sing with her, but I don't think our duet was ever officially released.

One of the craziest things about this newfound success was that I was meeting all these celebrities and artists I had grown up listening to, but now, they were listening to *me*, too. While doing a radio interview overseas, I passed Destiny's Child in the hallway, and they showered me with love and light and encouragement on my path. I'll never forget the kindness of Kelly, Michelle, and Beyoncé.

I'll also never forget the bitchery of another popstar I interacted with. When I went to *TRL* to promote my song on a movie soundtrack that we were both on, she sneered and snickered, looking me up and down. *Did she really just roll her eyes at me, or was I imagining that?* I went to give her a polite kiss on the cheek when I greeted her on set (as I had seen rich and famous people do), and she pushed me away from her with an outstretched arm. I didn't know what I'd done to warrant this kind of treatment, but I felt like she wanted to send me a message that I was not worthy of her attention or affection. The saddest part of the whole interaction was that this was a woman whose voice and vision I *idolized*. Growing up, I'd watched every single interview and video and behind-the-scenes tape that existed, recording her video premiers on a VHS so I could study her every move. My Uncle Dale, who had driven down from Foxborough to Manhattan to join me at *TRL*, had said hello to her in the hallway, and she literally just said "No." How she made us feel was an example of how I never wanted to make *anyone* feel—and a reminder to stay humble.

Since I had gotten some success in music under my belt, the obvious next step for me was to get into movies and television. Mom and I met with several agencies who were courting us to sign to them "across the board," meaning they wanted to represent me as a singer, a touring artist, an actress, and a spokesperson.

Basically, a whole brand. We went with ICM and started working closely with an acting agent named Brian. He was fielding offers for me to do a bunch of different things, but then he came across a script for a small movie called *Aquamarine*, where I would play a supporting but main-ish character. It wasn't the type of edgy content that I'd envisioned myself doing as an actress (like that 2003 Evan Rachel Wood movie, *13*) but the filmmakers really wanted me in it—and I really wanted an excuse to go to Australia. Plus, Brian thought it was something I could potentially shine in. Barry, on the other hand, was not feeling the vision. He had said he wanted me to get into film as well, but he hated the fact that it would take me far away for four months, that he wasn't involved in the decision-making, and that he wasn't so much as a producer on the movie. I think Mom liked that this was a way she could actively take some authority back.

In the span of just seven months, I filmed two movies, one after the next. First up was *Aquamarine* in Australia, followed by *RV*— where I got to play Robin Williams's daughter—in Vancouver, Canada. In *Aquamarine*, I once again felt a bit odd-girl-out-ish, but I never let it show. Emma Roberts and Sara Paxton were super lovely and kind, but they hung out together more often than they did with me. To be fair, they seemed to have much more in common with each other than they did with me. They both had two parents on set, and their upbringings couldn't have been more different from my own. I couldn't help but feel a little jealous of Emma's lineage and the perceived ease with which she navigated the world. How much better would my life have been if I'd been born with (what seemed like) a silver spoon? And a cheetah-fast metabolism? Those girls could eat all the toasted turkey, cheese, and avocado sandwiches they wanted, all day long, without gaining a single pound. Meanwhile, I noticed my jeans fitting tighter and tighter, my cheeks getting chipmunkier by the day.

I imagined neither Emma nor Sara grew up sharing a bed with their mom, flakes from the ceiling peeling off and falling into their cereal, dressing in five layers of clothes at home in the winter so they could keep the heating costs down. Even though Mom and I were in a different financial position now because of my fledgling success and her willingness to drop everything to support me through it, we both still felt strange around people who had grown up with money. Mom had always warned me that "the want of money is the root of all evil." She was always distrusting and judgmental of people who had money. And here I was, having fun acting and earning money being on set, but weren't these movies going to bring in *more* of this "evil" thing for us? Was that good or bad?

Filming *RV* was a totally different kind of experience, and it was cool to be around more veteran actors, especially since many of them embraced me as a younger niece kind of figure. I lived for the endless stories and jokes that Robin told. He was the King of Tangents. He spoke so intelligently and hilariously about any- and everything, as if he was channeling from another planet (maybe that's why he was such a natural for the part of Mork in *Mork & Mindy*). Robin was a class act; the first to arrive on set and the last to leave, and he knew everyone's name and their dog's name, too. Barry Sonnenfeld, the director behind not just *RV* but the *Men in Black* franchise and *The Addams Family* remakes, was a character himself. Neurotic and self-deprecating, he infused a lot of his own humor into the movie. I loved all the improv and witty banter between the OGs like Jeff Daniels, Kristin Chenoweth, Cheryl Hines, Robin, and Barry. I couldn't keep up for half a second, and I rarely even *attempted* to get a word in edgewise, but my eyes ping-ponged between them and I soaked it all in like a sponge, laughing like I understood the jokes flying over my head.

While we were filming up in Canada, Mom heard that Barry (not Sonnenfeld) had sent goons to my agent's office at ICM in LA, all to intimidate him and let him know who was running the JoJo show. After that, Brian felt a bit nervous walking around by himself, which made sense, considering that Barry allegedly had a number of skeletons in the closet by then. Mom, however, was pissed beyond belief and felt responsible for my sweet, innocent, musical theater–loving agent now questioning if it was safe to pull into his garage alone at night. (For what it's worth, it's now public record that years after this happened, Barry settled a $5.8 million judgment against him from a former artist/lover who claimed that he'd falsely accused her of having AIDS and blew up her car.)

CHAPTER 7

YOUNG LUV

I MET FREDUA KORANTENG ADU WHEN HE WAS SIXTEEN AND I WAS FOURTEEN. TWO YEARS earlier, Freddy had become the youngest professional US soccer player ever and had signed a million-dollar deal with Sierra Mist on top of the contract he got from Major League Soccer. He was getting paid far more than his adult teammates, but he was the "boy wonder" carrying the hope of MLS to take the game to new heights stateside. The hoopla around him was *wild*. He'd been a child prodigy in his native country of Ghana, but his whole life changed when his family won a green card lottery to gain American citizenship. When it became obvious that he was destined to be a phenom, a youth coach took the family under his wing, and Freddy's mother and brother recentered their lives around supporting his undeniable potential.

Within a few years of moving to the States, Freddy was being touted as the second coming of Pelé. A year or so after he stepped onto the field to play his first professional game, I made my debut on the charts. His agent reached out to mine to introduce us after we had both been featured on the same MTV show. Even me, a popstar who literally knew *nothing* about soccer or sports in general, knew who this kid was. I was intrigued by the prospect of meeting a fellow phenom, and when I heard he would be playing Gillette Stadium a couple months later, I decided to shoot my shot. I passed along my email address (or was it my AIM back then?) to his team, and we started texting back and forth on our Sidekicks.

Meanwhile, Mom had signed me up to be the headliner of the Rock & Roll Gymnastics Tour, featuring gold medal–winning Olympic gymnasts . . . and me. It was a weird setup, but apparently it was a good decision for us financially, and the guy Mom had started dating was the one putting on the tour. In my eyes, he was yet another creep, and I couldn't understand what Mom saw in him. Then again, by this point, she'd fully fallen off the wagon and Chianti had become a part of her nightly routine. The decision to put me on that whack-ass tour sure sounds wine-induced.

With all the dancers and my crew on one bus, and me, Mom, the tour manager, a label rep, and Stephanie on another, I had *intense* FOMO. I knew they were throwing all kinds of parties on the B-Bus and I'd never get invited because they thought I was too young. One night at the end of the tour when Mom was out on a dinner date, I snuck onto the other bus and asked the chillest dancer to make me a drink. Up until then, I'd only ever had sips of drinks here and there at one of Connie and Dale's kickbacks, but alcohol always tasted disgusting to me. Seeing how relaxed and cool everyone looked on the bus, dancing and socializing without a care in the world, I wanted to get on their level. So the dancer poured me a red cup filled with Captain Morgan and Coca-Cola, and I was *off.*

One minute, I was excitedly cheers-ing everyone . . . sticky, sweet drink sploshing around in my cup . . . and the next thing I knew . . . I was falling face-first out of the bus onto the carpet of the hotel's entrance. Another milestone: my first blackout. Mom and her then-boyfriend picked me up off the ground and carried my lifeless body into their room.

I only have flickers of memory from that night. There's a fuzzy impression of the look of sheer horror on Mom's face when she first realized what had happened, crying and freaking out as she looked at the front desk attendant, wishing there wasn't another soul around to see what had become of her only child. They put me to bed, and then I woke up in the middle of the night thinking the toilet was in the center of the room. It was very much . . . *not*. I peed on the carpet, and Mom and her paramour woke up to the sound of me relieving myself.

"I'm a failure. I've failed as a parent . . . I've lost her. My baby . . . look at her!" she choked out, as this guy comforted her. The next day, as I nursed my first hangover and contemplated all my life choices up to that point, she took away my Motorola Side-kick. I knew I deserved that, at the very least, but I was disappointed because it meant I wouldn't be able to keep up my texting with Freddy. It would be years before I even *looked* at alcohol again.

When Mom and I headed back to Foxborough to celebrate my birthday and the holidays with our family, Freddy and I finally got a chance to meet up, after a few months of daily texts and phone calls. I went to watch one of his games at the stadium, and even though he didn't play that day, just seeing him out there on that bench or warming up on the field excited the hell out of me.

The crowds went absolutely INSANE anytime his name was called. And he knew how to channel that energy and be a star. He smiled with his entire body, and although he had a small athletic frame, he still seemed larger than life—especially to fourteen-year-old me. I don't think I knew anyone who was born and raised in Ghana, let alone Africa, but I thought his accent, his humor, and the way bright colors made his skin tone pop all made him simply beautiful.

More than anything else, Freddy had *audacity*. No other boy I had ever met would say the things he would say to me. He was bold. Forward. He wasn't intimidated by me *at all*. If anything, I was by him. We hung out a few times and continued to talk all day, every day on the phone before he asked me to officially be his girlfriend. I hadn't even been kissed yet and I was still mad nervous! I felt late to the kissing game, but Freddy quickly got it out of the way for me. At first, I worried my lips might be too small to feel good for him, but he shut that down right away, telling me that they were perfect and so was I.

Freddy opened up a whole new part of myself that I wasn't yet aware existed. I felt beautiful and desired from the way he looked at me. We laughed a ton. We also kind of reveled in the attention that came from us being seen out together in a small town like Foxborough. "Are you a virgin?" he wanted to know. Um . . . well, YEAH. I had never dreamed of losing my virginity before sixteen. In my mind, that felt like the "right" age. And I personally wasn't in a rush. But after countless late-night discussions in the dark about it—him laying all that convincing on *thick* over the phone or via AIM under blankets from our respective cities—I started to feel more comfortable with the idea of him being my first. If Freddy and I were getting lunch somewhere, Mom and her new boyfriend would be sure to sit at another table and keep their eyes on us. I rolled my eyes at them, incredibly annoyed that *this* had to be the setup. *How embarrassing.* Mom tried to give me my space, but she also probably knew that he was already trying to convince me to have sex, and she felt protective of me.

See, he had been with girls before. He was two years older than me and had lived a very different life. It's not just that he was a teenage boy; he was also a superstar professional athlete surrounded by grown-ass men. But I figured that might actually be a good thing. At least *one* of us would know what we were supposed to be doing.

One day, a few months after that first kiss, while Mom was out on a run in the state forest, we finally *did it.* It wasn't quite what I expected, nor did it live up to the hype people made about it, but I absolutely felt like a *woman* the next day. I was one of the first among my friends to take it that far. I told Nene, bless her Jesus-loving heart, and she was scared for me, saying that this was too much all at once. She also didn't really like or trust him. We'd all hung out together a few times by then and she felt like she'd gotten enough to see right through his bravado. She was worried that he was only with me for the publicity, not my heart. But I wondered: Was I drawn to *him* for the right reasons? It was hard to be completely sure—everything was wrapped up into one. After we crossed that line, I felt the bond between us grow so much closer. We were in the deep end, and I felt like now I might die without him.

Mom said she would kill me if I had sex while underage. That it would be the worst, most disrespectful thing I could possibly do. So I obviously didn't tell her. This only put further strain on our relationship, inching out the distance that was already starting to grow between us.

Meanwhile, Freddy and I had been in communication the whole time I was filming *RV*, and he even came out to visit me in Canada when he had a break from futbol'ing. It physically *hurt* to be away from him. He had mentioned many times how important sex was to him, and since I wasn't there, I was going crazy thinking about him giving away what was now *mine* to other girls out on the road.

With the money we'd made over the past couple years, Mom was finally able to buy her first home, and we officially moved back full time to Foxborough. She also copped an iridescent Coca-Cola-colored hardtop convertible Lexus. In the beginning, she said she felt a bit uncomfortable and embarrassed to be driving one of the nicest cars in town, but eventually, she settled into her new persona as Momma D, a successful woman who was worthy of buying some nice things for herself. Built back in the 1950s, this house was modest but by far the loveliest, biggest place we had ever lived in. I remember the dark oak and the white accents, the backyard that led into the woods, and, most importantly, the semifinished basement that I could hide out in whenever she was getting on my nerves (or sneak down to when Freddy came over). After years of going back and forth between the East and West Coast, Massachusetts was once again our home base while I flew around the country to record the second album in Miami, LA, and Atlanta.

Money and success absolutely made a lot of things flow more easily for us, but not everything felt totally stable by the time 2005 rolled around. Barry and Mom's relationship was now pretty strained, and I could feel the tension. Barry also wasn't in the studio as much this time around, but I was totally fine with that. All I needed was Vincent.

Just like he had for *JOJO*, Vince assembled an all-star cast of creatives for album number 2. This time, thanks to the success of the first record, we had an even wider list of people to choose from, and Vince brought in Swizz Beatz, Sean "The Pen" Garrett,

Ryan Leslie, and Stargate to help us out. Mom had also gotten a phone call out of the blue from none other than the one and only Diane Warren. We were *shook*. Diane was famous for writing some of the greatest love and heartbreak songs ever. Matter of fact, this woman had single-handedly written nine number 1 songs and thirty-three Top 10 songs on the Billboard Hot 100, including Cher's "If I Could Turn Back Time," Celine Dion's "Because You Loved Me," LeAnn Rimes's "How Do I Live," and Aerosmith's "I Don't Want to Miss a Thing." There was simply no other woman who'd had such a successful, singular career as a songwriter, and here she was, calling up Mom to say she wanted to work with *me*. Mom thought someone was pranking her at first. To her, Diane's interest and investment meant that I had really made it.

That's not to say Mom was totally onboard with how things were going. She was increasingly voicing her concerns out loud that this "new style" of singing I had adopted ever since I became a recording artist wasn't good for me. That it held me back, kept me from showing off what I could really do. This messaging was in direct contrast with the feedback I was getting from the pros in our sessions, which was very much "less is more" and "save the acrobatics for specific moments, not sploshed across the whole track." But when someone as respected and prolific as Diane finally reached out, Mom had to acknowledge that I must be doing *something* right if the best in the business now wanted to work with me.

Vince told me he had just emailed me a song written by Billy Steinberg, Josh Alexander, and Ruth-Anne Cunningham called "Too Little, Too Late." I grabbed some headphones and flipped open my Sidekick to take a listen. I had never felt this feeling before, but upon hearing it, I instinctively knew in my gut that it represented my next chapter. It was catchy and pop-forward, but

I could also sing the shit out of it and show off my range, plus it felt like a "natural progression" (as the people around me kept saying) from "Leave (Get Out)" to the more R&B feel I wanted to push on my second album. Once he knew I was onboard, Vince set me up with Billy and Josh to cut the song ASAP. I felt such an urgency to get my voice on it and put it out in the world. I didn't want another artist to hear it and feel the way I felt about it and outbid us or, worse for my ego, be more famous than I was and thus a more attractive vessel for it.

That's one of the dangers of not writing a song that you want to cut; other folks might want it just as badly—and you are (rightfully) completely beholden to the whims of the songwriters and their publishers and what's ultimately best for their bottom line.

When it was time to record, we flew back to LA and I got into the studio to sing an endless number of takes. Billy and Josh had a similar kind of system going that reminded me of what it had been like to record with Soulshock and Karlin on "Leave," but to the ninth power. This time, I did like three hundred different takes of the song that were then broken down into smaller fragments and blended together into a perfect pop sausage of a track. Billy was a legend; he'd written "Like a Virgin" for Madonna and "True Colors" for Cyndi Lauper, among other smashes. It was a huge compliment that he thought I could carry this songbaby of his that I loved so much. Both he and Josh seemed to genuinely care and believe in me. Enough that they wanted us to write another song, just the three of us.

We got in a room together while Mom walked miles around the Santa Monica streets. I took out a leather-bound notebook with thick sheets of papyrus-style paper and a lapis lazuli stone on the front, and my special turquoise-colored ink pen fell out from inside when I opened it up to a fresh page. Billy wanted to get inside my teenage brain and asked if I had any poems or ideas

I might want to start from. I shared what I had and learned that it was a good place to start: coming into a session with ideas and things that I liked. A perspective. He said he'd also been working on some ideas and wanted to see if I dug any of them.

In the same vein as Elton John and Bernie Taupin, Josh came up with the chord progressions and then the whole musical composition while Billy was behind the lyrics and melody. Josh went over to a keyboard, chose a Rhodes sound to play with, and plunked out a beautiful, soulful outline of a song. Billy sang some melodies and a basis of lyrical ideas. We then went around the room and shared ideas aloud until we finished writing the song in a couple hours. Billy said that, in his experience, there was no need to force a song. It shouldn't be like pulling teeth. This one had come together naturally, and, to him, that was a good sign. He also took the time to school me on the industry. He reiterated how important publishing could be in my (or any artist's) career and that that's where the real money was. He told me I had something special and unique to contribute as a creative, that I should be a part of creating my songs moving forward. Mom had said the same thing for years, but it didn't hit me the same. You see, something I couldn't quite grasp until I was older was the distinct differences among performance, publishing, and master rights (but we'll get into that later). Anyways, I definitely wanted to be involved in the whole process, but my label always pushed back. It seemed like they wanted me to focus on being a vessel for songs, not a songwriter. I wrote tons of songs around that time, but somehow "How to Touch a Girl" ended up being the only one I had a hand in writing that actually made it onto that album.

I didn't push back too hard. Even though I'd been writing poems and lyrics in my journal for a while, I'd slowly become convinced over the past two years that being a popstar and delivering surefire hit songs was much more important than writing and releasing my own random shit. That's what I was laser-focused on: What-Was-Gonna-*Work*. I *never* wanted to go back to a "regular life," especially after getting such a sweet taste of the highs that success could bring. Still, I was grateful that Billy advocated so hard for me to have my pen on at least *one* song.

As empowered as I felt in the studio with Billy and Josh, the months leading up to the release of the second album exposed me to a whole new side of the business. While I was working with Scott Storch in Miami, six-foot-tall impossibly tanned and toned models strutted around the studio compound in six-inch stilettos, and everyone was rolling blunts right there in the lounge. Mom and Vince scolded people to keep that shit away from me, but I waved them off, especially when Freddy was around. I *hated* the idea of anyone treating me any differently than the real adults. It didn't help that the power dynamics had already started shifting. I was now providing for both Mom and myself. Plus, I wasn't a virgin anymore. It irritated the shit out of me that Mom and Vince didn't realize that they were in the presence of a *woman* now.

While we were making stuff in Miami, I learned that Timbaland and Static, two breakout creatives signed to Blackground, were working in the studio next door to us. I'd heard a lot about Tim; not only were we labelmates but his sound had changed the music world more than once. Still, it had become somewhat common knowledge in the industry that he and Barry had a sour relationship now—especially after Aaliyah's passing. Static was a total genius as well. He and Tim, along with Missy Elliot, had really come to define Aaliyah's later sound. The way he put lyrics and melodies together was so unique. When I was recording my first album, Static was the first person ever to tell me to use his studio time and engineer to record a song by myself. The way he treated me was like an uncle who believed in me and wanted to show me the ropes of this thing we both loved. He said he was going out to get some food and wanted me to have a song ready to show him when he came back. In twenty minutes, I wrote a song called "Bad Boys" and in another thirty, I had used what he taught me in our work together to record all the lead vocals, background stacks, harmonies, and ad libs. I felt resourceful, capable, and proud.

According to Vince, I was supposed to be having a session with Tim and Static, who were also in Miami working with Nelly Furtado and Justin Timberlake and had reserved a whole studio. My family always stressed the importance of being on time and respecting other people's lives and schedules no matter their profession or social standing, so I was a little offended when we ended up waiting around for hours and hours on the couch until they were ready for me to come in. I tried to pass the time by learning a video game on the console in one of the rooms attached to the main studio. Why would they play it so aloof if they *actually* wanted to work with me? But, after what felt like forever, I was finally in the room with Tim and Static.

Once their attention was focused on me, Vincent kept the pulse of creative energy beating steadily—playing music from previous decades that might serve as inspiration, queuing up funny videos online, ordering enough hot wings for an entire army. That man always knew how to steer the flow and lighten me up when I was feeling insecure. We tried out a few ideas until the wee hours of the morning when I left with two songs written and recorded. Sometimes, you end up forgetting how long you had to wait because all that matters is the end result. And even though the songs didn't come out for whatever reason, they were good. And

I didn't (and still don't) look at shared energy and creating something with amazing people as wasted time. Plus, a few years later, Tim reached back out and included me on a couple songs on his *Shock Value II* album.

Even though a lot of my time and attention went into working on that second album, I was very much in the full swing of being a teenage girl, so my hormones were going apeshit. Back then, all a man really had to do to occupy significant space in my mind was tell me that I was talented and beautiful. And mature and special. After that, I'd start asking myself, "Hmmm . . . should we fall in love?" Even though I knew Freddy cared about me, we were always on again, off again, plus I felt pretty self-conscious day to day and longed for male validation. I don't know if they could smell it on me, but there were a couple of men around this time who would slip those kinds of compliments into our creative sessions. They knew I was underage, but they still treated me like I was an adult, an equal. And *that* was what I craved most.

For example, when I was on a festival lineup during my first album cycle and this dancehall artist who was having massive international success with an undeniably catchy song told me that he wanted to take me back to his island and make me his queen, he wasn't joking. It made me feel so special to be the object of this grown man's affection. Or when a young (but not nearly as young as me) rapper chatted me up for *months* via Sidekick messages and short but sweet-enough phone calls, slipping me unreleased songs he *said* were about me but were probably more realistically about one of the dozens of women he was fucking on the road, since we never even kissed.

With the dancehall artist, Mom saw what was going on and how he kept putting his hands possessively across my lower back.

Shaking with anger, she walked right up to him and cursed him out, telling him he should be ashamed of himself. He denied knowing my age. With the rapper, Mom looked through our messages and threw my phone into the Hudson River (we were still living in New Jersey at the time). Since I had a business manager now who gave me my own credit card, I went to a Target and bought myself a prepaid phone that I hid in my backpack and continued the madness behind her back. Besides, I paid the bills. I mean, *technically*, the business manager did, but who was the one making us the money? I was. So why did *Mom* get to make the rules about who I could or couldn't talk to?

The closer I got to my fifteenth year, the further I pulled away from Mom. I felt like she was always disapproving of something or mad at someone (often me), hating everything about the music industry and threatening to pull me out of it and make me go back to public school. The truth was that she could've literally put a stop to everything at any moment she wanted to. It terrified me. She reminded Barry and Vince about that, too. Yet she never actually went through with it. She would just say, through tight lips, that "this could all go away at any second. I can stop this any time." I think, in many ways, she wanted it to stop, but felt we were in way too deep.

Barry didn't love the power dynamic any more than I did. Behind her back, Barry got in touch with my father and flew him out to LA. After Barry wined and dined him, Dad left convinced that he had to fight for custody of me. He now firmly believed that Mom was damaging my career and making detrimental decisions and that she was generally not mentally or emotionally stable (let alone qualified) to manage my career or even fulfill the role of being my primary guardian.

It was now an all-out war between Mom and Barry. He accused her of being racist, which was one of his favorite accusations to wield against white folks—on top of saying that she was an ineffective manager. I could not believe this was happening, and yet, other than the claims that Mom was racist (Mom is very much *NOT* that)—I agreed with him. To be honest, I'd been dreaming of emancipation. Mom always insisted on being right by my side at any given moment, within eyesight of every move I made. I couldn't imagine Dad cramping my style like that. They ended up going to court and fighting it out for me. I was torn, but because I worried that this might be the straw that broke Mom's emotional back, I chose to tell the judge I wanted to stay with her. I decided I would just have to tough it out until I couldn't any longer.

Things with Mom were *really* tough. I struggle with how to write about this, since I still want to protect her and her right to her privacy, but I hope that by sharing my experience, it could help someone else feel less alone. So I'll just say it: Mom threatened to end her life pretty regularly, particularly when I was a teenager, saying I'd be "happier" that way. I knew she had been through the most devastating loss imaginable when she was three, knew she considered herself an addict and was actively battling depression. But it made me fully furious and absolutely terrified whenever she talked like that. It was as if she wanted to even the score and show me how she felt growing up without a mom.

"You're acting like a disgusting, ungrateful, spoiled brat."

"This industry has sucked all the goodness out of you."

"You're fucking *ruined*."

Vitriolic verbal jabs like these were increasingly common, and they hissed out of her mouth even more easily when she was under the influence. She was "the only one in the fucking world who actually told me the truth," she said. Everybody was thinking it but didn't have the balls to say it, apparently. This was her truth, with or without a lychee martini. I knew she loved me; I never doubted that. But she also deeply resented—and possibly even hated—me now. I hated her, too.

Some of my extended family tried to take me under their wings, saying she was crazy and always had been, agreeing that emancipating myself someday might not be a bad idea. Others tried to reason with her, explaining that the distance between us was par for the course between a mother and teenage daughter. But Mom doubled down on the evilness of rich people and the music industry, and blamed the world for irreversibly corrupting her formerly gifted and talented but now ruined child.

As irritated as I felt, I still didn't want anyone around me to worry or overreact. Most of all, I didn't really want Dad or Barry to be able to use anything she said or did as ammunition against her somehow. But after holding it in for a while, I finally confessed to Connie that I'd recently talked Mom off the ledge in Paris while we were over there on a promo tour.

"Please, Mom. Don't do it. I *need* you. I love you. I'll be better—I'm on *your* side—I *promise!*"

I begged her to hold on as I picked up the hotel phone and dialed Father John, the priest at our church back home. He stayed on the phone with her for at least two hours while I cried and tried to calm myself down in the corner of the elegantly appointed room. It was too ironic to be in a space so beautiful, halfway across the world, living out my dream—and yet somehow finding ourselves in the middle of a nightmare. She wasn't well and I'd known that, but I don't think I realized just how bad it had gotten until we arrived at that moment in Paris. I felt myself tensing up as I tried to strike the delicate balance of keeping her alive and keeping everything moving.

My family threw around their own diagnoses of what might be afflicting Mom on a deeper level. As much as everyone had their theories, none of it mattered. She was my mom. Yeah, I was a teenager and I didn't want her around me all the time.

But I thought it was obvious that I never for a *second* wanted her dead.

CHAPTER 8

SHAKEY GROUND

WHEN *AQUAMARINE* AND *RV* FINALLY HIT THEATERS IN 2006, I CLOCKED A *MASSIVE* difference between the music industry and the film industry. There seemed to be an additional air of stability in movies and television compared to the shakiness back in the world I was coming from. Opportunities were funneling in left and right, and I could barely unpack my suitcase before we were picking up and heading off to the next event. Mom and I were put up at the Waldorf Astoria while promoting in New York, and the Four Seasons while press junketing in LA. It was fancy as fuck, and I loved soaking up all the action and new experiences.

Looking the part mattered more than ever. When I sang the national anthem at the Pro Bowl in Hawaii, I spotted a dress in a gift shop that I thought would be perfect for the *Aquamarine* premier. It was this pretty watercolor wash of dark greens, blues, and purples, with a colorful 3D plumeria sash that started up on my right shoulder and fell down to just below my left hip. It also had a somewhat risqué (for a teenager) low-cut neckline with a high slit in the skirt that I thought would push the boundaries of my age just enough for Mom to not shoot it down.

For *RV*, though, my publicist convinced us to hire a real movie star stylist, who outfitted me out in a white, thigh-skimming mini-dress with a sheer lace overlay that reached all the way up to my neck. With my long hair curled and cascading down my shoulders, and decked out in silver jewels and accessories from head to toe, I felt grown-up and beautiful.

I was so proud and excited to have some of my family with me at the premier; Uncle Dale and Uncle Scott (Mom's half-brother, who's not only hilarious but also a novelist and real estate agent) had come in from Boston to support me and "help" drink the free liquor at the after-party. It made my heart flutter to see Robin interacting with my people. He was never rushed. He took his time talking to them. He somehow remembered the littlest details. I also brought Freddy along as my date, and we got to walk the red carpet together for a minute. In that moment, everything was joyful. I could feel in my bones that superstardom was just around the corner. There I was, just fifteen, expanding my career as a music artist and actress, never running from hard work, supported by the boyfriend, the family, with the Hollywood starlet look.

I had *everything* going for me.

I didn't hear it from him directly, but I heard rumors that Barry and other members of the team were disappointed that I had walked so brazenly across the red carpet with Freddy. It was bad enough that I was with him, they said, but to now have professional photos confirming our relationship "looked crazy." It was impressed upon me that by "flaunting my interracial relationship everywhere," I was singlehandedly ruining the possibility and money-making potential of me being "The Great White Hope" I was intended to be. They said it would take a very long time for anyone who saw that to be able to get those images out of their heads. In other words, it was okay to be compared to a white R&B icon like Teena Marie, but it was *not* okay to be dating Rick James—and especially not out in the open.

What?!?! I was totally thrown off by the hypocrisy. I'd been surrounded by Black excellence for two years now, and I couldn't understand how I could be doing something so "wrong" by dating this respectful, unproblematic West African all-star. A female executive took the time to sit me down in the Universal office and convey some of the nuances of racism and even colorism, gently explaining that I might alienate more than one section of my fan base because I, a white girl, was dating a dark-skinned Black man.

The *last* thing I ever wanted to do was upset anyone, and this warning hit me hard. Although I had an awareness of the complicated history of race in America and beyond, I naively thought times had changed, enough that Freddy and I were part of a new generation where things were different. Where race wouldn't be at the forefront. Plus, no one in my family, especially Mom, had ever brought up any concerns about dating outside of my race. So, I didn't *get it*. But as I soon learned, and would continue to learn, the world around us was filled with unspoken prejudices and harsh realities, particularly in this country, that existed but were rarely outwardly acknowledged.

Thankfully, whatever controversy I'd stirred up internally at Blackground didn't seem to have any kind of effect on the box office. *Aquamarine* was adored by a lot of my preexisting fans and opened me up to an even wider audience. There are still people who come up to me today and ask if I am the girl from *Aquamarine*, which never ceases to be hilarious (and a wee bit cringey). I loved that I was able to infuse my character, Hailey, with some of my own quirks. Like me, she was from New England and rougher around the edges than the other main characters. A lot of girls told me they saw themselves in her. But seeing my face and body projected and stretched out onto movie screens, especially next to Emma and Sara, was kinda hard on my squishy ego. I felt like the big, boxy tomboy next to their lithe angelic perfection.

RV also did well at the box office; it was number 1 in its first week and stayed close to the top for several weeks. I didn't know whether either movie (or my performances in them) was objectively good or not, but it seemed like a lot of people were genuinely enjoying them. So who was I to judge? As an added bonus, Robin introduced me to his daughter, Zelda, at the premier, and we instantly hit it off just like he predicted we would. (She's still one of my closest friends to this day, and has even directed a few of my music videos, some of which are my absolute faves—shout out to "Save My Soul" and "Think About You [acoustic]"). I was so freaking pumped when they decided to come visit me on the set of my next music video, one that I was hoping would catapult me to even greater heights.

Everyone agreed that "Too Little, Too Late" was the best choice for the first single from my second album, *The High Road*. We shot the video at the UCLA soccer stadium (a not-so-subtle nod to my real life), but not surprisingly, it was suggested that I cast a leading man who had the same complexion as me. I felt like I was selling out and buying into the status quo of what I had been told was acceptable. But I also wanted to make sure that Barry and everyone else around me felt that I was taking what they had told me about the world and my career seriously—putting myself in the best position to "win big" again. Plus, I was worried about staying in his good graces, knowing I'd upset him so much with not just the Freddy stuff but the movies as well.

While we crisscrossed Europe on another promo tour, the Universal radio department kept us in the loop of what was happening domestically with "Too Little, Too Late." A few weeks after we'd sent the song out to radio, Jomo called me to catch up. While I was on the call with him, I noticed that I was suddenly getting a bunch of messages and asked him to hold on a second so I could check my email.

Apparently, the song had jumped from number 66 to number 3 in the span of a week.

My eyes popped out of my head.

"I mean, that shit sounds *amazing*, Jo, but there's just no way that's possible. I looked at the charts this morning," he said. "Hold up, let me look again real quick."

After a few minutes of holding my breath and then scrambling across several three-way calls, our confusion was cleared up: that shit was *true*. It was the single biggest jump in that chart's history—a record previously held by Mariah Carey.

The rush of dopamine that flooded my body in that moment could only be compared to the feeling of realizing you're in love. Mom and I cried. Tears of excitement and overwhelm. Per usual, she was trying to make sure I didn't get too hyped up—but too late, I was GEEKED. I'd been so afraid of being seen as a one-hit wonder, and now, that was officially off the table. We had another smash on our hands. Even when Freddy and I broke up (for some teenage reasons I don't even remember now), nothing could bring me down. Instead, I used all those feelings as fuel to propel me into overdrive. I wanted more than *anything* to capitalize on my moment.

Opportunities were pouring in left and right. I'd perform for Ryan Seacrest's show in LA on a Thursday, interview with Jay

Leno and do a performance on *The Tonight Show* the next night, then take a red-eye flight so I could make it to NYC the next day for more interviews and press. Mom started pushing back a little, saying she wouldn't agree to that kind of schedule unless it was ensured that I could get enough rest and have enough time to do my schoolwork. She refused to compromise just because TV shows had certain slots open. If they really wanted me, she said, they'd have to work with my schedule. Then again, she said she *might* consider it if they chartered a private jet for us. Knowing her, this demand wasn't because she wanted to ball out but instead because she genuinely wanted to make sure I was able to do my schoolwork and sleep. Because of her requirements, though, I ended up missing out on things and not knowing about it until much later. All I felt was even more tension in the air between her and whatever label representative was present. The corporate folks were at their wits' end trying to deal with her and, thus, with me.

Shortly after "Too Little, Too Late" came out, Vincent vanished into thin air. It was actually unreal. We'd been so close over the past four years, and his abrupt departure felt like a slap in the face from out of nowhere. He'd been buttering me up since my first album came out about buying me my first car, but I didn't get so much as a text from him on my sixteenth birthday. Apparently, things had become untenable between him and Barry. They had been working on other projects together, including one with Toni Braxton, who had just signed to Blackground. To make it even more complicated, Vince had gotten romantically involved with Toni's sister, Tamar.

Blackground/Da' Family (Vince's production company) had also just signed Ashley Parker Angel and were starting to set him up as another pop pillar on their roster. His first single "Let U Go" came out and did very well. They put him in the studio with Soulshock and Karlin (who had produced "Leave [Get Out]"), but for some reason, they never took the time to introduce us to one another. Now that Blackground was bringing in more money and successful projects, they weren't going to focus the whole staff's attention just on me, which was both a good thing and a bad thing. Barry was overheard saying he didn't need Mom and me anymore.

When it came time to release the second single from *The High Road*, Mom and I were passionate about it being "How to Touch a Girl." We thought it was important to show off my soulful roots and establish me as a songwriter, not just a singer. As usual, *everyone* seemed to have an opinion, but I don't even specifically remember what anyone else thought about it. Mom was right: when you're a star, most people just say a lot of empty words yet never get to the heart of what they really think if it differs from "what the star wants." But I was so swept up in trying to get the video shot, doing interviews and behind-the-scenes clips, and picking out diamond rings and bracelets and earrings from this random jeweler who came to set (and said I could keep them!), I didn't really have time to think about confusing viewpoints or really notice Vince's absence.

But I had to start making up excuses for him in my mind when things got more quiet. He was in a new relationship with Tamar and working on other projects . . . I should be okay with that. But had he really forgotten my *birthday*? And the promises he made to me? I couldn't have cared less about getting a big fancy car, but *he* was the one who told me I deserved to have one. All those Air Force 1s, the custom clothing and hats and jewelry, the epic dreams and long-winded pep talks—they suddenly just stopped. The big brother I'd always wanted and had gotten in the most unique of circumstances had now vanished into thin air. I reached out over and over, but I didn't see or hear from him for over a year.

This was harder than any breakup I could've imagined. I felt so abandoned. And confused. And when "How to Touch a Girl" failed to reach the same heights as "Too Little, Too Late," I felt even more discouraged. That was the first single I'd been credited on as a songwriter. An inner fire raged within me, competitive and relentless, propelling me toward adulthood. All I needed to do was make it just two more years and hit my eighteenth birthday so I could get out from under Mom's talons and misguided influence and make my *own* decisions—ones that were in line with what Barry and everyone else around us expected. I was sure that was the way to start winning again.

Mom and I had recently gone to a meeting with Mel Lewinter, the president of Universal, and laid down the law when it came to how my promotion schedule was going to go from there on out. She really wanted me to focus on finishing school and getting out of the industry, but those were *her* desires, not mine. She earnestly insisted that I was a brilliant student, that I could go to college and be anything I wanted. Mel told her in no uncertain terms that if that was the case, we should stop wasting everyone's time and not even try to make anything until I graduated college. Welp.

I was furious. Yeah, I *guess* I understood that she was trying to protect me in the long run—but at the cost of my career? What was wrong with this woman? What did she even know about *anything*? Frustrated beyond belief, I switched gears and focused on passing the time however I could until I could make my third album as a legal adult. No more of this missing the moment or pissing off the label shit. *No thanks.*

With the third album on hold, I now had time to obsess over other things—like my love life. I turned my focus to Freddy and couldn't stop thinking about what he might be doing in his new city. He'd switched teams since the breakup, but we stayed in touch. He even wrote me flowery emails, outlining just how badly he wanted to get back together.

We were on, then off, then on again, and before long, Mom and I were on a plane heading out to Salt Lake City to visit him and his family. Initially, things felt amazing, like time had changed us both and we were getting to experience more mature, 2.0 versions of each other. But it didn't last. He had a frenemy who was on the team but benched at that time, and he had no problem telling me *everything* my ex had been up to. Even when he was trying to convince me to give us another chance, Freddy had been messing around with several other girls.

One day, when Freddy stepped into the bathroom to take a pregame shower, I picked up his phone and a text message came through. Scrolling through that thread, I saw things I wished I hadn't. Something took over me. I went to the photo section of his phone and saw even *more* shit I shouldn't have seen. The air left my lungs as I slumped down onto the floor. I immediately called Nene and we came up with a game plan. I would pretend everything was fine—something I had gotten alarmingly good at—until after his game, and then I would let him *HAVE* it. I was done. I deserved more. The truth, at least.

Look—I may not be the biggest sports fan, but *trust me* when I say that this was the longest, most *boring* soccer game in history. He wasn't even playing; it seemed like he rarely did anymore. Tucked up there in the family section, I felt like everyone was looking at me, feeling bad for me. Like they *knew* what he was up to, *knew* that he had probably been with or tried to get with at least one of the girls I made eye contact with. I can't remember if they were daughters or nieces of the coach or owner, but it doesn't really matter. It was never about them.

After the match, I watched him sign autographs and we dropped his sweet-as-pie mom off at her hotel before heading back to his place. As soon as we shut the front door, I exploded, screaming out the details of what I had seen and heard. All I wanted to know was the truth, to not look and feel like a fool. When someone takes your ability to make an informed decision away, it adds even more insult to emotional injury. His "friend" who spilled all the piping-hot tea said he'd be waiting outside for me if I needed any support or somewhere to go. What a Judas.

Freddy tried to find any way back into my good graces as I packed up my stuff. I had Judas drop me off down the street where Mom was staying, and I cried, curled up next to her in a little heaving ball, well into the night. I wondered if this was life imitating art. My two biggest songs up to that point had been all about getting cheated on, and now I knew firsthand how shitty that truly felt. More than anything, I had reached my limit of feeling like a dumbass and was ready to put that relationship in the rearview mirror.

For the first time, I started consistently pouring my heart out into a journal. Uncle Scott had encouraged me to keep one for years, and I'd finally taken it up after turning fifteen, scribbling out my irritations and ruminations from a bunk on tour. The margins were lined with favorite lyrics from artists that inspired me, like Joni Mitchell, James Taylor, D'Angelo, and Erykah Badu. I wrote down poetry and whatever I could remember of my dreams, and kept a log of what I was eating.

Sometimes, I'd be listening to music on my iPod and start thinking of female responses to male songs. One of the first ones I wrote was a reaction to Sean Kingston's big smash, "Beautiful Girls." The song annoyed the *shit* out of me, but it might have been his ballsiness—the nerve to sing the word "suicidal" over and over again in an auto-tuned doo-wop style—that perked up my ears. I imagined how an even more confident, slightly older version of myself might respond, and lying stomach-down on my bed, I wrote some cheeky little lyrics into my phone in ten minutes. I sang it to Nene over the phone. She and her family had moved to Florida by then, but we were constantly calling each other long-distance and even sending handwritten letters through the mail. She wasn't into music the same way that I was (I mean, even now she sometimes still claps on the one and the three), but she absolutely loved it, and I took that as a really good sign. Especially because I couldn't put out a new album anytime soon, I needed my fans to know I was still here, still relevant, always thinking of them, and wanting to put music out there. So without overthinking it too much, I recorded it and put it up on my Myspace.

Blackground had lost their distribution deal with Universal, and I was trying to learn patience as the days ticked down to me being eighteen. I assumed they'd have secured new distribution by then, and I could focus on finishing school in the meantime. Brian at ICM was still getting scripts sent to him for roles I might be interested in, and one offer from Lifetime caught his attention. *True Confessions of a Hollywood Starlet* was loosely based on the idea of "what would happen if a newly sober Lindsay Lohan went to high school in Fort Wayne, Indiana, when she was seventeen?" People had always said that I looked like her, so I thought leaning into it might work, might be cute. Still, some of it hit too close to home; there were a number of aspects of the script that plucked at the strings of my insecurities. This girl sensed her cache diminishing rapidly and was embarrassed to have to disguise herself and live a regular suburban life after doing a stint in rehab at her mother and manager's request. By the age of seventeen, she'd already developed a bad reputation due to her alcoholism and unprofessionalism, and now no one would hire her as an actress. This thing was not going to win any Oscars, but I knew a lot of people still watched and loved these Lifetime movies. So I did it. Not gonna lie, the payday was a big factor; Brian negotiated by far the biggest single sum I had ever collected in one fell swoop.

After filming in Canada for a few weeks, I came back to Massachusetts and looked for a condo. My eighteenth birthday was right around the corner, and in addition to this paycheck from Lifetime, I'd be coming into a percentage of all the money I'd made as a minor, which up until this point had been stored in a thing called a Coogan account. (A Coogan account is a kind of blocked trust—usually in the SAG/AFTRA credit union—that holds 15 percent of a child performer's earnings until they reach the age of majority. It was put into effect in 1939 to protect kids from the sad reality that some would be taken advantage of by their parents or career handlers. Mom had been very cautious and cognizant of making sure that wouldn't be my story.) Finally, the money would be mine, and I couldn't *wait* to have access to it.

Dad and I had been talking a lot. I loved just shootin' the breeze with him on the phone. When he was in a good place, he was one of my favorite people to talk to about anything and everything. It just felt *easy*.

I'd been telling Connie and Dale about how consistent Dad had been sounding and how excited I was to see him in person after what must have been almost a year. When I got back from filming *True Confessions*, Connie said I should invite Dad over and she'd make us all a nice family dinner. It had been years since they'd seen each other anyway. I could barely contain my excitement, thinking that after years of tension (and Dad perhaps being a little bit jealous of the big role Dale played in my life), the two of them could reconcile and we'd all get to share hilarious holidays *together,* devouring Connie's lasagna and passing filthy jokes around the dinner table like mashed potatoes.

When Dad pulled into their driveway, I couldn't wait to go out to the car to greet him, but I realized immediately something wasn't right. He seemed a lot slower than when we had been talking on the phone. He sounded off. But he still smelled like himself—six sprays of Obsession—and his hair was thick and black as ever, freshly combed to the back. He walked with a cane now, and I helped him into the house, hoping I was just reading too much into his behavior. He came in, and I tried to chalk up the awkward exchange between him and my aunt and uncle to nerves. This meant a lot to him, too. It was just a couple hours. He wouldn't ruin it by getting high. Right?

Dale reintroduced him to my little cousins, Riley and Tanner, who he hadn't seen since they were babies, and took everyone into the living room to catch up while I helped Connie get the food onto the table. She asked if he seemed okay to me.

Fuck, I thought to myself, knowing that she saw it, too.

Dad sauntered off to the bathroom, and it became even more obvious when he got back that he was a lot more lethargic, slurring his words, leaning in his chair like the Tower of Pisa. Ri and Tan had taken their pizza into the living room so they could watch TV, but Dad, Dale, Connie, and I all sat down at the table, and it was awkward as *hell.* Connie and Dale kept trying to volley conversation back and forth, but it was so obvious that Dad just wasn't holding on to any of it. Mortification rose in my chest as I sat there, burning, wondering if Dad could feel anything at all. He got a few bits of saucy lasagna into his mouth and on his mustache before nodding off, nearly landing face-first on his plate. I didn't want to cry, but I couldn't stop the tears from falling, even as we all tried to pretend he wasn't as obviously high as he was. Connie made him an extra-strong coffee before he finally headed out.

We were supposed to drive back up to New Hampshire together for the weekend, but I knew I had to tell him I couldn't go.

"Dad, I want to go with you. But you're high as *fuck*."

He laughed and told me that I was wrong. That I was being crazy and dramatic. But I wasn't. I felt sick to my stomach, and I didn't want him to leave without me, but I just couldn't see any other option. I'd already made up my mind that I wasn't going to tell Mom what had happened, but the hurt felt fresh and deep. I slept on Connie and Dale's couch. In the middle of the night, I tiptoed over to the makeshift bar on their porch and made myself a cranberry vodka, trying to numb any of the feeling I had left. I noticed the porch light shining on his face in the car—he'd fallen asleep there. It put me at ease to know where he was and that he was okay. In the morning, when I peered out the front window, he was gone.

Personally, things were complicated, but musically, things were starting to look up. I had made plans to get into the studio with my piano player, Jordan, who had become a close friend and also lived in Massachusetts. I adored my band, which was composed of current and former Berklee students who all played their asses off and were beautiful inside and out. Jordan was a virtuosic musician who immediately felt like my long-lost brother and musical soulmate. We bonded over our love for neo soul, and he was always inviting me over to the home studio he'd built with his brother. As his mom brought us snacks, he showed me all kinds of deep jazz cuts I had never heard before. He also recorded me doing the remixes that I'd started writing and putting up online. We'd spend day after day in the studio, listening to stuff we loved and then making stuff we wanted to listen to.

It was such a turning point for me. Up 'til then, I was so focused on releasing the next hit, I hadn't really stopped to think about the kind of music my soul actually *wanted* to make. Working with Jordan sparked something new in me. At eighteen, I was just starting to come into myself creatively, and even though you'd think success would bring a certain amount of freedom with it, I hadn't actually felt that free since I was a little girl playing around with watercolors and brushes. With a new album in the wings, I figured I could keep working on stuff with Jordan on the side and then loop in the label when we had something really special. I was hopeful we could integrate some of these new songs into my third album—or, at the very least, release them as a separate side project. (Two of my fave tracks, "All I Want Is Everything" and "Wait a Minute (For Your Love)," didn't end up making the cut in the end, but I ended up including "All I Want" on my first mixtape, and I think "Wait a Minute" might still be up on YouTube somewhere.)

Though I was now officially eighteen and ready to start working on my third album, things were still super tense at the label. Someone Mom and I both trusted and respected had left Blackground by then to work elsewhere, but stayed in touch with us regularly. Right around the time I approached the finish line of being a minor, I reached out to ask for her comanager recommendations. Johnny Wright, of N'Sync and Backstreet Boys success, was at the top of my list, as well as circling back with Larry Rudolph, Britney's lawyer, who sometimes managed, too. She hit me back with some names of her own but wrapped up the list by saying that she actually wanted to get into management and would love nothing more than to focus her new company around me. I was *stoked*. She felt like home in so many ways: a maternal mama bear in her interactions with me, yet a badass lioness in business overall. Plus, she knew my backstory and had been around since the beginning, *and* she had strong connections and experience in the industry. I figured we—meaning me, her, and Mom—could all build something special together as I stepped into the next phase of my life.

I didn't want to totally take Mom out of the equation when it came to my career. I thought she had some great ideas, and together, we had defied *all* odds—but it was undeniable that working with her was getting harder by the day. At this point, her baseline was cynical and pissed off. Our relationship was a *field* of land mines. If either of us said something that could even be slightly misinterpreted, an explosion was all but guaranteed. One time, after a performance somewhere down South, we got into a physical fight in the hotel lobby, shoving one another with tears in our eyes. Maybe she was drunk, maybe she was just tired of my shit, like she said. I don't even remember the details of it now—just the fact that it happened and I hated it. I felt like one of those girls on *Maury*—and *not* the kind who showed up on the episode with talented kids.

I looked for escapism wherever I could find it. A few months prior, I had started dating my guitar player, who was older than me but far less experienced in life. He was a sweet Alabama boy, a devout Christian, and a phenomenal musician. My family adored him, including Mom, even though she hated that I was still a minor and he wasn't. Keep in mind that I was just a few months shy of eighteen at the time, and I gave a total of *zero* fucks. As far as I was concerned, I was on my way *out*. Plus, this boy wouldn't hurt a fly. With adulthood on the horizon, I had a car, a credit card, and I was always on the edge of running away. I was a lot like Mom in that way—never above doling out threats, even though neither of us ended up acting on them.

In anticipation of me hitting the big 1-8, Barry opened up a budget for me to officially start recording my third album. Mom, my new comanager, and I flew to Vegas to work with Danja and Esther Dean, two creatives I knew and loved. After getting rave reviews for his work on Justin Timberlake's new music, Danja was touted as the next Timbaland (which made a lot of sense since he was Tim's protégée). Esther was one of the industry's newest and favorite topliners, composing lyrics and melodies for everyone from Ciara to Pussycat Dolls to Christina Aguilera and Robin Thicke. Though she was technically my comanager, this person was now taking the lead when it came to my career and having all the conversations that Mom would have normally had. I imagined it was for the best since she had a better relationship with the industry, anyway. Fortunately, Mom never said she had a problem with it, even though I could see her tucking further and further into herself, getting quieter by the day.

Ever since I was little, Mom has made faces while I sing. It's something I've always been hypersensitive about, whether I'm performing live in front of an audience, or on TV, or in the recording booth. I think I take it so seriously because I respect her so much as a singer. And whenever she feels like I'm not reaching my full potential or if I'm a little flat or holding back, I can see the internal cringe creeping up all over her face.

When it came time to record for the third album, I now had the balls and the you-can't-fuck-with-me-energy to ask her not to be anywhere in the studio where I'd be able to see her face (and feel her criticism). The older I got, the more dead-ass I became about this. I did not want to hurt her feelings, but the truth was, I couldn't bear to see those grimaces, especially for these sessions where I really needed to keep my head in the game. It wasn't like I couldn't sing around anyone—My Manager (as I will refer to her going forward, or M.M. for short) and Katie from the label were there, too, but their presence didn't make me feel self-conscious, so I was fine with them staying. Katie was a young protégée of Vivian Chew (a music industry veteran), who'd moved from Milwaukee to New York to work in music; in a lot of ways, she felt like the big sister I never had but always wanted. I really hoped Mom would understand, but she took it as a personal attack.

While I was in the booth singing what Esther and I had just written, the onslaught of texts began.

"Be sure to enjoy your life with your new mother."

She was clearly talking about M.M. She also started shooting off quotes from the Bible, like Matthew 16:26: "For what is a man profited, if he shall gain the whole world, and lose his own soul? or what shall a man give in exchange for his soul?" Her texting style was frenetic and kept coming in one after the next. I was in the recording booth trying to sing but I couldn't look away. She reiterated that I was ruined and that all she'd ever wanted was my love, and now I was going to "get what I [always] wanted": her gone. As she typed out her goodbyes, I felt my blood turn ice cold. It was like Paris all over again. I walked out of the booth with a fake smile, politely telling the producer, engineer, writer, and execs that I would be right back, and then I walked from the studio level of the Vegas hotel we were working at to the elevator to go check on my mother upstairs—afraid of what I might find.

The door to her room was locked and dead-bolted. I was banging and yelling through the wood that divided us. After what felt like a long time, she finally opened up and stood in front of me: naked, tiny, and soaked from tears. The bathwater was running and she had the hair dryer turned on.

All around us were several pieces of paper covered in her handwriting. After texting me, she'd taken the time to write out a goodbye letter, explaining how I'd be happier this way. She said that all she'd ever wanted was to be close to me, to be my mom, but I had just thrown her away like she was no better than trash.

Seeing these words, my sobs turned into full-blown rage, and I started legitimately fighting with the naked body of my frail forty-four-year-old mother.

"Mom!!!!!!!!!! NO!!!!!!!!!!!!!!! I love you!!! Please stop this!!!!!! I love you. Don't leave me!!!!! *WHY ARE YOU DOING THIS, MA?*"

The screams ripped out of my throat, painful and all-consuming. I turned off the bathwater and the hair dryer and sat with her on the floor, holding her and stroking the top of her head as she struggled to get a hold of her breathing. I assured her that M.M. would and could *never* be her replacement as my mother. As I reminded her, I'd wanted them to comanage me *together*! I knew she hated the industry; she was very outspoken about that, but I also felt like this was my purpose, like I was destined to make something of myself as an artist. I didn't want to give that up, especially since I'd already come so far. But if she needed me to make a choice, I would. I would always choose her.

I don't remember how the episode ended, but when I look back on it now, all I can think about is how I kept begging her to stay alive. It felt like we were up there for hours, going back and forth in that room. She said I should go back down to the studio, but I didn't trust her. I was confused and it was as if I was look-ing down at us from the ceiling of the room, outside of my body. I couldn't tell if it was a test or not, but it wasn't lost on me that all these people were downstairs waiting for me in the studio. I hated keeping people waiting (and Mom always stressed how rude that was). I didn't expect anyone to understand what was going on upstairs, and I was terrified to leave her alone.

With every ounce of strength I possessed, I made her *promise* that she wouldn't hurt herself. That she'd stay here on Earth in this life with me. It felt like she was mad that I'd intercepted her plans, but she reluctantly agreed and I finally left the room.

Those Vegas hallways are long as *fuck*. It feels like you're walking in a twisted fun house—especially when you don't know what you're in for at the end. By the time I reached the end of the sixty-first floor near the elevator, I'd had a full-blown panic attack and called Connie, collapsing into a heap on the carpet. Somehow, I made it back downstairs to the casino level and saw M.M. and Katie walking toward the elevator. I hung up with Connie and told them everything that had just happened, and then I went back to the studio to finish recording the song. As I write it out now, it sounds chillingly callous, but I didn't know what else to do. I was on autopilot.

On the way back home to Massachusetts, Mom wouldn't speak to me—not just on the plane but on the drive to and from the airport. And I mean no words.

Nothing.

As soon as we got back, she disappeared. My boyfriend, Connie, Dale, and even Dad (who I hadn't spoken to in months) all stepped up and helped me try to find her. At the time, I was applying to colleges and trying to hit all those deadlines, but for that first week she was gone, I honestly didn't know if she was dead or alive. It was hard to focus on *anything* else—especially my future. Stephanie helped me finish my applications and essays, even though it seemed pointless. Finally, after what seemed like forever, Mom's boyfriend called to let me know that she was okay and just needed some time. I was hopeful that he could talk some sense into her and calm her down.

Two weeks later, she returned. I came home one night with my boyfriend to see her passed out in the living room, with an empty bottle next to her. My sweet boyfriend carried her upstairs and helped me put her to bed.

In a sick way, I *had* gotten something I'd wanted for a while: for the two weeks she was gone, I got my first taste of living on my own. But I was so angry and exhausted that it was in this way. I wondered if this was her trying to punish me and teach me a lesson, but it also clarified that I needed to leave that house as *soon* as possible, terrifying as it sounded.

My family supported me and said I had to put myself first, reminding me that it was my life and I was not responsible for my mother's issues. I knew they were right, but it was still impossible to grasp, especially after I'd read that five-page letter she'd written for me in Vegas. Damn near every day, I had flashbacks that floored me all over again.

When it finally came time to move out, I didn't just take my belongings; I brought a nice party mix of rage, shame, guilt, and numbness along with me, too.

CHAPTER 9

SPIRAL SZN

THANKS TO MY REALTOR (AUNT CONNIE), I WAS ABLE TO FIND AND PURCHASE A condo in Boston. I loved the energy of the city and wanted to be in the middle of all the action. This was another unforgivable slight as far as Mom was concerned. In her eyes, Connie was yet another outside force getting in the way of our relationship; she even accused Connie of doing it not only to get a commission but also because she wanted to replace her as my mom. In Mom's dark headspace, nobody, not even her own sister, could be trusted.

A week after my birthday and closing, I moved into my loft in an up-and-coming part of the city that we knew was about to be popping because all the gay boys were moving there. Historically, it had been a rougher Irish working-class neighborhood. The building was a renovated printing press from the 1900s with a dining room that used to be an elevator shaft. With high ceilings and shiny, cracked concrete floors, my new home also still had all its original beams and pipes, which were exposed throughout the unit. It had integrity and charm that reminded me of the type of artist I wanted to be. I was in love.

All that was left was for me to put my own finishing touches on it. Uncle Dale, who had started a painting company, came through with his motley crew and turned each wall a different bright color, even painting the exposed pipes fire engine red at my request. My new home felt like my own little creative sanctuary. I had all my Berklee pals over, and the space was constantly filled with music.

And booze.

So much booze.

Once I turned eighteen, people didn't mind buying for me. Since my first intro to rum and coke back on the tour bus, I hadn't had much alcohol until I turned eighteen. I may have had a drink or two here and there, but nothing for real. Still, whether it was a family gathering or a backstage party, I saw the way alcohol loosened people up and took the edge off. (A good chunk of family on both sides would probably be classified as functional alcoholics.) I felt like I'd waited my whole life to be initiated into this adults-only club of liquid chill. Plus, whenever I went out to the bars and clubs on Newbury Street, I rarely got carded. I knew I was a local celebrity, and I *definitely* played into it whenever trying to get my drink on. I quickly realized that my favorite drink was the next one. Alcohol made me not give a *fuck*. Without it, I gave so many fucks that it physically hurt. There was just no better, freer state than totally out of my mind.

One of the regulars at my new place was my friend Jill, who I'd met at my fourteenth birthday party—the only person I'd kept in touch with from Foxborough other than Nene. Jill was three years older than me and a total rebel. She'd been bullied even more mercilessly in school than I was, and when Connie invited her to my birthday shindig, she came to help us set up and we hit it off. I loved that I could tell the girls who were mean to her to fuck right off when they tried to get into the party. Four years later, we were about the same size, so we could share clothing and bras, and she had this metallic-blue Toyota Celica that she would pick me up in whenever we wanted to go out and cause a ruckus far away from the suffocation of suburbia.

Now eighteen (me) and twenty-one (her), we were finally escaping the small town we'd grown up in and pushing the limits of our well-being. We were pissed at the peers who had made our younger lives hell and at our parents for not acting how we thought they should, and we were generally raging hormonally. At my pestering, she was finally going to cosmetology school and pursuing a career I really believed she could thrive in. After all the hair and makeup experiments that she'd done on me and her sisters over the years, it was obvious to me that she had what it took.

After she'd finish the school day, she'd come to my place, we'd take her Adderall, smoke Camel Crushes, and pregame before going out to party, boozing it up at an Irish pub or sitting court-side at Celtics games, carrying purses that were big enough to hold our sugary flavored-vodka-filled water bottles. Whenever ballers from either side took notice of us, I got off on the fact that I was actually in a relationship (with that sweet guitarist) and could only flirt back.

Being desired was like a drug to me, but my one and only experience with my professional athlete ex had scarred me to the point where I wasn't looking for a repeat event. I wanted to be wanted—but that's as far as it went. Still, after the games, we'd hang out with some of the star players—who were usually from different parts of the country, unfamiliar with this town—and take them all over Boston. Picture nights of going round for round, taking tequila shots with seven-foot-tall hoopers, trying to prove that I could drink them under the table. Spoiler alert: I couldn't. The nights often devolved into me crying on someone's strangely broad shoulder about Mom or Dad or Vincent. *Hot.*

When it came to making a decision about pursuing higher education versus continuing in my career, I still wasn't sure what I should do next. The thought of having a degree to fall back on outside of music sounded smart. I had already seen how uncertain and unpromised all of this shit was. And who knows, maybe I'd find my tribe and make some cool, smart, eccentric friends in college. But I questioned whether I'd be able to tell whether someone liked me genuinely or not.

When I got my college acceptance letters back, I knew right away that the Harvard letter was too thin to be an invitation. Looking back, I had delusions of grandeur to think I could get in, but I can't say I was totally shocked; my SAT scores just weren't great—I fully froze and spaced out during the taking of the test, and it was also my first time back in a real school setting since middle school—even though I maintained pretty close to a 4.0 throughout high school. As a senior, I had made a point to get involved in charities that I believed in (like the Boys & Girls Club of America) and logged as many volunteer hours as I could. You might think that being a popstar could've counted as another extracurricular activity; alas, it did not.

To be perfectly honest, I got a lot of help with my schoolwork toward the end of high school. And by "help," I mean that people would write outlines for me, sometimes even whole papers, and then I'd simply rewrite them in my own words. Sometimes I didn't even *bother*. I was coasting and generally was treated as if rules didn't fully apply to me. I was already working and making money and providing for myself and others. What was the point? When I struggled to conjugate verbs, an adult close to me suggested I just pay someone to do my Spanish work. Just get it over with. It was all a means to an end. I was also really lacking in the math department and could never seem to grasp any of those concepts, no matter how many ways Stephanie would try to explain it to me. She eventually stopped trying. Mom never knew about any of this, but nonetheless, she was right to think I wasn't being pushed enough to reach my academic potential. She still believed what that online test had determined about me as a child: "Genius." But I knew I wasn't. What I was, at this point, was impatient and undisciplined with no structure whatsoever. As always, I justified all this cheating and shortcutting to myself, saying that the whole point was for me to graduate so I could get into a good college. But if Mom had known any of this was going on behind her back, it would've broken her heart.

After meeting with several of the schools in the area that I'd applied to—Harvard, Boston College, Boston University, and Northeastern—I verbally committed to Northeastern University and declared that I would be in their sociology program, focusing on cultural anthropology. I've always been interested in understanding more about how human beings are influenced and organized by cultures, systems, and societies. Another big factor was that Northeastern seemed to understand and celebrate that I already had a career and was willing to work together with my team to create a schedule that was partly on-campus, and partly virtual/distance learning. This was obviously way before COVID, so they were ahead of the curve.

As the time drew closer for me to matriculate and live the college girl life, I started having serious conversations with M.M. about what the next few years would look like. Was I really about to go to school and slowly bleed out my precious youth (the most valuable currency in entertainment), or did I want to go all in on my career? I felt she would support me in whatever direction I decided to go in, but then she put forward this question for me to chew on that I just couldn't get out of my head.

"Do you think you'd be happier going to college now and coming back to music in four or five years? Or do you want to go for music now, while you're in your prime, and go back to college when you feel like taking some time off down the line?"

When it was put like that, I felt the smart choice was pretty obvious. I had all these thoughts and feelings about what being an "adult" now meant. This *was* my prime, right? *Would* it be irresponsible to the career I loved and the fans who kept me going to pivot and go all Scholastic Sally now? I didn't want to lose the goodwill of the people who believed in me. What if I failed harder in college than I did with that second single off *The High Road*?

Around the same time I was mulling over what to do next, Lady Gaga was taking over the world and blasting into the stratosphere. Vincent had signed her about twelve months after he was allegedly iced out of the JoJo equation by Barry. Over two years after his disappearance from my life, I saw his familiar face right next to Gaga's, splashed across MTV and every magazine you could think of. This chick was *everywhere*, and she deserved it; there was no denying that she was fucking incredible. But it still stung whenever I thought about him.

M.M. reached out to him—hoping to help ease some of the pain I felt from his abandonment, but also to see if we could work together again. This time, Blackground would be out of the picture since *he* (Vincent) held the first line of power in my convoluted contract. She knew I was still deeply in pain when it came to him ghosting me. And to see him return with not just a shiny new thing but *THE* biggest artist in the world? Yeah, it pretty much crushed my spirit.

Vince seemed genuinely thrilled to be back in touch and was very eager to explore the potential of working together in a Barry-free environment. When Gaga went out to LA for a gig, he got tickets for M.M. and me and stood by my side as Gaga took the stage. He was acting like my big brother again. Trying to pick up where we had left off. I felt all kinds of mixed emotions—comfort, anger, confusion, and elation—now that I was finally standing next to him again.

A few songs in, he yelled to us over the music that he had to go take care of some stuff at front of house and that he'd be in touch later. I did my best "cool girl" impression as we hugged and congratulated before kissing him on the cheek and saying goodbye. *Would* he be in touch? Or had I just gotten another reality check of how people will lie to your face in this business? That show really was bittersweet for me. I was electrified and inspired by the force of nature up there on that stage, clapping and bopping along to the music with the crowd. We ran into a lot of industry folks we knew, and M.M. made sure to position me in the best light and protect me in my shaky emotional state. Under the lights of that venue was a flurry of metal and glitter and songs that were destined to be smash hits—and apparently, *Gaga wrote them.* I was in awe. She was at times futuristic and at times nostalgic, this petite young woman with the audacity to push herself past the edges of the pop world and beyond. She was just four or five years older than me and yet totally in command of her voice, her body, the audience. As the extent of her talent really started to sink in, it became clear in my heart that he was never coming back to me. Without warning, tears started pouring down my face. I felt like I might pass out. I didn't want to make a big deal out of it, but I knew I really had to go.

As we made our way out through the crowd, people turned to look at me and I could hear them whispering to each other "Is that JoJo?" Nope, it's just the shell of a person who Vince *used* to call JoJo. The girl who *used* to be "the only thing that mattered" to him. I kept my head down and tried not to let anyone see the panic attack brewing inside. On the long car ride back to west LA, I didn't want to be dramatic, but I couldn't take it anymore. I curled into a ball in the passenger seat, trying to calm myself down, as M.M. spoke life into me.

"You are a once-in-a-generation talent, Jo," she said. "*Everybody* who knows you knows this. You're a world-class singer—your star quality is undeniable. Your life and career are just beginning! *None* of these little bitches have even a *sliver* of your authenticity and soul! You're not a gimmick! You're going to have the last laugh! We got this! I got you!!! Don't compare yourself to someone whose journey is different to yours. FUCK Vincent! We don't need him!!!!!!"

I had never played sports before, but damn it, she had a way of gassing me up and getting my head back in the game. I decided then and there that she was going to be my new Vincent. And as long as she believed in me, I was going to be okay.

By the summer of 2009, it had been almost three years since the release of my second album. Blackground still didn't have distribution or the structure to put music out. To say I was growing impatient would be an understatement. It was around the time when a lot of social media platforms—like Myspace, Twitter, and YouTube—were getting super popular, and I jumped at the chance to connect with my fans. I didn't want them to feel like I'd just forgotten about them.

I started off posting random cooking videos or song covers I'd recorded at Jordan's studio (like a response to T-Pain's "Can't Believe It") and even blogged here and there. People had been asking me where new music was, and I was feeling increasingly embarrassed that I didn't have an answer for them. It was too complex to understand let alone explain the inner workings of a nonfunctioning label. But I shared what I could: I had to wait for Blackground to sign a distribution deal to release my next project, which I wanted to call *All I Want Is Everything*. Until then, even the idea of an official album was on hold.

A couple months later, after no movement whatsoever, we officially initiated a lawsuit against Da' Family (Vincent's now-defunct company, pre-Gaga) and Blackground to nudge them to make a move (at M.M. and my lawyers' suggestion). We had a simple request: secure major label partnership or let me go. The clock was ticking and we weren't playing around. It seemed like Blackground had burned bridges to every major label distributor, thanks to Barry's hot temper and not-so-clean reputation. I didn't have the legal rights to my voice due to the contract I had signed at twelve. And according to that same agreement, if I wanted to put out new music, I couldn't do it without a distributor on board, which meant that I was constantly stuck in a holding pattern until someone in control decided to shit or got off the pot.

Little did I know, but something was brewing with Interscope and Jimmy Iovine. I'd heard they hated each other, but apparently over the past year, Jimmy and Barry had kissed and made up. Timbaland had his revenue streams split between Blackground and Interscope, and now, hot off the success of his second album (and a slew of chart-topping duets with people like Nelly Furtado, Justin Timberlake, OneRepublic, Nicole Scherzinger, and Keri Hilson), Jimmy wanted the whole shebang.

But, of course, it wasn't quite as simple as that. Even though Vincent (who was now taking over the Interscope building with Gaga) had moved on from Blackground, he and Barry were still mortal enemies, whether or not they admitted it. There was also an opportunity for Aaliyah's posthumous catalog to be acquired through a new long-term partnership between Interscope and Blackground, and for one of Jimmy's artists and producers to work on it. I knew I was a bargaining chip in the negotiation as well, but I didn't get the sense that Jimmy really wanted me—more like I came with the whole Blackground package.

This is what I understood about the culture at Interscope: it wasn't uncommon for those in power to be constantly critiquing their female artists' looks and bodies and sex appeal. Whereas today, executives would never dare sit around a table and openly voice their judgments of an artist's desirability out loud, this was the late 2000s and early 2010s, when cancel culture and body positivity movements didn't yet exist. Apparently, some of their biggest stars worked out two to three times a day and watched everything they put into their mouths. They sauna'd and lipo'd and deprived themselves of everything to be on the covers of magazines. It seemed like a pleasureless existence, but that was the cost of being a big star.

I was a little nervous about the pressure of even trying to compete with these older, more conventionally beautiful goddesses, especially since I knew I'd gained a little weight after being back home in Massachusetts. Still, the thought of calorie restricting seemed far-fetched as I was deeply content eating anything and everything I wanted, bingeing late into the night. Ice cream sandwiches, Subway wraps, Baked Lay's—I'd often go to bed with a comforting assortment of sugar and carbs laid out next to me. I think I'd picked it up from watching Mom be "good" during the day—drinking only water, coffee, and working out—and then go on all-out binges at night. A food coma could be as effective as a sleeping pill.

Ultimately, though, I wanted to do whatever I could to get back on top, and if that meant trimming down, fine. I'd heard Adderall could help me lose weight, so I added that into the mix using a friend's prescription. Then I started chain-smoking while taking it, perhaps because the pills made me crave cigs but also maybe in protest when I realized that my voice was no longer my own. I'd suck the nicotine into the back of my throat as hard as I could until I felt it rolling and rumbling through my lungs. It tasted like rebellion.

I was irritated and angry and felt like I didn't deserve to be in the holding pattern I was in. But coming across as bitter, I was told, would be the final kiss of death for my career. "Looking good" and giving people something to believe in was part of my job. So I stuffed it down. All that mattered was that I could take this shit all the way back up to the top of the charts. I hadn't deferred from college to settle. From now on I would do whatever they needed me to do if it meant I could get my train back on track.

While the execs were exploring a potential partnership, M.M. flew out to Boston to see how I was doing and listen to the music that Jordan and I had been making for *All I Want Is Everything*. More than anything, I think she wanted to get her eyes on me and make sure I was *really* okay, especially after I called her several times from my car, drunk and sad and tired of waiting in the wings. I'm not even sure how I made it home sometimes.

There was a lot that felt out of my control at that point, and music (and food) was pretty much the only thing that made me feel good. I was excited to show M.M. all the music I'd been working on, so I rented out the best studio in the city and Jordan brought in live horn players to put the final touches on one of our favorite songs. Eagerly anticipating her approval and pride, I set the mood with lighting and snacks and went to the soundboard to put our new music on blast.

What we had created was this soulful yet modern sound, inspired by all the incredible musicians around us, the city we lived in, and the young love I was a part of. It was a big departure from what had made me famous, but I wasn't afraid. You could hear my earnestness and purity ringing out in every song, my influences, my developing skills, my sense of self expanding. This new music was *dope*. I had started prepping M.M. for what she was in store for, especially since it was such a big switch-up, and to her credit, she lovingly bopped her head along to each of the songs as I played them. But I could sense her apprehension traveling almost like goose bumps up my skin. We'd known each other for so long that I was almost as attuned to her as I was to Mom. I felt all her energy shifts, tightness, openness, concern—and I knew that deep down, she wasn't into the new stuff like I was.

Here's the thing about being an artist who has experienced some success: most people don't want to tell you the truth to your face when they disagree with you or don't like something you're doing. They'll coddle and pussyfoot around the issue, and often, they'll never really say what they feel directly. Why? Because they don't want to stir the pot and get thrown out of the kitchen.

So even though I could feel that M.M. wasn't diggin' it, I also knew she wasn't going to shit on the new sound I was passionate about and working hard on. And it wasn't just about access. She truly loved and cared about me, and I know in my heart that she could see how excited I was. Remember: I wasn't even in my twenties yet. She knew I was trying to find myself, and even though this new sound fit me and the person I was becoming, it probably wasn't going to be easily digested by the mainstream. What's more, with her marketing background, I bet her wheels were spinning the whole time, wondering: "What would we possibly *do* with this?"

Sensing her doubts, I switched it up and played songs from a whole *other* project we had started working on, which was a fusion of pop sensibility, dance, and hip-hop—all with an undercurrent of musicality that was deeper than what I was known for. I wanted her to approve of something I was making, and I just knew this would likely be more up her alley. I wanted her to believe in what I did—that Jordan and I could do anything. We could even do it from Boston!

Fortunately, she was a lot more receptive to these tracks, especially this trippy, sticky song called "In the Dark." I'd been experimenting with different ways to write songs for years, but my favorite stuff originated when I was alone and working on poetry inspired by real life. I'm a massive Joni Mitchell stan, and apparently she started with lyrics and then shaped the melodies around them. And that's how this particular song came to be.

A couple months after I turned eighteen, I was on a break from my guitar player boyfriend. We were kind of on and off at the time, as we had been riding the emotional roller coaster of his guilt (since we'd had sex before marriage), plus some other not-so-great stuff (we'll get into that in a minute), and I felt that I should probably be single anyway.

There was a man twice my age who I considered a mentor-type figure out in LA. He was unbelievably cool in my eyes. Smart, funny, respected, connected, worldly. Since I was now without a boyfriend or much male attention in my life at all at that point, I was regularly confiding in him and leaning heavily on him emotionally and creatively. In other words, I was getting super attached.

He was the one who told me it was the flyer, skinnier choice to have a drink with a single big ice cube in it. No extra calories and no time wasted. We started getting closer and closer every time we drank together: a hand on the lower back, a suggestive whisper over loud music, a deep look into the other's eyes that lasted longer and longer. It all came to a head one night after we went out in Hollywood and went back to his place, where he made me another vodka on ice to sip on as he played me his new album. Before I knew it, I was straddling him, fully clothed, and we were going back and forth about what we were going to do about all this tension that had been building up between us.

He seemed conflicted, but the pressure coming from inside his jeans suggested that he was tempted. He told me that years earlier, his father had asked him, "Son, in this life, are you going to be a protector or a predator?" I meeeeeeeeean . . . knowing I had this much power over him made me feel invincible, like I'd rendered him incapable of making any other choice than whatever it was I wanted to do. And what I wanted to do was have sex.

So we did. In the moment, I felt everything I wanted to feel: powerful, beautiful, desired. But afterward, I felt alone and like I wanted to get home before the sun rose.

I started putting my thoughts down on paper and came up with lines that eventually wound their way into that song:

"This ain't the first or last time
We'll meet up this late at night
To let our fates intertwine
Casually, I'd rather be
Detached from all tragedy
This don't need to be defined
And I know that it's wrong (I do, I do)
Baby, keep holdin' on (I do, I do)

Yeah, I know that it's wrong (I do)
When the sun comes up, I'll be gone
I only know him in the dark . . . "

That arrangement was one I went back to for years whenever I needed a cocktail of comfort, guidance, and connection. This was a new favorite outlet of escapism for me. An option where I could dissolve all my worries and fear and hope and intensity into the flesh of another human being, where I could feel totally unjudged and taken care of. Held. Supported. I loved losing an hour, a day, a weekend in making LOVE. It was a beautiful, calorie-burning way to get closer and distract myself from reality while ascending to another dimension. I was never a one-night-stand girlie. If anything, I was a recycler. If I felt safe with you and we had good sex together, I might leave the door open. So if both parties were single and feelin' it . . . it was on.

In my late teens and early twenties, some men took the way I viewed sex as an invitation to try to have it with me. I was propositioned more than once by people I was working with. And while I loved knowing I was desired, I didn't want it to go farther than that. I didn't *want* to be thrown against a wall of a studio and kissed on the neck and feel someone's unwanted hand between my thighs. One time, M.M. and Katie came to rescue me from a session where I had discretely texted them from a corner of the room, saying this producer locked the door, wouldn't let me leave the studio, and was trying to get me to drink more than I wanted to so that I couldn't drive. He wouldn't take no for an answer.

Fortunately, he doesn't work in music anymore. Fuckin' *creep*. But it's kind of like the head of a Hydra: one head gets chopped off and then ten more snakes grow back in its place.

Let me give you a little backstory on how I landed in this sexually free / dumpster fire of a season of my life. On December 31, 2008—just eleven days after my eighteenth birthday—I got invited to Katy Perry's New Year's Eve party on a studio backlot in Hollywood. I'd been working in LA at the time, and I met up with Emma Roberts and a couple of other girlfriends so we could all go to the party together. It was so awesome to be a part of this cute little girl gang. Since *Aquamarine* had come out a little over two and a half years before, it was also nice to get back in touch with Emma and share some of the real-life shit we were both going through in our coming of age.

We pregamed before the party and kept it going all night. As the clock was about to strike midnight, I realized that, damn it, I wanted to *smooch* someone. My boyfriend was in Boston playing at church, and I was so drunk, I started asking myself, "A little kiss isn't a big deal, right? I'm eighteen . . . we're not married . . . isn't this what I'm *supposed* to be doing right now?" Trust me, I'm not trying to play victim here or anything—what I did was categorically wrong. But this is what was going through my very, very drunk mind at the time. Surveying the partygoers, my eyes landed on this guy I thought was hot in a nerdy, hipster way. Fueled by alcohol and Adderall, I was primed to stay up all night and down drink after drink without feeling sick.

I stumbled over to him and, in the most seductive voice I could muster, I asked "Hey, do you wanna kiss?"

His smile melted me. "Fuck yeah, I do."

Just *look* at my power.

We made out for the rest of the night and stayed in touch after that.

A few months later, I was back in Massachusetts and he was in Connecticut for work. I drove out there to link up with him, telling my boyfriend that I was going to watch a friend from LA perform and that Nene was going with me. This guy was a kind-of-known DJ in his midtwenties, and I was excited to see him in action after learning as much as I could about his background on the internet (not that I'd asked him, since I was too scared to seem like I cared or was even interested; I had a boyfriend after all).

Aunt Connie said that I was playing with fire and shouldn't go—but IF I went, I shouldn't drink. Well, the likelihood of that was zero. Getting out of my mind was imperative, and the truth was that I needed *something* to make me feel comfortable and cool enough to be in his orbit. I was embarrassed about the nonmovement in my career and uncomfortable in my skin. This guy was totally sober and straight edge, yet he had this laid-back confidence that I could only scratch the surface of if I was under the influence.

When I rolled up to where he was playing out in Connecticut, I took a few sips from my alcohol-filled water bottle, chewed a stick of Big Red gum, and felt somewhat more prepared to say hello to him. We grabbed a bite together at one of the casino restaurants, and then security set me up with a table and bottle service girls. I loved the music, the lights, the drinks, the flirtation. But I was still deeply uncomfortable. First off, I *knew* I shouldn't have been there. I had a boyfriend. Second, did this guy actually take me seriously? Or was he just looking at me like some stupid teenybopper? And third, I *hate* getting in trouble— and I was still under twenty-one. What if someone at the casino found out? I drank more and more to shut down these intrusive thoughts, deciding that nothing sexual would happen and that maybe if I just kissed this guy here and there, I'd get whatever it was out of my system.

But, of course, that's not what ended up happening. The cranberry vodka sodas kept flowing, the music locked me in a trance, the hot skinny local girls working there kept coming over to take shots with me, and before I knew it, I was waking up in a sun-drenched hotel room, naked and alone.

Flashes of the night kept coming back to me in blurry fragments. I wasn't sure what was real or imagined. I have a vague memory of barely being able to hold myself upright but going back to his room with him. And then—nothing. I threw the bed-sheets back to see if my clothes were tangled up in the sheets. It was obvious what must have happened.

I looked down at my phone and saw I had a text from him:

didn't want to wake you before I had to leave. stay as long as you want, last night was fun ☺

I called Nene in hysterics. She stayed on the phone with me and calmed me down before telling me to check the bathroom trash can, where I found a used condom.

"At least we know you're not pregnant, Jo . . ." I appreciated that she was trying to find the silver lining in the midst of my break-down, but I couldn't help feeling like theworstpersonintheworld.

How could this thing have happened? This thing that I did but had absolutely *zero* memory of? I was mortified. I'd only been with my two boyfriends before this, and I also considered myself pretty prudish and deeply shy around men—at least, without alcohol in my system. This was a huge reason why I drank like a fish, to override my tension around them.

The guy had texted me at 6:00 that morning when he was on the train to the next city on tour, assuring me that the room was mine until checkout. *What the fuck.* How could this fully sober man ten years older than me not realize that I was blacked out? Was I not sloppy?

"Fuck. Fuck. Fuck. Fuck. FUCK!"

I cursed and paced around the room. Maybe he had just tried to put it in, but it didn't work. Maybe I had passed out and we didn't actually "do it." I was an irredeemable idiot, I decided, but I still needed to know. With Nene's coaching and prayer, I found the guts to call him and, in the chillest, calmest voice I could find, asked him to tell me what happened because I remembered nothing. He sounded so surprised as he told me that I was essentially "begging him for it."

"Wow, no . . . I couldn't tell you were blacked out," he said. "I mean, yeah, maybe you were drunk, but you seemed fine and you wouldn't let it go. . . ." He then confirmed we had sex, which was still somehow nearly impossible for my brain to process.

I went back to Boston and tried to live with this secret buried inside for as long as I could. But, incapable of keeping this in for any meaningful length of time, I told Mom everything. It was actually the moment that started bringing us closer again. And it's as if I knew it would. It was something she could personally relate to and advise me on. She shared several stories of things that had happened to her during blackouts over the years, what she remembered leading up to them and their aftermath. Part of me was sad that we both had this similar trauma and predisposition, but another part was relieved to be connecting with her again. She was there for me, comforting me, and finally letting her guard down. It felt like she was my mom again. I curled up into her arms and collapsed into little girlhood, back when our dynamic had been right-side up. As a big, bad "grown-up" who had willingly put herself in a position to cheat on her boyfriend and now couldn't handle the weight of the intense guilt she was carrying, I was grateful to be cared for by her like this.

I knew that I would eventually have to tell my boyfriend what happened. At the time, he lived in a tiny walk-up with three other musicians in a kind of dangerous part of the city near the Pentecostal Evangelist church he served at and the one I had started attending with him. That was the place where I got saved for the first time and felt loved and accepted by the whole congregation and all of the musicians. Since I started going with him, I'd become a little self-conscious of what I thought was appropriate church garb; during one memorable incident, I even had a cloth laid over my skirt because it exposed my knees and was deemed indecent and distracting. Clearly, I was the trashy token sinner in this building of respectable and saved believers. The teachings, consistency, and community of that church meant so much to me back then, but I was still figuring out where I fell on the religious to spiritual spectrum. Hell, after visiting Salem once when I was seven, I thought I would grow up to be a Wiccan. I wasn't ready to tie myself down to any specific doctrine just yet.

One Sunday, after a particularly moving sermon about truth and courage, I felt the guilt rising like bile in my throat, eating me up from the inside. I knew how it felt to have valuable information withheld from me. And it was inexcusable for me to be putting a person I loved in a position where they didn't have the facts. My conviction level was at an all-time high. He was a good, honest God-fearing man and he deserved more from me. After we got back to his place, I ended up telling him what had happened in Connecticut. I shakily blurted out slivers of the truth, attempting to paint myself in the least deplorable light possible. He tried to be understanding and forgiving. Christlike. But what I had done served as a fatal blow to the relationship.

After hours of back-and-forth, he started demanding answers and asked to look through my phone, scrolling through all my conversations with the DJ. That was when he'd had enough. He threw all the stuff I had at his apartment into the street below. It was like a 1990s music video where the female artist has been wronged by a no-good cheating man—but now, in an ironic twist given my discography, the genders were reversed.

The guilt consumed me and became my new identity. I didn't fault him for leaving. From my vantage point, I was a disgusting mess—an embarrassment—and knew this was exactly what I deserved.

CHAPTER 10

WILD WEST

NOW NINETEEN, I STRUGGLED WITH THE COMBINATION OF FEELING LIKE A WHORE WHO WORE a scarlet letter wherever she went and being sold the idea that somehow all these jazz musicians and church kids in Boston were making me "forget" who I really was. Who was I? I was dying to know. I now craved a fresh start, and I knew if I wanted to be taken seriously in the business—to *really* compete in this game— I'd have to move to LA. I rented out my condo in Boston, packed up my stuff, and moved in with M.M. for a few months until I found a spot of my own. I felt like I hadn't taken a break from writing and recording in forever, but I couldn't wait another second to get back in and keep trying to make the music that would take me to the top again—but in a fresh, 2010 kind of way.

No one could really agree on what direction I should take with my next album. Some people advising me thought I should follow the same formula of "Leave (Get Out)" and "Too Little, Too Late" (aka more on the pop side), but I pictured myself taking more of a Justin Timberlake-esque approach. I'd admired how he pivoted and prioritized artistry and writing post-N'Sync, carving out his own sound with Timbaland and Pharrell on *Justified* and then *FutureSex/LoveSounds*.

In that spirit, M.M. set me up in sessions with Chad from the Neptunes, The Stereotypes, Neff-U, Kenna, Tank, and some other creatives who I could really explore with, people who were super down to help me make and shape music that was unique and soulful but still "pop." We wanted to do something that really showcased my vocals, personality, and versatility. I wanted to make sure we infused some more musicality than I had previously displayed. Different time signatures, genre melding, world influences. Apparently what I gravitated toward and what was mainstream were not one and the same, but it was my nature to want to explore and take chances.

After we made an album's worth of songs, I was eager to get feedback from Barry or Jomo, but neither of them would speak to me directly. Instead, M.M. talked to them and then told me what they liked or didn't like. Okay . . . so, they liked a few of the songs. Great. So, what were the next steps? I always had questions but rarely got any answers.

Far from home, I also couldn't stop thinking about my parents— even though we were three thousand miles apart and Mom was no longer making unintentional faces of approval or disapproval from across the vocal booth. A big part of me felt nervous without Mom by my side telling me what she thought about things, while another part was relieved to finally be experiencing the autonomy I craved. I put on my most put-together front in the studio, trying to move my career forward, but I was constantly worried about her. Both of our drinking habits were pretty consistent (and excessive) in those days, but I chalked mine up to some college-age rite of passage, whereas I classified hers as straight-up alcoholism.

Dad wasn't doing much better. When I'd talk to him on the phone, his speech was slurred and sometimes completely incoherent. There were periods of time when one of them would be doing great but the other would be pretty unstable. Then it would switch up all of a sudden—and I couldn't predict when that might be. I felt like I was constantly bracing myself for a phone call saying that something bad had happened to one of them; every time my phone rang, my chest tightened up. The inconsistency kept me on shaky ground, and it felt impossible to gain my footing.

I had my first studio panic in Miami after getting a series of frantic calls from Mom while I was there working with Jim Jonsin and Rico Love. I tried to pull myself together and go right back into the booth, doing my best job disassociating so as not to waste the time we had together—I knew Blackground wanted a single out of these sessions, these guys were hitmakers and I felt lucky to be in session with them—but I just couldn't stop myself from crying. Nervous I was going to faint, I slid down the wall to the floor where I sat sobbing while trying to follow their instructions to breathe. Then came the hyperventilation. The freezing cold in my lungs.

In. Out. Slowwwww down. In. Out. In. Out.

When they asked me what was going on, I opened up a little bit about how scared I was about my parents and my career, but I quickly felt guilty, and that was all it took to shut me up. I wanted to protect Mom's image in their eyes. Just like she'd always tried to protect me.

These were definitely not my glory days. I felt like I was living out Omarion's lyrics: "I got this ice box where my heart used to be." Icicles were pressing down on my organs and stabbing me in the chest, my extremities were tingling, feeling like the anxiety might kill me. The drinking helped dull down my emotions, and whether it was alcohol or weed, I stayed in an intoxicated state as much as possible, even during the day—which made me care less about *everything*. But I continued the cycle, drinking to escape reality and then making decisions that were ultimately embarrassing (at best) or had horrible consequences (at worst).

I lived out my college-age years (and . . . a few years after that) as a kissing bandit. It felt sexy and freeing to be under the club lights, music blasting into my eardrums, countless friends and acquaintances all around me. All of them beautiful and reckless, too. Alcohol was quickly proving itself to be the perfect fuel whenever I needed to fill up my bottomless pit of insecurities and satiate my craving for validation. It didn't matter if it was a bartender or a famous actor. I'd be out with my girlfriends, and all of a sudden, I'd lock eyes with a rando at a club like Voyeur or Hyde and try to entice them with my booze-goggle gaze. That, or I'd straight up go over and pursue them. Anyone I was curious about, I would just go up and shoot my shot. But if they wanted to go further than kissing and grinding in the club? Well, I loved saying no. I felt powerful, knowing there were men who thought I was cute enough to mash tongues with, men who lusted after me. I became addicted to the distraction, passion, sparks, loud music, lust, beautiful people, and access that other people my age, back in my small town, didn't have.

As much as I was out in these streets smooching strangers, I was also working my ass off. From the ages of nineteen to twenty-four, I wrote and/or cut over two hundred songs, striving for perfection and acceptance in the process. On top of songs I was making that felt like me, anything the label sent that I thought was even halfway decent, I would record, putting my all into every second of it, every syllable of a line, even if whatever it was wasn't quite my taste. M.M. said it was smart to keep an open mind, and since I was wrong about no one liking "Leave," that made total sense. Playing and creating and making things was a treat in itself, but I also wanted another dose of bona fide outward success. Based on how shameful I'd acted in relationships and how M.M. often said she had to reel me in and protect me from my own musical taste, I internalized that I didn't know what was best for me as a core truth.

I damn near *lived* in the studio during those years and loved every second of it. But I hated sitting on the sidelines without any fucking clue as to what the plan or the problem was. I was nineteen; weren't all those hurdles of my minordom behind us? I was irritated I had put off college for this. By now, it had been almost four years since my last album came out, and Blackground still couldn't provide a real timeline of when I would be able to release music again. I was pretty sure it had something to do with their deal with Interscope not being ready, or budgets not being opened, or maybe Barry and Jimmy getting into heated arguments that scrapped any and all progress. But the truth was that no one was telling me the truth about *anything.* All I knew for sure was that artists who had once opened for me and publicly and privately looked up to me had now taken what I considered to be my spot. If there was an artist out there—and there *was*—who was prettier and skinnier than me, a bona fide star, could act and sing her ass off, *and* was in a power couple plus the machine of Disney behind her . . . how could I possibly compete?

The music industry was—and still is—in many ways a very small fishbowl. Behind the scenes, there were all these songs I was working on that were getting amazing responses from people and then they would never come out, but I'd hear a very similar vibe or melody or concept that another artist managed to release. For every step I took forward, it felt like I was falling four steps behind, like I was always looking like I was late chasing a trend when I had been the one pushing things forward in the first place—without getting any of the recognition once it hit. Fuck it *all*.

In December 2009, Interscope hosted their holiday party in Santa Monica, and I unintentionally got wasted in front of everyone, dancing sloppily with another one of their new rap signings, dropping it low and splitting my tight blue satin dress right up the center of the butt. Thankfully, I was wearing underwear, but M.M. was humiliated and tried to cover not only my ass but my reputation as well. I was too drunk and emotionally numb to feel ashamed—or much of anything at all. After all the wild-ass stories I grew up hearing about everyone from Stevie Nicks to Lindsay Lohan, I suppose my behavior was pretty tame that night. But M.M. held me to a higher standard, and I could see her real concern and disappointment crystalizing day by day.

Rappers had been putting out mixtapes since the beginning of hip-hop. After a few years of industry limbo, I was so exasperated by the lack of forward movement with my music that I thought, Why not put my own "mixtape" online, directly to my fans, and cut out the middleman? My team and I investigated the legality of it all, and, lo and behold, if I wasn't standing to make any profit from it or make it available in a traditionally commercial way, I'd find myself totally in the clear.

According to my contract, Blackground owned my recorded voice. So basically, if I ever used my voice in a melodic way that had any kind of monetary commercial benefit, I had to ask for their consent. *However*, if the producers and cowriters I was working with agreed to let me release our creations for free and directly to the internet, then, somehow, I was within my rights to do so. This loophole felt like a godsend. Luckily, the people I was creating with were like family and were immediately down to be a part of my going rogue.

Another thing that had been happening was songs that were intended to be official releases were somehow getting leaked. (Look, if it was from me, I swear to God I would just tell you. But it *wasn't*.) Songs that we agreed would be official singles like "Keep Forgetting to Forget About You" and "Paper Airplanes"—as well as songs I wrote for other artists or cut and never intended for anyone to hear—would find their way onto the internet. This was *so* unfair to my collaborators too. We spent countless hours and days on these songs, so to have them leaked recklessly to the internet made me worry they'd stop working with me. (It persisted like this for years and, honestly, I started to wonder if someone was intentionally trying to sabotage my career. Or just drive me insane.) On any given day I'd wake up to fans rejoicing online over getting to hear new music—they didn't know it wasn't coming from me. The whole thing was confusing yet *kind of* encouraging because of the great responses a lot of the songs were getting. But underneath it all I felt confused, violated, and heartbroken that music I had worked so hard on wasn't being given a fair shot.

Fans started catching on that things were not going well behind the scenes. I began dropping clues about my frustration across social media. A "#FREEJOJO" movement was already brewing, and the release of my first mixtape, *Can't Take That Away from Me*, added spice to that concoction. In the first week of its release in September 2010, the mixtape was streamed/downloaded hundreds of thousands of times—a first-week number I'd never experienced before with any of my previous albums.

Just like I'd hoped, fans *loved* the project and took real ownership of it because it came directly from me to them. It represented one of the first times that I took full control over how I presented myself to the world. When it came time to shoot photos, I chose the photographer, location and set-ups, clothing, hair and makeup, and all the press shots.

One of my favorite things we did was shoot a video for "In the Dark." M.M. and I combined our resources, financially and creatively, to make it happen. Shot in gauzy grayscale, the video featured lyrics that splashed unabashedly across the screen and two blindfolds: one for me and one for my very hot love interest. It was more risqué than the music I'd released up to that point, and I was excited for my fans to meet this new, sensual, grown-up side of me.

Coming in at eleven tracks, *Can't Take That Away from Me* was a touch of the more experimental stuff I was into at the time, with a good dose of the edgier pop that was intended to be on a main album release. The title was a tender "fuck you" to the powers that be; essentially, I was saying: "No matter whatever weird shit is going on behind the scenes, you can't take my voice or my relationship with my fans away from me." It felt vindicating to have the industry see me make a way for myself when some people had already written me off after taking too long between releases. I refused to just wait and sit there while the execs fought among themselves; this was my career and my passion, and I wouldn't let *anyone* take that away from me.

Around this time, there were little songwriter/producer cliques in the major music cities. In LA, a lot of us would congregate at this producer, Sham's, house in the Hollywood Hills. Every artist of that time that you could imagine would roll through there, and we'd have a chef making Caribbean food while one of us mixed up the drinks and laid out the shots. It was basically nonstop writing, recording, and partying. I was also told around then that I was finally making music that was in the lane that M.M., Barry, and Jomo thought was perfect for my official reintroduction. So all the partying and rough-around-the-edgery was helping my artistry? *Woooooo!*

After much thought and planning with my hairstylist/glam artist twin cousins (Lisa and Chrissy, who had moved from MA to LA a couple years after me), we dyed my hair jet-black and put in extensions for drama and length. I'd also accumulated a handful of tattoos (a treble clef on my ring finger, a turquoise cross behind my ear, stars on my foot, and the words "love & music" on my hip) over the past few years and started dressing in ribbed undershirts, distressed denim, and studded combat boots, signaling that I was a badass and ready for battle. The deal between Blackground and Interscope had *finally* gone through, and Barry was now setting me up with one of my favorite producer duos, Pop & Oak. One or both of them had come up under The Underdogs, and I *LOVED* the way they produced me and crafted lyrics and melodies.

To start us off, Barry handpicked a song for me that he had actually already paid for (I would obviously be responsible for recouping this cost) called "The Other Bitch." And . . . well? No.

I'm so much hotter than her, but I guess you disagree
I thought that girl was a joke, but she's laughing at me
Come to find out that I'm the other bitch, and you never
    loved me
She was so above me

Yeah . . .

I just didn't think it conveyed the best message for my return. It felt disingenuous coming from me. Everyone involved listened to my concerns and heard me out, but also didn't shy away from reminding me that I had initially hated my very first single and that I "run from hits," as M.M. put it.

I mean, is that what I was doing?

It's not like I had ever said no to cutting a song that had gone on to become a hit for someone else.

I tucked my tail between my legs and sang the living shit out of the song, infusing all of my frustration, desperation, and confusion into the delivery. The whole thing made me feel a little stupid, but since everyone else seemed to love it, it was clear— once again—that I had no idea what would put me back on top.

After taking so much ownership over my mixtape, the loss of control I felt when it came to this new album was even more palpable. I'd always felt a bit ganged up on in meetings with some members of my team and the labels, and back then, I just wasn't strong enough to stand up for myself and fight for what felt right in my gut, especially if I knew I'd be standing alone. I was so focused on pleasing everyone else, making sure they thought of me as a good, solid, hard worker. I was starting to feel really disconnected from the whole process because I didn't love this new direction, yet I didn't see another way forward other than to agree with it and say yes time and time again.

What was the point anymore? What was I even fighting for?

After voicing my objections to "The Other Bitch," M.M. told me Barry wanted to talk to me in person. See, that's how it was now. They spoke to each other, and then she relayed his sentiments to me. I guess it was easier that way?

This time, he summoned me to meet with him one on one at Blackground's LA offices in the Valley. I drove myself over there, belly full of butterflies. I hadn't seen him in person for quite some time by that point. He'd once been a very real presence in my life, but over time, it felt like he'd become more of an urban legend. Someone who I heard was doing all these nefarious things behind the scenes but someone that I rarely actually connected with.

Immediately after I walked into the building, he put me at ease, welcoming me to take a seat in one of the unique chairs in his spacious office adorned with Afrocentric artwork and his artists' plaques. Even though I was a bit anxious, it was so good to see him in real life again, and I couldn't *wait* for him to get to know me as a young adult, finally free to work even harder. I was so ready to get down to business and hopefully get a real sense of what the next few years might look like for me in his eyes.

We discussed the songs he loved, and I reiterated the issues I had with "The Other Bitch." Barry nodded thoughtfully and offered a compromise.

"Well, how about we take the word 'bitch' off the table and call it 'The Other Chick'?"

Uhhhh . . . okay . . . yeah.

I barely had time to process that before he started talking to me about the importance of me looking and feeling my best. Aaliyah had been so visually stunning, he said, that it *really* helped to support the music. Her frame was perfect, an easily digestible complement to the dance moves and the songs. This man was such a good talker; I swear he could make a dolphin feel like it could live without water. He was explaining what made up the total package in such a soft and inoffensive way but was clearly insinuating that I fell short.

My pride sank into my stomach. I took note of everything that I had eaten the past few days, and I wished I hadn't had that stupid banana nut muffin earlier in the morning. Aaliyah represented a sort of aesthetic perfection. She was everybody's type. When it came to her, everything was *beyond* on point. This woman had style, grace, charisma, and real talent. Every time I passed by pictures of her in the office or the studio, I subconsciously compared myself to her. But it's like I wasn't even comparing myself to a real person anymore but rather to this mythic goddess who had once existed on Earth. I knew I'd never be the girl who gets mistaken for a model in a crowd. But I also knew I wasn't "a big girl," which was something that everyone deemed unacceptable for an artist like me.

Still, I understood what Barry was saying.

"It's time to step it up."

Often when I get overwhelmed or anxious, my words start getting shorter and my energy starts getting tighter, coiling up inside of me. I tried to unwind myself and explained to him that I wasn't mad about being told to lose weight, but that if we could just be honest, I was "the picture of health" (well, minus the binge drinking and smoking cigarettes . . . but wasn't I doing a great job of hiding it?). I was a size two, maybe a four on my heaviest day. He knew I had already been working out hard as hell with a trainer five days a week.

I felt like I was fit! Regardless, I wasn't measuring up to their visual expectations. And if I wanted an extraordinary life, I couldn't be ordinary. I just wished he would speak plainly and not in this flowery language, which was a bit of an insult to my intelligence. He seemed a bit taken aback by my directness but smiled as if he had taught me well and was perhaps a little proud of me for holding my own across from a grown man. By the end of the meeting, I agreed to go to the weight loss doctor he recommended. I went on a strict protocol of weigh-ins, injections, and five hundred calories a day, plus supplements. I learned all about nutrition and intermittent fasting and how this shot they wanted me to take would trick my body into thinking I was pregnant, taking the food that would normally be reserved for a baby and instead allowing me to excrete it out.

In his mind, I know Barry truly believed he was setting me up for success and wanted me to have the best shot at being a superstar. That's something I could appreciate even if it temporarily made me feel even more less-than.

So I just swallowed everything (the massively oversized supplements, anyways) and kept my head down. I didn't want there to be a *single* thing the label could say I didn't do or try. I wanted to win with them.

Those things made me feel *invincible*, like the pill in *Limitless*. They were better than Adderall because they didn't sharpen the already sharp edges of my personality. Even better, I was able to shed some weight, and, once I did, the label was finally ready for me to shoot a music video for "The Other Chick."

Well, I shot the video and WHAT DO YOU KNOW? It never came out. (LOL!!!) We even had the famous "Beats by Dre" placement in there, as was mandated for all Interscope artists to do back in 2010. As I write this, I *still* don't know why it didn't see the light of day. Then again, there are *several* unsolved mysteries when it comes to that period in my life. I'd ask for answers but get talked around in a circle. I was in a perpetual cloud of confusion.

Here I was, doing what the execs had asked of me. I was now a size zero, my face was less chipmunk and more gazelle, I was carrying measured-out quantities of strawberries and almonds in my purse, chain-smoking cigarettes in my car on the way to the next studio session where I'd inevitably write and record more songs that no one would ever hear.

Finally, I decided the insanity had gone on long enough. I talked to my lawyer about it, and he advised me to file for bankruptcy. That seemed like the best solution and one that could actually get me out of this otherwise ironclad contract. My Manager agreed that *this* was the plan that made sense, as we had exhausted literally every other option.

If this sounds strange to you, trust—it sounded strange to me, too. But as my current lawyer explains it: a recording contract is a personal service agreement where the artist provides a service for a fee. If you get into a bad contract where there aren't clear outs to protect the artist from the label side, you have to sit on the sidelines until the label acts—even if they're defunct, they legally have the right to approve or disapprove everything you do with your voice. I'd signed a seven-album deal, and since I wasn't being allowed to put out full-length albums, the label wasn't exercising the next option of their contract (triggered by the previous project), so I could never satisfy the terms of the agreement and be done with it. The option period would last indefinitely, and if you don't get to release an album, well—the term never ends. With certain types of bankruptcy, obligations to a personal service contract can be released. By filing, you're saying: "I have debts that I can't afford to pay. I'm in a service agreement that has taken away my ability to earn outside of this and I'm being starved out since I'm not making any money, but I'm still stuck under this exclusive agreement where a label is no longer functioning as it needs to." Bankruptcy would essentially have potentially cleared out the agreement (*if* the court sympathized with me).

But I'm telling you—I just could not *fathom* doing it. And I didn't *understand*, even when my lawyer at the time tried to explain it. People who come from blue-collar families like mine do not file for bankruptcy in their early twenties. Especially when they're NOT bankrupt. What would people think? My aunts and uncles would worry or pity me or judge Mom even *more* harshly for getting me into this deal or think I spent all of my Coogan account like some child-star stereotype.

If you're born into wealth, I think there's this unspoken safety net that the rest of us just don't have. A confidence that if you don't see abundance in front of you at the moment, you will in the future or you can just ask someone for it. That's a different concept of resources than the one I grew up with. I was terrified that filing for bankruptcy would mean I'd never have money ever again and that I'd have to scrub toilets for the rest of my life. *That's* where my mind went. The lawyer I had back then was just trying to teach me what rich people do. But my youth, poverty mindset, and concern with appearances prevented me from grasping it as a real option.

So, I needed something else. My lawyer said we could sue even though, to him, the contract looked ironclad. But I had been twelve years old when I signed it. All these adults had been around to ensure it was the best possible deal. *How* could that be the case? My Manager found two litigators who were willing to represent me on contingency (meaning they made no money upfront and would only collect on the back end after the case was settled). I sobbed, sitting across from the litigators, explaining that all I wanted to do was move forward. I wasn't looking to make money from a suit or go after damages. I just wanted to stop feeling like my life was at a standstill. Leaving Barry and Jomo was not something I looked forward to or wanted. Shit, I'd put *college* on hold to try to make things work and continue my career with them.

Still, enough was enough. And after I gave the go-ahead, the litigators drafted up a lawsuit that was ready to go if Blackground continued to not make right on their end of the deal.

CHAPTER 11

FEEDING THE HUNGRY GHOST

ONE MORNING, HUNGOVER AS FUCK AFTER A LONG NIGHT OF WRITING-TURNED-partying in NYC, my friend Billy called to tell me about this song he'd just heard: "Marvins Room" by Drake. It reminded him of me, since Billy knew all about the idiotic situationship I had been self-medicating with for the past few months. Screaming matches outside of Serena Williams's house where I had taken the boy to a pool party. The verbal-turned-physical assaults we descended into whenever jealousy and alcohol combined to rear its ugly head. Fighting while drunk driving as he whipped my cocaine-white BMW through the canyons. Me yelling from the sidewalk up to his apartment where he lived with his mom when he wasn't answering my texts, even though the TV in his room was blaring. The boy pushing me so hard down to the concrete of a parking garage that I needed chiropractic adjustments.

After Billy sent it to me, I listened to the song over and over again and imagined what it would be like if my boyfriend ever tried to move on from the dangerous space we were inhabiting. I began to write. My ego pulsated as I spit out lines like:

> *"I ran into your homeboys*
> *They're all fuckin' idiots*
> *You're not even my boyfriend*
> *But you're trippin 'cause I'm in the club*
> *Yeah, that's right, I'm dancing*
> *And something cool is in my cup*
> *Imma send a sexy picture*
> *To remind you what you're givin up."*

Outside of my friends and team, I don't think people knew that this was the way I thought and spoke, but fuck the "JoJo" image—*this* was the most "Joanna" thing I'd written up to that point. I was so tired of that boring-ass, tried-and-true marketable image that had been crafted for me, one that I'd so easily stepped into. "JoJo" was a good role model, someone who always knew the right thing to say, a less-troubled version of many of my pop-star peers around that time. But me, Joanna? I *was* troubled. I *was* dealing with shit. And what I was writing now reflected my raw, hungover, ego-bruised, Adderall-fueled thoughts. Within an hour of typing into the notes section of my phone, I had the lyrics to my "girl version" ready to go.

Later that night, I landed back in LA and went to Travis Garland's studio where he and his girlfriend, my makeup artist Carlene, often hosted me to write, record, and hang out. Jordan, who was now splitting his time between LA and Boston, had created a track that sounded just like the original. Travis then laid down some sexy "fuck boy" vocals in the beginning, and I talked my shit. *"Fuck that new girl that you like so bad . . . she's not crazy like me, I bet you like that."* Surprisingly, M.M. *loved* it, so we sprang into action with our friends at Rap-Up.com (the same people who put out my mixtape), and they agreed to host it online for us.

Hundreds of millions of listens later, it quickly became obvious that people liked this new sound coming from me. Even Drake DM'd me, saying he dug it. The radio started playing it organically, and it became a part of the pop culture conversation online, too. In the midst of so much uncertainty and fear in my career and personal life, it felt good to have this glimmer of positive feedback and attention—even if it was a product of me at my most toxic.

Two months later, we released "Disaster" as the first official single from my long-awaited third album. Sure, I liked the song and knew it was catchy and that I sounded good on it—but it was still hard to talk myself into it. The truth was that it basically repeated the same formula as "Leave (Get Out)" and "Too Little, Too Late"—and that *bugged* me. With artists like Gaga and Rihanna forging their own lane and constantly evolving their sound, I hated how middle-of-the-road and, frankly, *basic* this "comeback" was shaping up to be. It didn't seem like there was enough time or space or resources for me to be able to experiment. And now I was being heavily persuaded to get in line because this was the only song we'd cut so far that Interscope would get behind.

I was confused. This track was *SO* different from the edgier sound that people were currently responding to from me on the interwebs. But then again, I could really relate to the lyrics my friend Gino wrote:

> "*'Cause the walls burned up when our love fell down*
> *And it turned into whatever, now we're sayin' never*

Feel the fire 'cause it's all around
And it's burning for forever and always
We gotta let it go and be on our way
And live for another day
'Cause it ain't the same, my baby
Watch it all fall into the ground
No happy ever after, just disaster"

The relationship I was in was a fucking mess, and *none* of it was sustainable. The fighting in the streets. The drinking and smoking. M.M. having to get in between us. Having to make phone calls when threats were spewed.

So I slowly but surely walked away, channeling all that energy into the song, shooting a video, sending it over to radio, and going back out on tour to promote it. I was so stoked to be on the road with Joe Jonas, a pal from the *TRL* days, as he embarked on his first solo effort away from his brothers. It felt like a safe, wholesome reprieve after such a dark season. My fans probably didn't know just how badly I *needed* this back then. Performing live was one of my favorite things in the world, and it felt like food for my soul to get out there again. My Manager and I held on tight to the belief that if I could just leave Blackground's shenanigans behind, I would be one of the biggest stars in the world. Gotta say, though, being the first performance slot of that tour, right before Jay Sean, was an exercise in humility. In many ways it felt like I was starting from the beginning again.

In every city we stopped in, I did interviews and performed live for every radio station that would let me and my guitar player into their studios. We were getting amazing feedback from people at pop radio, making me feel like we had another hit on our hands. But then, a couple weeks into the launch, Barry allegedly had some aggressive and threatening words with a department head at Interscope. "Disaster" premiered on the Billboard Hot 100 at number 87 and then fell off the chart the next week. *Womp.*

It could have been a coincidence. Then again, maybe not.

Maybe the title could have predicted how it was gonna end.

After that, it was more of the same. More confusion. More dodging when I tried to get answers. More time spent talking to boys who had nothing really going for them but a willingness to do what it took to make me feel desired. I loved when a guy couldn't believe that "someone like me" would ever even look at "someone like them." Meaning: someone who either lived with their mom or had several roommates.

I also had an affinity for older men who told me I was "different than other girls my age." Call it "daddy issues" if you please, but I wasn't the only one. As all the men around me in Hollywood got older, it seemed like the ages of their girlfriends never quite followed. There was one such figure like this at the time who had developed quite the reputation with popstars and movie starlets, and yes, I'm talking about *him.* Over the years, men like him were the ones who taught me how to drink whiskey and how to get into the hottest clubs through the back doors, the ones who doled out unsolicited career and fashion advice, which I imagine made them feel as needed as it made me feel chosen. Right alongside alcohol, the opposite sex was another favorite gateway to numb out any and all of my unwanted emotions.

One time, Solange Knowles invited me to her birthday party at a West Hollywood mansion. I always thought that she and her whole family were so amazing, and I was excited to get the chance to be around them. The fact that her parents were helping guide her and her sister's careers, and both Solange and Bey were phenomenally talented, and they all seemed to really get along? How did that

WORK? They were doing the impossible—and I couldn't wait to see that for myself.

M.M. helped me summon the courage to say hello to Beyoncé, who remembered me and remains the most radiant human I've ever interfaced with: gracious, kind, and incandescent. I took a picture with Solange and felt like we both looked so pretty and colorful in our little dresses. I had observed her interacting with other people at the party, and every time, it seemed like she was having these fascinating, free-flowing conversations. I never really knew what to say to fellow artists other than to compliment them (and only if whatever I had to say was true). Being around a talented peer like her shined a light on my social and artistic hang-ups, and it wasn't long before I started to get in my head. I questioned absolutely every physical movement and every word that came out of my mouth. Did the drinks help or hurt? I could never quite tell.

As My Manager and I walked around the pool, a vodka cranberry in my hand and a club soda in hers, we kept running into industry executives who asked why "they didn't have me" (I assume they meant on their label roster) and wondered when/how I was getting out of the Blackground deal so they could "take me to the top where I belonged." I'd play up my humility and disbelief, but this type of conversation was what I had come to expect and the very thing that kept me going. Someone even referred to me as "the caged bird," saying that folks could observe me from outside the cage and hear me sing, but I wasn't able to do what I was meant to do: *fly*. Whenever they'd good-heartedly ask about when I was planning to put out new music, I'd let M.M. take the lead and explain the circumstances of my shackles. I would then nod and furrow my brow or shrug, adding a word or phrase here and there for added effect, but when it came down to it, I didn't wanna mess up the "sell." Her strength was marketing and my strength was singing. And our new pitch—my new identity—was that I'd been a victim of bad people and a bad industry.

People couldn't seem to believe what a clusterfuck I was in. There was a lot of goodwill out there for me, and it felt like the whole industry and the world were out there rooting for me: the underdog. M.M. and I had been good to folks over the years, and we kept believing that if we could just hold on, we'd come out of this whole mess stronger than ever. But every time we repeated the story of me being powerless and at a standstill, I felt it in my body: victimhood. Awkward and uncomfortable, feeling bad for myself, like my heart had worms crawling around inside of it, eating me alive from the inside.

Like many women in the industry, and many women in general, my looks became an even more constant source of anxiety for me during my early twenties. By the time I was twenty-one, I had 32Ds. They had naturally developed into what I would have given *anything* for back when I was stuffing my bra with those "cutlets" for the "Leave" video. I can't lie; up until that point, I thought my boobs looked pretty damn great.

Then, one day while I was surfing the internet, I saw the picture I had taken with Solange at her party on some blog. In the comments, people were all talking about how saggy my boobs were. I mean . . . yeah. They were not sitting. They were tig ol' bitties that kinda hung a bit. Even though I felt beautiful when I'd worn that dress, as soon as I saw those comments, I instantly regretted not wearing a bra, too. Soon, I regretted wearing the godforsaken thing at all.

I also felt a lot of shame that I hadn't been able to protect myself from these kinds of comments with perfection. I didn't usually look at gossip-y sites like this, nor did I actively seek out negative feedback, but I honestly think at this point, I needed an excuse to take a break from life—and so I found one. With so much out of my control, I felt like one of the only things I could really do while I was waiting was to financially invest in improving myself. It was either going to be piano lessons or rehab or *this*. *This* was the most appealing because it was damn near instant and would knock me on my ass for a week. After a few months of thinking about it and talking to other women who had recently gotten the procedure, I decided to get a breast augmentation. The doctor I went to told me that my best option for a nice, lifted effect without possibly damaging the feeling in my nipples was to add a small implant to fill out some of the skin enclosing my already-large breasts. I hoped for the best, even though I didn't feel totally comfortable with the idea of my boobs being heavier than they already were.

Other than when I got my wisdom teeth out, this was the only time I had ever been under anesthesia. The recovery involved some of the worst physical pain I'd ever experienced, but I very much enjoyed the hypnotic effect of the drugs they prescribed. In fact, I felt myself loving them a little *too* much—not caring about much of anything, just watching TV and sleeping on and off all day. I also felt closer to my father as I inhabited his preferred state of being. I loved that I had a valid reason to stay in bed all day and not answer anyone's texts or calls. Disconnected from the world of my own expectations and outside pressures, I felt like I could finally relax.

And my tits? Well, they felt like rocks for the first couple weeks, but then they softened up and looked pretty nice. Was the result worth the money? Nah, I don't think so. Should I have gone to rehab instead? Probably.

Meanwhile, Barry and Jomo had been holding on to some never-before-heard Aaliyah vocals for years and were finally ready to open the vault. After a prolonged period of shopping the project around for the right producer, Noah "40" Shebib and Drake agreed to take on the priceless files. In a last-ditch effort to try to make things work with Blackground, I optimistically went out to Toronto and started working with 40. It really seemed like the perfect fit. My version of their song "Marvin's Room" was still a conversation in the zeitgeist after going viral—all this before that was even really a thing. So I got looped into the deal with Aaliyah's long-lost tracks, too, and I decided to make the most of it.

That's where my next single, "Demonstrate," came from. 40's production was special and the song made me feel all kinds of ways. It was deep, musical, and unique yet accessible. I had decided since putting out my remix on "Marvin's Room" that sensuality and sexuality were the new weapons I could yield to make "my thing." 40 called up Canadian artist Dvsn to write with me, and even though I loved their music, I just couldn't get the pressure out of my head during that session. It felt like my whole career depended on whatever songs came out of it. My nerves were higher than a whistle note, and I just couldn't stop thinking that these guys were probably thinking I wasn't beautiful enough to "sell the music." I wanted to feel like my best, most focused self and didn't want to have an appetite, so I took Adderall and became even *more* intense than I naturally am—if you can imagine that.

After I got back to LA from Toronto, M.M. told me that 40 didn't really like working with me and that his manager thought I was whack. Alrighty then! Luckily, though, everyone seemed to love the two songs that came from those sessions and were willing to embrace this new, more sensual R&B direction because it came with an OVO cosign.

We were all set to film the most opulent-looking video I'd ever been a part of at a big fancy mansion in LA. Leading up to the shoot, Jomo started talking to me about looking the part, taking the baton from his dad. I hit the gym harder than ever and dosed myself with friends' Adderall, no longer under the expensive guidance of that witch doctor, I mean, *nutritionist*.

But my binge eating at night was still something I looked forward to. Like I had grown up seeing Mom do, I all but starved myself during the day and then gorged on everything I could get my hands on once I was alone and away from anyone's judgement. I was hyperfixated on food: what would I eat, how many calories and fats and carbs were in each bite, and how soon could I get back home at night to eat in peace. Eating around other people took the pleasure out of the equation, so I stuck to salads until I could be in the quiet solitude of my apartment or hotel room. Salty, sweet, salty, sweet. I would eat until my emotional state changed. It put me to bed like a Xanax would. I just needed something to take me out of my mind. And the pattern of telling myself I was going to stop but not being able to eroded any sliver of self-trust I still had. I was still working out a lot, but I felt ashamed. I couldn't get over this idea that I was letting everyone down because I wasn't as thin as I "should have been," but I couldn't bring myself to stop the bingeing, either.

The day of the shoot, I was on edge. My cousins were there doing my hair, and Carlene was on makeup duty. They all did their best to keep my spirits up and keep the vibe light. But I was bogged down by a gray cloud of anxiety that I couldn't do what was expected of me, that I never knew what was next for me, that I had been effectively getting whiplashed over and over for the past few years. During the lunch break, a camera crew came over to interview me and ask about my upcoming album, dropping the lawsuit, Drake, and so forth. I felt like I was going to cry. What I was able to summon were slightly passive-aggressive answers that barely covered up my embarrassment over not having more concrete answers to share. People just said words around me. What was the truth?

Back on set, My Manager rushed over to the DP (director of photography) to adjust camera angles, looking at the monitors and then back at me with concern. I was triggered and taken right back to the moments when Mom would make "those faces" while I was in the recording booth. Or when she'd tell me to suck in my stomach right before going out onstage. I *must* be fat and ugly. Too unattractive and large to sell this music. M.M. made them change the lighting and the angles they were shooting me from. Everything had to be shot from above now. I started hearing all these whispers around me and wasn't sure if they were in my head or not. So I took someone's Xanax and drank a bottle of white wine to drown these negative thoughts out as I tried my best to push through the rest of the shoot.

A couple weeks later, we got a rough edit of the video, and *everything* was picked apart. M.M. reassured me that every female artist goes through the same level of making sure they're presented in the best light if they have a team who actually cares—and that she was just trying to protect me. She hated that she had to be the one to relay all the negative things that Barry, Jomo, and Jimmy were saying. But according to "everyone," the styling was wrong. The leading man looked "too feminine and not into me." The hair and makeup weren't hitting the mark. My legs looked unflattering, sitting atop that chandelier. I was too pale; I should have gotten a darker tan. My face was way too intense whenever I was delivering the lyrics. I wasn't being sexy enough—scratch that, I wasn't being sexy *at all.*

The video was eventually scrapped, and I later found out several people who worked on it didn't even get paid, including the director. I was livid. It wasn't that I was particularly attached to the shoot, but I couldn't stand that my reputation was being fucked with in *yet another way*, all because of the whims of someone else. If anyone was going to fuck with my reputation, it'd be *me*.

CHAPTER 12

LIFE PRESERVERS

BETWEEN HAVING TO CALL THE POLICE A COUPLE OF TIMES THAT YEAR TO DO WELFARE checks on Mom in Massachusetts and flying back to New Hampshire after getting the news that Dad had OD'd, I was barely hanging on to my own sanity.

I needed professional help.

I started seeing a therapist, and after a few weeks of telling her all about my life, I went on antidepressants. Dr. Janice explained that I was experiencing situational depression but that my true *essence* was not depressed. She said that anyone in my shoes would need a life preserver and that getting on an SSRI could be that for me in this season of life.

Janice sported bouncy white-blonde hair, dressed in bright colors, and had blue eyes like deep pools of spring water. Whenever she'd open the door to let me into her office, I wanted to immediately burst into tears because I was so relieved to be in her presence. This woman was pure sunshine. She offered me tea and biscotti at the beginning of every session, and I never *once* felt

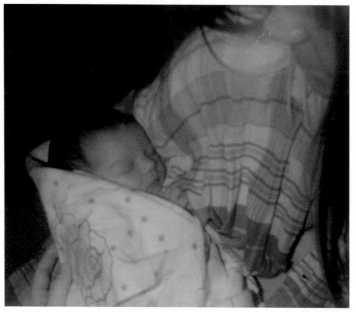

Newborn lil' baby me with Mom

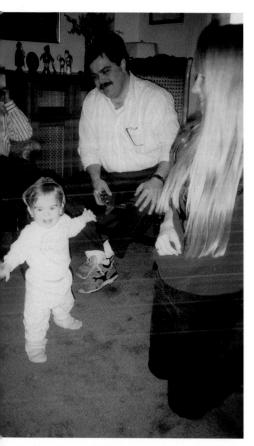

Rockin my mom's signature haircut
(with my hamster)

Bein' a toddler with Mom and Dad
(and I think that's cousin David?)

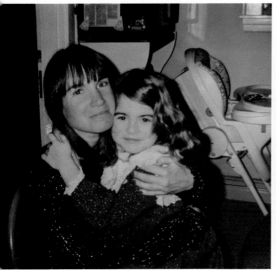

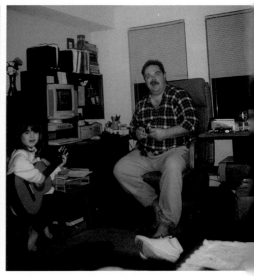

Not sure where we were but Mom sure is pretty ☺

Dad and me jammin' and making faces in Nashua, NH

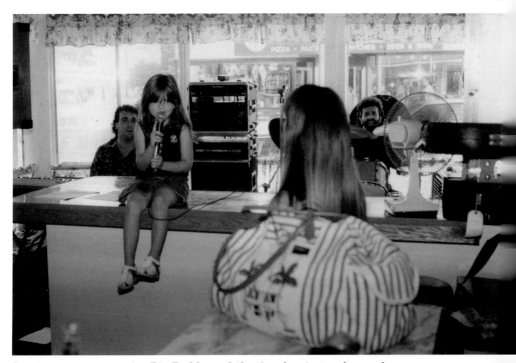

Singing to my mom at a Big Daddy and the Accelerators rehearsal

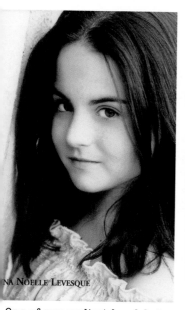

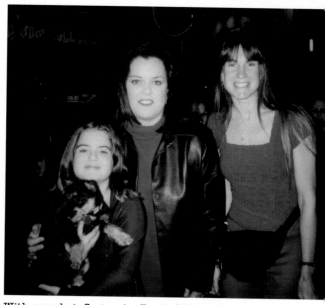

One of my earliest headshots
taken by one of my mom's
housecleaning clients

With our dog, Sugarpie, Rosie O'Donnell, and
Mom in NYC

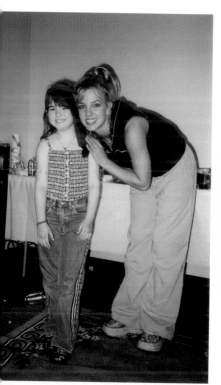

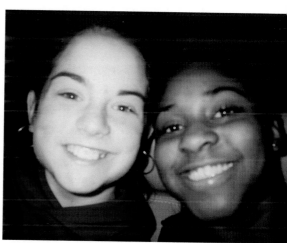

With Charlena aka NeNe

With Queen Britney Jean Spears in
Mansfield, MA at the Kiss108
Concert, backstage

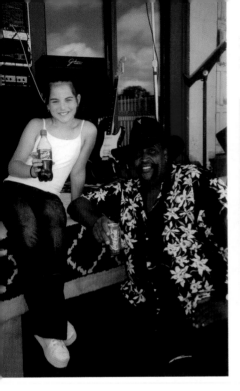

Big Daddy (Darwin Phillips) and me pretending to shoot a Coca Cola ad

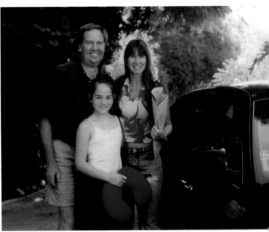

Mom's cousin Stephen with Mom and me after we moved into his home in La Habra, CA (those are printed directions in the envelope)

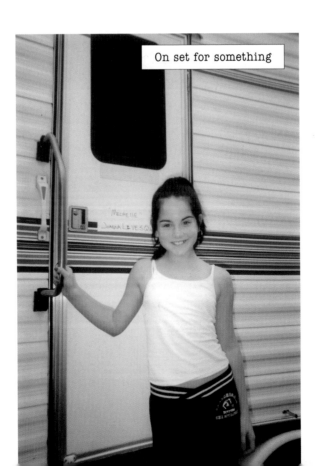

On set for something

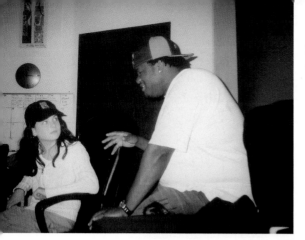

The very start of 1st album vibes with Vince

With Vince at a big fancy NYC studio

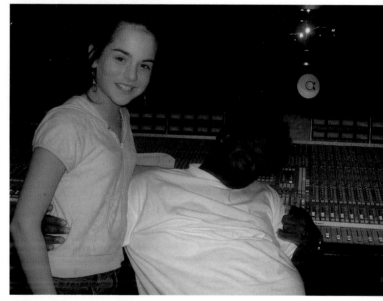

Feelin' myself in a big chair at the studio

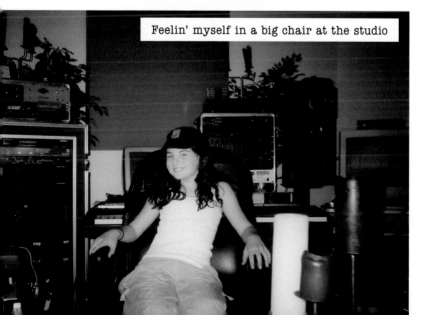

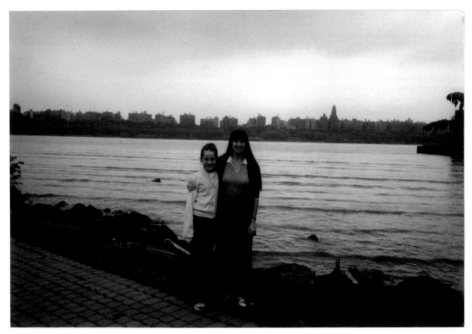

Mom and me in Edgewater, NJ on the riverwalk

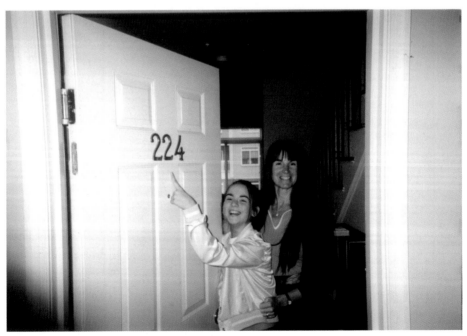

Move-in day at our apartment in Edgewater, NJ

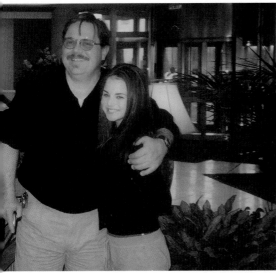

ad visiting me at a hotel after a performance
omewhere in New England

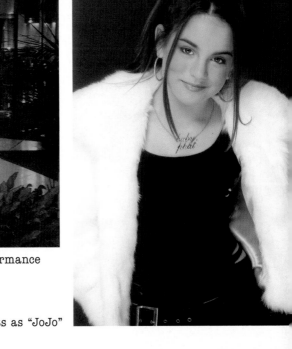

One of my first photoshoots as "JoJo"

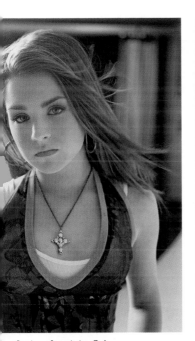

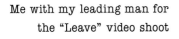

photo shoot in LA

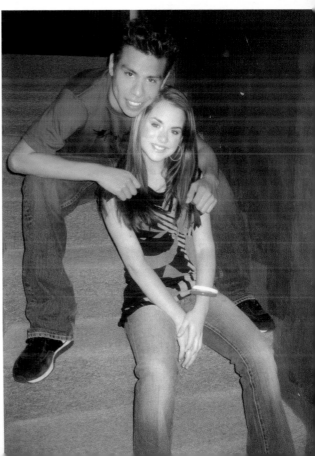

Me with my leading man for
the "Leave" video shoot

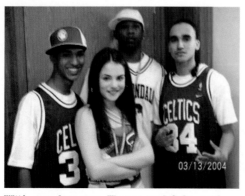

With my dancers, Kanec and Solo, and Eli, the head of promotions for Blackground

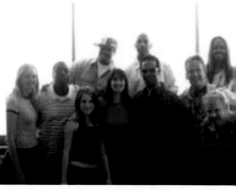

With Mom, Barry Hankerson, and staff from Blackground and Universal

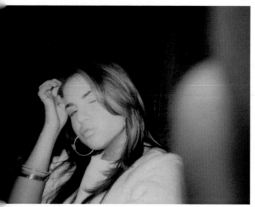

Bein' 14 with my highlights and my hoops

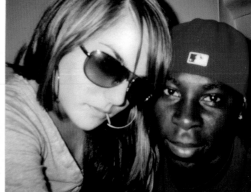

With Freddy Adu

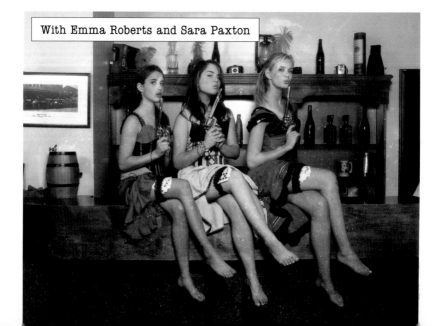

With Emma Roberts and Sara Paxton

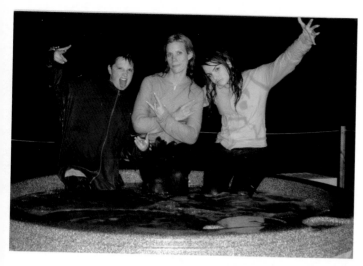

With Josh Hutcherson and Cheryl Hines on the set of *RV*

With Robin Williams, Josh Hutcherson, Hunter Parrish, Alex Ferris, and Chloe Sonnenfeld in Vancouver for *RV*

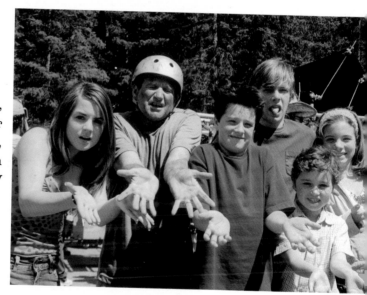

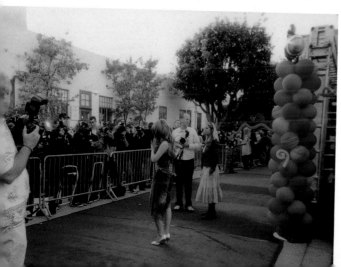

At the premiere for *Aquamarine*

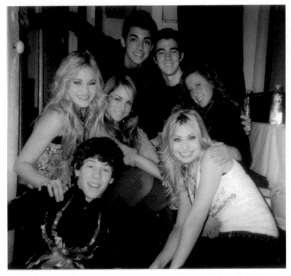

With the JoBros, Aly + AJ, and my friend Jill backstage in Boston

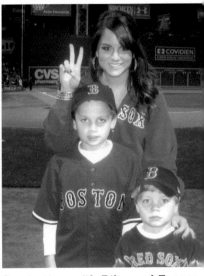

Cousin time with Riley and Tanner before singing the national anthem at Fenway

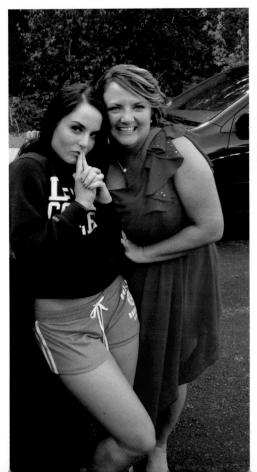

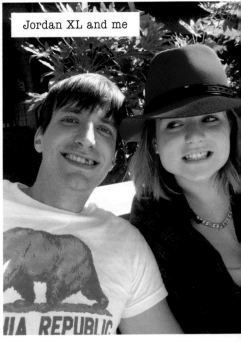

Jordan XL and me

No idea of the context but here I am looking mischievous while Aunt Connie looks adorable

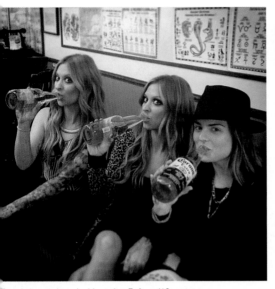

Bout to get a tattoo in LA with my
cousins, Lisa and Chrissy

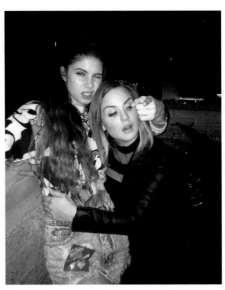

Leah Labelle and me

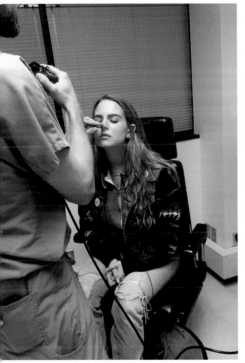

Me at the Ear, Nose, and Throat doctor
in 2016 after losing my voice

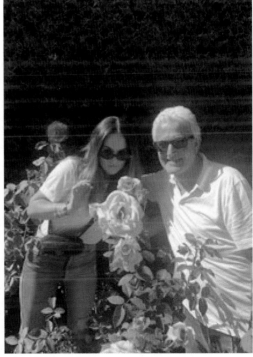

Billy Steinberg and me in his garden

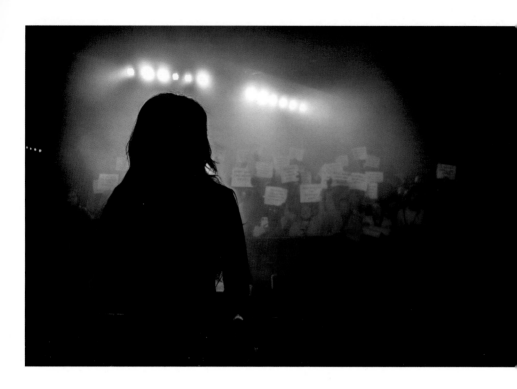

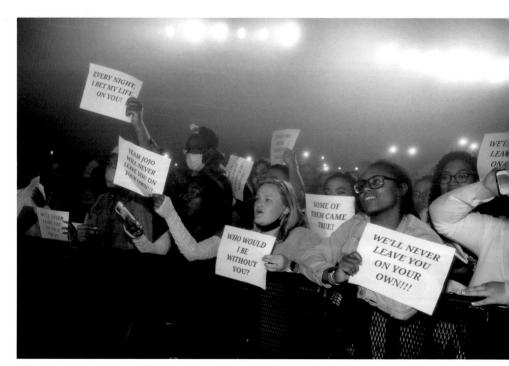

The most loyal, thoughtful, amazing fans in the world... #teamjojo ♥

Photo credit: Doug Krantz

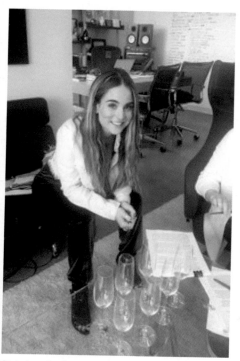

Signing to Interscope

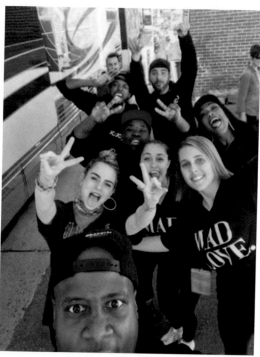

Pullin' into another city on the Mad Love
Tour with some of the crew!

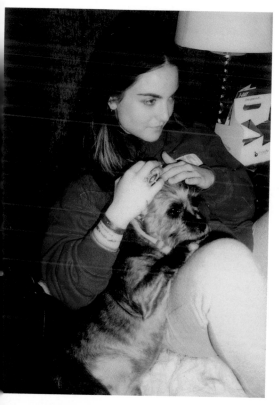

Me and Zelda at her birthday party

My baby, Agapé, and me at the
studio listening to a take over
the loud speakers

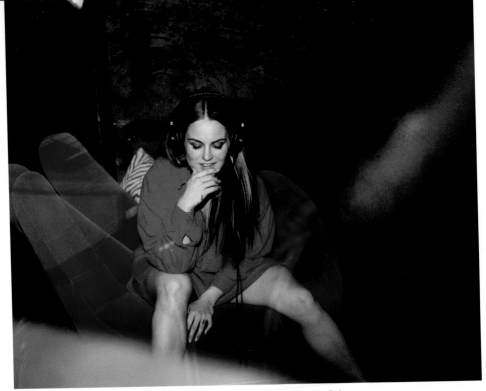

Listening back to my 2018 re-recordings in a studio in LA

Photo credit: Doug Krantz

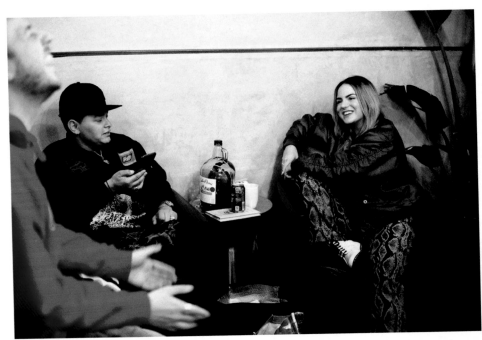

In the studio with Lil' Eddie and Lido

Photo credit: Doug Krantz

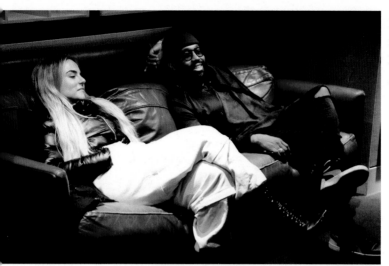

Listening back to music with PJ Morton

Photo credit: Doug Krantz

Doug Krantz, Katie Gallagher, and me on set of the video for "Worst (I Assume)." Katie hates pictures so I'm honored she let me include this one.

Photo credit: Alfredo Flores

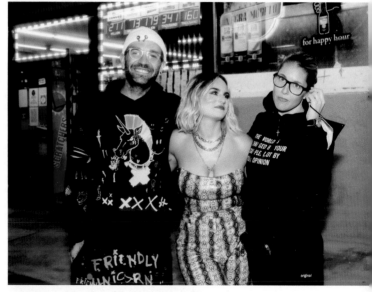

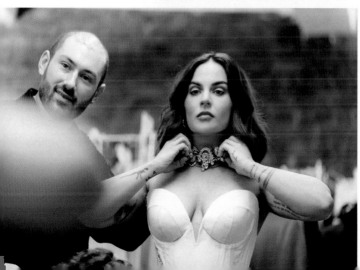

In a wardrobe fitting on the road to playing Satine

Photo credit: Avery Brunkus

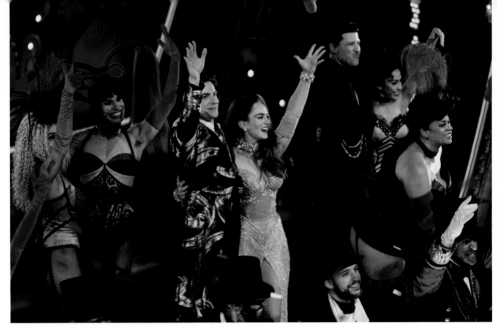

With the cast of *Moulin Rouge! The Musical* on Broadway

Photo credit: Avery Brunkus

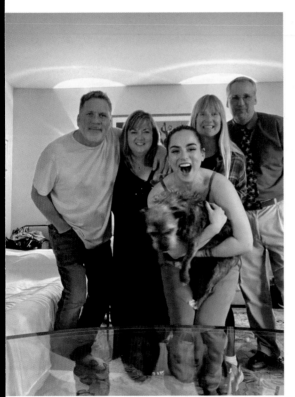

After opening night of my Broadway debut w/ Uncle Dale, Aunt Connie, Mom, Uncle Scott, and Agapé

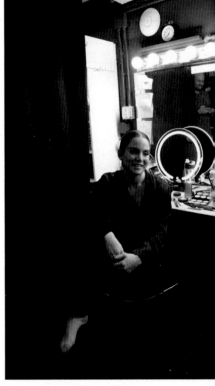

Backstage chillin' ♥

like she was in a rush or judged me for the treats I ate or how much honey (not calorie-free Splenda) I added to my drink.

I knew Janice had clients back-to-back, but somehow, she made me feel that I was the only one. She spoke to me in different ways, sometimes mirroring my own harsh humor and slang but also like a wise, loving, and nurturing Southern grandmother. When she looked deep into my soul, I felt her sincerity in every fiber of my being when she told me: "No child should have had the pressure on them that you did and still do. In spite of this, it's a *miracle* you are as wonderful and loving as you are." I revealed all my deepest fears to her—of becoming like my parents, of never reaching my full potential, of letting addiction and depression overtake me. I also shared that alongside these fears, a big part of me felt undeserving of what I had, the success I'd achieved so far, the money that was in my bank account.

I lived in constant fear that my life could change in an instant. At any moment, I just knew I was going to get the phone call that one of them had died. If it was Mom, it would've been because I had made her so sad that she just couldn't take it anymore. And if it was Dad, it would've been because he loved being high more than he loved being present for life.

I was now fully in this lawsuit with no end in sight. Yet I had to keep things on good enough terms with people at the label in case they were able to get it together and make things between us work again. I was expected to stay skinny and wait—for however long it took. "Stay ready so you don't have to get ready," as one of my former trainers loved to say. To add fuel to the fire, I tried to keep up with a roster of guys in my phone and put-on like I was some kind of player, but to be honest, all I really wanted was to be distracted from reality and bank up as much dopamine as I could.

Back then, alcohol sometimes seemed like my saving grace, but it really only made everything else that much worse. I hate to say it now, but I'd drink on an empty stomach (when I was being "good" and restricting calories)—feeling like I had a high tolerance and thinking I was fine to drive—and get behind the wheel. I'd be flying down the highway and start bawling my eyes out the second I saw a cross on the hillside, blasting Kirk Franklin's "Help Me Believe" and "Hide Me" as loud as the stereo would go. I was so scared and so sad. I've never had suicidal ideations, but at the same time, I felt like it might just be better if something happened and I was no longer alive. At least all of my music would be released into the world. I couldn't see a light at the end of this tunnel. I was consumed by melancholy and a perpetually inflating/deflating ego.

Oftentimes during those drives, I was totally blacked out, but the people around me said they couldn't tell that I was even fucked up. Every time I made it home and didn't injure or kill anyone (including myself), it was only by the grace of God. Sometimes, I would wake up and have absolutely no idea how I got to where I was, lucky that I'd only scratched my car or somehow lost the rearview mirror. Janice made me promise to stop. I wanted to, so I told her I would. But I didn't know if I was actually strong enough to keep any promises to anyone—let alone myself.

The guilt and tension that lived within me felt unbearable. Thankfully, as the Prozac took effect, the edge of those feelings dulled—just enough for me to keep trying. I beat myself up for not spending my time more constructively. Instead of going out drinking with friends, I wished I had the discipline and energy to spend more nights at home learning how to play piano or produce my own music. But all I wanted to do was feel a sense of comfort and relief *immediately*.

It was as good a time as ever to back away from the cliff's edge, get back in the river of life, and figure out where I'd left my life preserver. I wasn't ready to die, and I certainly didn't want to be the reason anyone else died either.

It was during this time that Janice asked if I had ever tried yoga. There was a colorful yoga studio near my apartment in Mid-City one of my girlfriends went to that looked inviting. It always sounded like some bougie LA shit and something I probably wouldn't like. Still, I knew I needed a change, so I started attending classes. No one was more surprised than I was that I enjoyed it so much, to the point where sometimes I'd even go back for a second round at night. Don't get me wrong; yoga frustrated the *hell* out of me. I wanted to "get it" and be great at it instantly— and I definitely wasn't. It was humbling, to say the least. But more importantly, I liked knowing that there was something I could do with this one body and mind I was given beyond turning them into some package to be consumed and critiqued by the powers that be.

As an added bonus, the yoga community was instantly welcoming; it was a total 180 from the Hollywood scene I'd come to know. It was reminiscent of religion but markedly different. Every time we arrived at our mats, the teacher instructed us to focus on ourselves and our bodies. No one had to look like the person to their left or right; we just had to show up exactly how we were, right in that moment.

As comforting as that was, it didn't immediately compute for me. For the first few months (probably years, honestly) of my practice, I was in a silent competition with everyone around me in whatever yoga class I took. No matter how calm I may have looked to my classmates, inside I would be burning up with rage and shame when I couldn't quite nail an inversion or hold a tree pose as long as the teacher. Sometimes, I thought I'd surely taken a step forward in my strength and flexibility—only to find myself back at the beginning the next day when I couldn't replicate that progress. I came to realize, though, that yoga is much more than the physical actions; it is about commitment, compassion, and fortitude. Slowly over time, the practice—the *real* yoga—started gently working on me.

Around the time I was introduced to yoga, a mutual friend, Francia Raisa, introduced me to Selena Gomez and we all started hanging. Sel came to a few of my studio sessions, and I swung by hers to hang out or write together. It was a breath of fresh air to be around someone who had started in this industry at such a young age, just like me, and was still so down to earth and open. I can't lie: I felt the occasional twinge of pain or jealousy at the outward differences in our lives and careers, but then I'd quickly reel myself back in: the level of fame she had was overwhelming to me. She couldn't go *anywhere* without security flanking her and fans mobbing her at every corner. It just seemed like there was no sense of freedom for her to explore the world and be wherever and whoever she wanted to be. I imagined that must be suffocating. It made me grateful for the relative anonymity I had whenever I walked down the street.

For Galentine's Day, Selena invited me to Taylor Swift's house so we could all celebrate. Taylor had this arts and crafts section set up where we took pictures of ourselves and slapped them on this cute questionnaire where we described our best qualities (and our worst ones), the things we were looking for in a guy, and the reasons why we were currently single. I snuck outside to the In-N-Out truck on her lawn to grab a burger, fries, and Diet Coke, but also went out there to text the guy I'd been obsessing over at the time. This whole "girl's night" scenario at Taylor's, reclaiming the saddest day of the year for single folks, was the best possible distraction from the complete unavailability of this fuckboy.

This was such a big departure from the female popstar polar-ization of the 1990s and early 2000s. It was the 2010s now, and the "girl boss"/"girl gang" vibe was having a real moment. Earlier in my career, I'd been conditioned to keep girls like Selena and Taylor close but never let them really know what I was doing, going through, or thinking. To be "strategic." But I wasn't. I some-times wished I could be, but I simply liked who I liked and didn't like who I didn't like. While some of my peers could "play the game" like their lives depended on it, I never could quite figure out how to posture and politic and not feel like a big huge phony in the process. I genuinely enjoyed these girls, and although two of them were among the most famous women in the world, we had the shared experience of starting out very young, and I was happy to be let into the fold, part of a group. We stayed up late, wore sweats and no makeup, laughed until we cried, and ate copi-ous amounts of french fries. It was awesome.

Taylor was sweet and complimentary, and she seemed excited that Selena had brought me along with her. She mentioned deep-cut songs of mine she liked and kept saying how fucked up the lawsuit was, the fact that I couldn't put out music. I don't remem-ber if she already knew what was going on from social media or if I'd told her about the situation, but she was—in no uncertain terms—letting me know she was on my side and believed in me.

I appreciated Taylor's kind words, but I thought I could see in the eyes of everyone else at the party that they felt bad for me. Maybe they thought I was never going to get out of this limbo. Or that it was too late for me even if I did. Maybe they could tell I didn't have the money or the parents who could help dig me out of any holes I might find myself in. Maybe they saw the imposter in my eyes. Then again, perhaps that was all my own projection.

CHAPTER 13

UNCONDITIONAL LOVE: AGAPÉ

BY 2013, I KNEW THAT DAD WAS GOING TO DIE IF SOMETHING DIDN'T CHANGE. HE WAS constantly in and out of the hospital, the methadone clinic, the rehabilitation facility. His weight was skyrocketing, his stomach was hard and round like a watermelon, and his activity was at an all-time low. He barely even went outside.

I was at a Color Me Mine in Studio City with my girls Leah and Denise, brushing turquoise paint across a ceramic spoon holder, when I got the call from my Aunt Sally that Dad was back in the ICU. I was scared and sad, but I was also fucking *pissed*. Whenever Mom was good, Dad was bad—and vice versa. She'd just gotten back on the wagon and was committed to her sobriety again, but I felt like I couldn't really lean into what a win that was because (1) I didn't know how long it would last and (2) I was super worried about Dad. I was jealous of all my friends who didn't have to deal with this, whose parents had careers and fulfilling lives and homes with a dining room and a bedroom of their own and whatnot.

I wondered if maybe Dad's environment was the problem. Ever since he and Mom split up, he had either shared living spaces with a roommate or stayed by himself in a studio apartment. He lived off social security checks and hadn't worked in years. His diet consisted primarily of peanut butter and jelly sandwiches, a couple gallons of orange juice and 2% milk per week, and pre-made food from the gas station or Hungry-Man frozen dinners from the grocery store. It broke my heart. I wished I could cook for him and see him every day. I truly had no idea how he was occupying his time besides watching DVDs and getting high on medication.

After months of focusing on my own health, I fancied myself some kind of wellness guru. I was getting really into working out and eating mindfully—juicing, yoga, Pilates, sweat lodges, intermittent fasting, adaptogen lattes, hormone-balancing tinctures . . . stuff that people back home looked at me like I had three heads when I brought up. Whenever I would drive up to New Hampshire to spend a day with him, I would—with his permission—empty the fridge and cabinets and fill them with all new healthy things. Fresh produce and healthier-but-still-easy frozen options from the local Market Basket and vitamins and supplements from the GNC near his building. He was receptive to it. He wanted to change. Maybe he just needed to get out of the Northeast; after all, he'd lived his whole life there except for his stint as a cook in the navy. Maybe the people he hung out with were bad influences. I racked my brain like a parent would over their teenager, trying to think of ways to help him get back on track.

For over a year, I'd been faithfully going to a church called Dream Center in Echo Park, and I knew they had a rehab program. Addicts could live there and serve the church while they worked to turn their lives around. Every Sunday, I bawled my eyes out as ex-gang members, victims of human trafficking, and former drug addicts shared their incredible stories of redemption. After another incident landed him in the hospital, I floated the idea of Dad moving into the Dream Center, and, to my surprise, he was really open to it. Pastor Matthew—in all his good-hearted glory—said he would personally oversee Dad's journey and look out for us throughout the whole process. When Dad let go of his apartment and came out to LA, it seemed like sobriety might just be on the horizon for him after all.

At the time, my chosen brother/musical husband, Jordan, and I were living together in an apartment in Westwood. Jordan could tell how optimistic and excited I was, and he was wonderfully supportive as we got things set up for Dad. We prayed about it together and were so stoked to have some East Coast fatherly energy out in LA. I pictured Dad coming to meet me at the studio or taking long drives where we jammed out listening to music on the Pacific Coast Highway. I could feel that things were going to be different this time.

Dad landed around sunset at LAX, and I picked him up to take him to his new living space at the church. It was just nice to have him next to me—his big paw hands wrapped around his coffee Coolatta with half-and-half and Sweet'N Low from Dunkin'—and I thought about how, on the other side of this stint, our relationship would be better. He would learn to love himself, decide that he wanted more out of life, and then be by my side as I tried to do the same in my own way. We talked about him working for me one day after he mentioned how great he'd be at tour managing. He couldn't currently walk very far without a cane, nor could I see him comfortably fitting in a tour bunk, but I humored the idea. After all the emotional ups and downs of having Mom as my manager, I didn't *really* want Dad to work for me—I just wanted him around. But I knew that in that moment, he needed something to look forward to, so I agreed that we could totally figure something out. During the drive, he told me I was his only reason for living, and I felt my throat close up. I know he meant it as a beautiful thing, but I didn't want to be his *only* reason; it felt like too much pressure.

When we pulled up to the imposing white-and-mustard-colored building on the outskirts of downtown LA, it was like dropping my kid off to college. I could tell he wasn't thrilled about where he would be living and that the actual building IRL hit a little different in person than it had online. There were multiple people assigned to each room, and he would have to work to earn his stay. Food and in-and-outs and phone calls and all that would be monitored, but he knew all that going in; it was another version of rehab, a place he had been *many* times before. As I drove away, I looked out my rearview mirror and I finally allowed myself to believe that change could be possible for him—for us. Miracles happen every day. This was going to be the beginning of a new and beautiful life for Dad and for me.

The next day, I got word that Dad had left his room in the middle of the night and no one knew where he was. My heart sank into the floor as I fell out of bed and banged on Jordan's door to wake him up. Springing into alertness, he talked me off the ledge as I ran through all of the worst case scenarios.

Had Dad somehow ended up a few miles from Dream Center on Skid Row, looking for Oxy? Had he instead gotten hooked on heroin since it was cheaper and easier to find?

Had he stumbled into the wrong alley?

Was he now lying dead in a garbage can somewhere?

Had his organs been harvested to be sold on the black market?

Could anyone take one look at him and think any of his organs would be viable to sell???

We jumped in the car to drive around the neighborhoods adjacent to the church—me in the passenger seat with my cortisol spiking, and my big bro behind the wheel. Hours of driving around LA went by before Dad finally reached out. My hands were trembling as Jordan and I looked down at the phone—Q-Tip's "Vivrant Thing" taunting me through the ringtone—and I picked up the call, staying totally silent as I waited for him to say something. I used yoga breathing exercises and tried to unclench my jaw as I listened to his apology spill out.

"Joanna? Are you there? Jo . . . I am so sorry. I'm SO sorry. The people there were seriously crazy. I was hearing screaming in the middle of the night. It was just so uncomfortable, Jo . . . I couldn't do it. I'm *sorry*. I was scared. It's so big, there's too many stairs for me to climb . . . and there are gang members, these men with face tattoos and real mental illnesses . . . I don't belong there."

I was choking back tears when he confessed that he'd taken a taxi to the airport and was already heading back to New England. I asked him what he was going to do, where he was going to go since he'd already let go of his apartment. He said to let him worry about that.

The world was spinning around me. I'd built this fantasy up in my mind, and within twenty-four hours, it completely shattered, like a glittering, delusional disco ball hitting the cold, concrete floor and bursting into a million fragments of glass.

I couldn't believe I'd actually let myself get my hopes up. He was disabled and walked with a cane, but in that moment, all I could visualize was pushing him to the ground. I was hurt and disappointed and felt so *stupid* for thinking that this could be the solution he needed. I wanted to physically hurt him for breaking my heart.

I gave up on trying to help him for a while after that, but we still stayed in touch. What was I going to do? He was my dad, and no matter what he did or didn't do, I loved him. His sisters recommended that we give him the tough love approach and disengage. But I just couldn't bring myself to do it.

Meanwhile, things were moving along with the two litigators we'd hired to comb through the fucking contract. They'd recently discovered a loophole in New York law that said you can't hold a minor to a personal service contract for longer than seven years. Mine had already exceeded that by three years. In other words, the contract was now null and void.

It was close to Christmastime, and I was in NYC for a Broadway musical workshop. The director/writer of the cult classic *Jawbreaker* was turning his movie into a musical, and Liz Gillies, Frankie Grande, and I were all part of the first cast read-through.

Just a day or two after my twenty-third birthday, I was at a friend's apartment in Midtown when my lawyer called to tell me the news: the fight was *over*. Blackground—aka Barry—had accepted that my contract was no longer upholdable, and I was *free*. We celebrated with champagne and screaming and a whole lot of crying.

After all this time, what did it even mean to be *free*? I could now sign my rights away to *another* company? That's all I knew how to do. That was the only goal in my mind back then—I didn't really take any time to consider what my other options were. I signed with Atlantic Records a few days after getting out of the previous deal, and dove into making new music before the ink had even dried on my new contract.

Aaron Bay-Schuck was my man. He was the A&R guy behind Bruno Mars's game-changing success with *Doo-Wops & Hooligans*, and he wanted to use his leverage at Atlantic to help me get back up to the top. I was fucking *stoked*. He loved what I'd made with 40 up in Toronto and another song called "Obey" that I wrote with my bro, Lil' Eddie. Best of all, he wasn't afraid of going in the pop-but-still-heavily-R&B direction that I craved.

Aaron sent me a bunch of songs that he either wanted me to finish writing or just cut, and it was feeling like we were *completely* on the same wavelength! I stayed in the studio day in and day out, laying down what I thought were my absolute best vocal performances. I would come out of the booth vibrating, feeling like I had just left my *soul* in that MF.

I was coming for blood.

Randomly, I'd also gotten really into boxing. It seemed like all the tough girlies were doing it, and it made me feel like the ultimate scrappy badass. Around the time of filming that music video for "The Other Chick," I'd started training with various boxing coaches and sometimes enjoyed watching single-player fighting sports. It's not unusual for me to stumble upon something and then suddenly become completely obsessed with it.

Anyways, there was a big fight coming up for Floyd Mayweather, and I thought his new, younger competitor was kinda cute. I looked the guy up on Instagram and saw that he followed me, so I followed him back. He asked if he could call me, and right away, we started chatting and planning a meetup with my crew when I was performing in his city.

Within minutes of being in each other's presence, he unloaded his devastating life story on me. This poor guy had been dealt the roughest deck of cards and was literally fighting his way into another reality. To a much lesser extent, I understood how he felt. He cried on my shoulder within the first few hours of meeting up in person.

This was someone who needed more help than I could possibly be equipped for—but I was strangely drawn to him. I tried to stick it out for a couple months of casual dating to see if somehow things would magically get better. But he got *hit in the head* for a living. I figured his profession and mental state were even more unstable than mine. Plus, he had a jealous streak, and beyond that—it generally annoyed me that he *always* wanted to be together. As much as I craved love and affection, this was just too damn much. I had to cut it off.

Not long after that random dalliance, I did end up getting into a relationship with a new guy. I wasn't expecting to, but *no one* made me laugh like this kid. We'd pretend to be dinosaurs, geek out on conspiracy theories, listen to the quirkiest most "out there" music, watch all the artsy documentaries.

I felt like a little girl again.

This guy also became like a brother to one of my oldest friends from middle school in New Jersey, LeMicah, and they made plans to get an apartment together. We'd pack a picnic and some wine and walk down the road to the house of this producer I'd recently been introduced to (Austin Brown), where I ended up making another mixtape and finding the creative community and musical freedom I had been craving. He was my muse. Even though we *were* smoking a lot of weed, there was no outward dysfunction or abuse and I, for one, celebrated that as a big win.

My boyfriend and I also adopted a dog, who instantly made a huge impact on our lives. She was a long, strong-bodied, brindle-coated mutt who looked like a mix of Falkor from *The Never-Ending Story*, Toto from *The Wizard of Oz*, and a human. She'd stare deeply into your eyes like she was trying to impart some mind-bending message into your soul. There were a million other rambunctious rescue dogs at this shelter who eagerly ran up to the front of the crowded cage when we walked into the room. But my eyes immediately went to the one precious little pumpkin who shook quietly in the back corner. I was curious about her. She was beautiful, and I wondered what she had been through. Why was she separate from the other dogs? I know this sounds silly, but there was a depth to her. You know how some dogs don't seem to have much going on between the ears? Looking into her eyes, I felt like she really had all these thoughts and insights about this life. I asked if I could spend some time with her in a playpen. She had the sweetest disposition, and after maybe thirty minutes of gaining her trust and gently showing her I would never hurt her, she took to me like I had birthed her myself. She deserved a powerful name, so we decided on Agapé, which means "unconditional love" and perfectly summed up how I felt about her. She was my *baby*—she still is.

I just loved that concept of unconditional love. It was pure. It's what I aspired to experience and to give to others. In that spirit, I named the next mixtape *Agap*é, too. My creative friends Austin Brown, Tommy Parker, Scott Bruzenak, and I dove in so deep on that record, crafting an eclectically cohesive sound, feeling unlimited by genre or political A&R process. My Manager wasn't too thrilled about the lack of clear hits on it—that's just not what my goal was with it—but she saw how happy I was and probably knew she *had* to let me fly in the interim of everything. That Agapé era was healing.

After two years with this boyfriend, I thought we'd be in it for the long haul. If you would've asked me then whether or not he would ever cheat on me, I would've laughed you right out of the room. One afternoon, though, I accidentally (swear to God) picked up his phone because we both had the same case and no password lock. I don't know what I was expecting to find, but it was definitely not graphic pictures and conversations between him and this girl from church. The way they were communicating would *NOT* have been pastor-approved . . . but I digress.

Shocked to the core, I looked over at him, napping peacefully in my bed, the glow of LA's golden hour washing over him like an album cover. Naturally, I woke him up by throwing his phone directly at his head. Like my first single almost ten years earlier, but with much, *much* more profanity this time, I told him to promptly "GET THE FUCK OUT OF MY HOUSE!!!!!!"

Poor Jordan, who was chillin' in the bedroom next to us, heard *everything*. My mind flashed back to my guitar-player ex and the look of hurt and disbelief that was in his eyes years ago when I told him I'd been with someone else.

This must be my karma.

In the weeks that followed, making music, going out with friends, and sanding off my feelings with alcohol kept me busy as I tried to grasp what life might be without him. If *this* guy could hurt me—a Christian, with little *actually* going for himself other than slick words and potential, who'd always said he wanted to marry me and take care of us and build a family together—who *wouldn't* hurt me?

Dr. Janice helped me realize that I had chosen someone who was in that position because it seemed like the safest bet back then to get my need for comfort met. He'd been willing to "cocoon" with me. We spent our free time making love, getting high, listening to music that I *actually liked*. I didn't realize what I was doing, but I now see how much I craved someone who was fully dedicated to making me feel good while also encouraging me to embrace my nonmainstream predilections. But what about *him*?

Perhaps he needed someone to look up to him so that he could feel more like a man.

I'll never know for sure.

But I subconsciously decided that from then on, I would cut out the middleman—and break my own heart before anyone else did.

CHAPTER 14

OLDER, NOT WISER

AS THE SUN SET OUTSIDE THE WINDOWLESS STUDIO, THE INSIDE STARTED TO RESEMBLE a dark private room in a strip club: red lights, bass-heavy beats that thumped through your chest, thick swaths of weed smoke, half-eaten lemon-pepper wings and waffle fries, Styrofoam cups filled with liquor or "purple drank" covering every surface, thick women grinding around in tight clothing, and men getting lap dances while their sunglasses fogged up.

Aaron had recently put me into sessions with a producer I'd known for a long time, someone I'd developed a casual friendship with over the years. Jordan and I had also invited this guy to come with us to church at the Dream Center a few times, and we all shared our family/industry/relationship woes over tableside guacamole post–church service. He'd just come off a string of big crossover hits for female artists, so working with him felt like the perfect fit musically.

In the studio, our conversations always seemed to veer toward sex and relationships. Our intensifying friendship was fun and not overly frisky, but I had become genuinely curious about him and wondered if he was curious about me, too. I was in a heart-break hallucination after breaking up with my ex, and he spoke to a part of me that didn't give a flying *fuck* about anything.

One night after our first session for this new project, we were out drinking Hennessy Sidecars at Bar Marmont when he casu-ally mentioned that he had a bag of Molly in his pocket. My ears perked up at what clearly sounded like a dog whistle for trouble. I used to judge artists when I'd hear rumors about them sleeping with one of their producers. But I can't overstate how much I didn't give a shit about *anything* in this moment.

Late nights back at the studio with him descended into some-thing out of one of The Weeknd's music videos. He lived walking distance from where we recorded, and we'd start the evenings either at the studio or his place, drinking tequila sodas and dropping a single pill into the glass, enjoying the music we'd been making and talking about how magical it all felt. One night, the effects took hold of us, our eyes lowered and fixated on one another, and things took a devious turn.

Suddenly, the man I'd only known as a colleague and industry friend was now fucking me on top of the studio console where we'd been making all this music just moments before. The drugs made me feel like nothing was off-limits. Let people see us. *I don't care.* Forget the condom. *I don't care.* Film it. *I don't care.* Yeah, I think girls are hot, I'll call up a girlfriend and invite her to join in on the fun. *I don't care.* Molly to come up and indica to come down.

After a couple weeks of this, I felt like a full-on fiend. I wasn't just chasing a high from the pills; I now felt a sense of needing him to want more from me than just sex and hits on the radio. He'd look deeply into my eyes as he dove in and out of my body, asking, "If this isn't love, what is it?" I couldn't tell whether he was genuinely confused or just saying reckless sexy shit for dramatic effect, trying to edge me closer to ecstasy.

As much as I wanted him to *want* to come over to my place or take me on dates, I just couldn't ask him out loud to do any of those things. It was embarrassing. If he wanted to, he would . . . right? I figured it was best to keep things "light" while we made music. Maybe he had a girlfriend and was lying about it? Maybe I was good enough to fuck, but not to date? Any fragile self-confidence I had remaining had been irradicated by the recent cheating. Maybe I was trash.

Even if deep down I wanted something more meaningful, my actions prioritized instant gratification—and this guy was more than happy to oblige. We would lie in his bed after a long day of making music and just as long of a night of debaucherous hedonsim, and he'd tell me all about how he was the only producer that truly understood me and could take me where I needed to go. This dude *loved* to play Usher's "Superstar" on repeat, singing: "*I'll be your groupie baby. 'Cause you are my superstar. I'm your number one fan. Give me your autograph. Sign it right here on my heart,*" while stroking my body and telling me how much he loved me.

"I'm the next Timbaland. He told me that himself, actually. I'm next. And you're a fucking superstar, Jo. You're my Aaliyah. But you're muthafucking JOJO. Do you understand how amazing that is?! To have the skin color you have, but sing the way you do?"

Woof.

Pretty sure Tim and Babygirl were more like brother/sister and were not lovers . . . but sure, whatever.

In his long-winded MDMA comedowns, he pontificated on how us fucking and knowing each other on this level was a key ingredient when it came to this whole project being the most amazing it could be. Even in my clouded state, I knew that was flawed logic. But I just let the man talk.

I'd lay my head on his chest, looking up at him while tracing the lines of his six-pack with my long almond-shaped fingernails. When he had been saying too gahtdamn much for too gahtdamn long, I put a finger over his lips and climbed on top of him to start another round—hoping I could shut him up and go back to getting what I convinced myself I really wanted.

The more I got to know him, the worse of a person I deemed him to be and the more I hated myself for acting desperate and naive. M.M. knew what was going on—because I told her, and I'm terrible at keeping secrets about myself, especially when I know I'm doing something wrong—but even in knowing that she disapproved, I still didn't want to cut off the energy we had between us.

I was in a full-blown addiction to love and validation, sex and stimulation.

Everything was whirring so fast. I honestly thought Aaron would love the new stuff we were coming up with. But after he heard it, he said he thought that this music was not headed in the right direction. Where initially, we thought this guy would produce a whole EP for us, now Aaron wanted me to work with different producers. I trusted him and was down to pivot. (I was actually kind of relieved.) It had become an insane environment where everything was simultaneously way too much and not enough.

One afternoon, after not speaking for a couple weeks and fully detoxing from the situation, a mutual friend told me the producer was in the hospital. He'd continued partying after we stopped hooking up, and his body had finally said, "Enough is enough."

It wasn't lost on me how far I'd pushed the limits of my own systems—just like Dad had done so many times.

The only difference was that, for some reason, I was lucky enough to walk away without making a trip to the hospital first.

About four months after signing me to Atlantic, Aaron got an opportunity to become the president of A&R at Interscope. He called to share the news, and I could hear in his voice that even though he was thrilled, he wasn't sure how I would take it. As cool as it was, the reality of the situation was this: he was no longer going to be able to work on my project, and someone else would be taking over his role. I pinched my feelings off and stashed them deep, deep down.

What kind of a person would I be if I made this about me? I should be *happy* that my friend got the opportunity of a lifetime at age thirty-two.

We talked about the possibility of me following him to Interscope once he got settled there, but I was still under contract with Atlantic and had been working on a strong batch of songs that everyone seemed to feel great about. It didn't make sense to cut ties now. Surely, I'd find another champion inside the building.

M.M., Katie, and I flew to NYC to meet with Atlantic and come up with a plan to put out a single and finish the album. After a couple months of industry musical chairs, a new A&R had been officially assigned to me. He was smart and kind and brought some good songs to the table, but he lacked the sense of urgency and understanding of my taste and R&B roots that Aaron had gotten. My team and I started to get antsy and concerned. Now that I didn't have my original person repping me at the label, it was like every Tom, Dick, and Harry was encouraged to voice their opinions about what they thought I should do.

What had seemed like smooth sailing at this new label quickly turned into choppy waters and endless confusion about what direction people thought I should be going. I came in with a vision, but I don't even remember what it was anymore. It (and my confidence) had been subtly eroded for so long that at some point I just plain abandoned ship. I was consistently advised to "stay open and just try what they want you to try. You never know! You *know* you always change your mind. Once you cut a song, you might end up loving how you sound on it and feel differently over time."

OK, I was starting to feel insulted. I was always open. But what had "going with the flow" gotten me lately? If my own team wasn't fucking with my vision, then what the fuck? I told myself I must be the problem and became determined to find a sound that everyone would agree on and approve of.

Under Aaron's tenure, I'd rounded up twenty-five or so songs that were strong, edgy, vocal showcases. I'd flown to Europe to work with some of the best dance/crossover creatives because I really wanted an international influence in the mix, too. People like Ina Wroldsen, MNEK, Steve Mac, and The Family. After those sessions, I felt clear and energized—like we all felt strongly about the direction I was heading in. But the new regime and I just weren't seeing eye to eye, and I couldn't help but feel like My Manager was more on the label's side than mine. I would get so frustrated, *dying* to understand what it was they didn't like about what I was making. Genuinely. So I could use that information and grow from it. But no one was shooting straight with me. If Aaron had thought what we had was good enough before, what was the source of this new disconnect with the rest of the label?

I'd heard so many stories over the years of company chairmen telling their artists they needed to go back to the drawing board and keep trying, so I didn't take it personally. But was that what was going on here? Or was it industry politics and dick-swinging, where everyone needed to put their own little stamp on something to deem it worthwhile? What would satisfy them enough so I could put music out? All they said was that they wanted "hits."

Well, ya don't fuckin' say.

That's what we *all* want, isn't it?

I didn't get why expensive-ass songs made by famous producers and writers (or producers and writers who already had deals at my label) were automatically perceived as better than something dope made by someone without as big of a name. In my heart, I just couldn't accept that playing it safe with a right-down-the-middle sound was a better bet than taking a chance on something I really believed in.

But I did accept it. I hate that its true, but some of the music I released was a result of people telling me what they thought I should do and me wanting everyone's approval, begrudgingly putting my own instincts last. I retreated inward and assumed a posture of defeat. Not only did I not hold the purse strings; I just had no fight left in me. It wasn't fun anymore. According to M.M., every decision was of the utmost importance. I was free of Blackground now, yes, but that also meant, according to her, that the wrong choice could be the final nail in my career's coffin, and this time it would be fully on me. I didn't want to make the wrong choice. So I deferred to others around me. My eyes lost their sparkle as I tried to grin and bear it. "Push through" became my mantra.

My Manager had made it known that the way I presented myself wasn't cutting it. So she started styling me—just for everyday stuff like meetings or last-minute performances. (It was far cheaper than having a stylist on retainer; that shit is insanely expensive.) I knew she just wanted to present me in the best light, but there was a way she spoke about it that made me feel like my "lack of taste" disgusted her. I wanted to *understand* what was so wrong about the way I dressed myself so I could correct it. Did I really have to throw a T-shirt away if it got a little stain on it?

That felt wasteful. Did I always need to keep my hair long, with extensions for added fullness, and down? That felt boring. Were my arms really too big to wear a tank top without a jacket? That didn't make sense to me at all because when I looked in the mirror, I usually saw someone who was slim. And also? WHO. REALLY. FUCKING. CARES?

Growing up, Mom had been my role model when it came to feminine beauty—and she didn't give a *shit* about fashion or freshness or ironing a blouse before wearing it. She looked amazing to me, and she washed her face with Dove soap, dyed her own hair with $11 box dye, and threw colorful outfits together with thrift store items. She never bothered with fancy creams or Botox treatments, and she had a "less is more approach" when it came to makeup; I rarely saw her wearing more than mascara, concealer, and a wisp of blush. I think that's also why Mom always looked so good for her age. She knew what she liked and what worked for her.

But Mom wasn't in the entertainment industry—I was. That was the difference. M.M. said that because I was a grown woman now, I needed to learn about all that next-level superstar female artist stuff if I wanted to compete. "Everything matters," she'd say. And I hated that I believed she was right. Whether or not I agreed with it or wanted it to be true, it was. Humans respond more favorably to things that are well-presented. People get better treatment and attention when they look their best. She just knew much more about image stuff than I did. In talking about how stylists were missing the mark with me she'd say, "They may know what works on models, but they don't know what looks good on *your* body." Even when I did book a stylist for a shoot or something, she'd find a way to sway me toward whatever it was that she thought I should wear. If they dared to push back with their opinion, it never ended well for them; they wouldn't be welcomed back for more work with us.

Things with My Manager and I were complicated at this point. But I knew she truly cared about me. Like a daughter as well as her client. (I also knew that agreeing with her was necessary in order not to have an argument.) But our personal styles were so, *so* different. Her closet was full of designer purses and shoes, and her hair was always freshly pressed and perfect, hands and toes polished, her shirts steamed and tucked in. I looked up to her and her commitment to presentation, even though sometimes I railed against what I perceived as ridiculousness. After passive-aggressively acquiescing to her time and time again, I was truly starting to forget what my personal style even was. Ever since I was a kid, I'd been proud of my eclectic taste—musically and stylistically—but now, this word that I'd once found so charming and complimentary was suddenly balked at.

"'Eclectic?'" she'd chortle. "Now is *not* the time, Jo. But I promise—just stay the course and we'll get to that. We'll get to *alllll* the artsy experimental shit you love. First, we have to build you up into a consistent figure who the public will embrace taking that journey with."

She'd always bring up other artists as examples. Rihanna was one of her go-to's; before Rihanna transformed into the risk-taker she's known to be now, she'd stuck to a cohesive and identifiable style every album cycle, winning fans over each time, evolving slowly but surely over time. I didn't love it, but I guess M.M.'s logic kind of made sense to me.

And more than anything, I wanted more sense—and less confusion.

When I walked into the meeting with those label execs in 2015, charged with energy and openness, I had been meditating and yoga-ing and working out and gaslighting myself in preparation to present my music and my best, most marketable self. Truth was, I resented these fake-ass meetings, where a bunch of people from various departments listen to full lengths of your songs and pretend to like them and just pretend in general. But I was eager to show everything I was bringing to the table and how much of a team player I could be. The powers that be smiled and said flowery words—compliments someone like me might want to hear—yet they still felt like I didn't have "the song." Of course they didn't tell me directly, though. The truth had to go through My Manager.

After the meeting, the company's copresidents sent a demo called "When Love Hurts." They said it was produced by one of the hottest producers and was a "no-brainer" (the industry *loved* this term at the time). They called it the perfect fusion of dance and pop.

The only problem? It was just not at *all* the kind of dance music I was into.

This song had a cute energetic vibe but when it came down to it, it felt annoying and vacuous to me. If I cut it, the execs said they were ready to put it out as the first single from an eventual album. They'd give me a plan and a timeline. They'd "throw the building at it" in terms of resources (which was another overused term I've never actually seen come to fruition).

Mind you, at this point, I was twenty-four. In a few months, it would be a whole *TEN YEARS* since my album *The High Road* came out. M.M. told me that the chairmen had been playing nice with me, but that the reality was, *this* was the *only* song they would push.

I really couldn't fucking believe it. I felt backed into a corner and saw no other option than to convince myself that I liked this song.

Which I didn't.

How would I spin this shit into silk in my mind? I thought the message that "love hurts [and] that's how you know it's real" was stupid at best, dangerous at worst, and it sonically went against everything I thought we were trying to do—namely, to make songs that felt tailored to *me*, that only *I* could deliver. This felt like the quintessential "insert female artist here" kind of song. Totally void of identity.

But *surely* these people who have had multiple successes at the highest level in the music game know better than I do. Right? After all, I hadn't had a bona fide radio hit since I was a teenager. Nothing made me feel more insecure than that. So I put my faith in their vision and tried to figure out how to modify it in a way that I could live with.

My Manager had the idea to have me record a soulful intro for the video version of the song and, when doing it live, mash it up with Sylvester's "You Make Me Feel (Mighty Real)," which I loved. It made me feel grounded in myself again. She also suggested releasing three singles at once to give my fans a taste of some of the different sounds still to come from me. We wanted to make up for lost time. This calmed my nerves a bit, thinking I could showcase more depth on other tracks while still delivering the pop hooks and top-notch vocals. Atlantic could focus on "When Love Hurts," but maybe, just maybe one of the *other* songs would get such a strong reaction from my fans that they'd have no choice but to pivot.

We shot visuals for each of the songs, but I felt the most disconnected from my body and my own taste during the "When Love Hurts" shoot. I'd been wanting to dance more, but I ended up feeling as uncomfortable as I looked, not nearly prepared or practiced enough to nail it on the day. I just didn't believe myself to be the right vessel for this song—and it showed.

When I looked at the camera playback, I was mortified, thinking this was going to be my reentrance after all these years. And yet I rolled with it and tried to find ways to like it and wear it as my own. I trusted my team and tried to be optimistic that they were right. But there were simply too many cooks in the kitchen, all with a cacophony of opinions. There wasn't any room for mine. And even though I was trying to be *something* . . . I still didn't know what or who I wanted to be. I resigned to repackaging myself into some version that the label would accept, even if that meant outwardly abandoning the things I liked.

Since I had agreed to let "When Love Hurts" be the first single, I made them promise we could do videos for the other two songs. On the shoot for "Save My Soul," another one of the songs from the tringle (what a cringey word), I got super drunk. I'm sure a huge part of the reason why was because I was so miserable and disappointed by my lack of artistic courage overall that it seemed like alcohol was the only thing that could help me not give a fuck. My friend Zelda made her directorial debut, and we filmed in the desert with a mix of our visions and friend groups. M.M. was livid with me when she found out I'd been drinking. There were label reps there, and when we got into the van to head to set, she called me an addict.

"Send me to rehab then!" I shouted, really kind of wishing that she would. "You think I do fucking heroin? I can't have some drinks with friends?"

It was now 1:00 A.M., and it seemed like everyone else on set (besides her and Zelda) was either high or drunk. All I needed to do was stomp around in the sand and be emo to the camera. So what if I'd been drinking? Being drunk helped me not care about all the judgmental eyes behind the lens, all the pressure I put on myself to get this right and score another hit on the charts. All I wanted to do was escape the discomfort of being in my own skin in my own life. I wished I was stronger. M.M. was mad at me, but no one was more mad at me than myself.

During this time, I had started dating this complete free spirit of a man who was twelve years my senior. This Older Man was also an East Coast transplant living out in LA, and because he was in the music industry, too, I'd run into him multiple times since my late teens. He dressed in bright garments, wore loud hats, rolled spliffs using the guts of American Spirit cigarettes, and listened to the wildest, most out-there jazz I'd ever heard. We started out as friends and then slowly transitioned into drunken make-out buddies, eventually landing ourselves in an open relationship. Since I had lost all faith in men (and myself) at this point, I needed something fun and low stakes. This guy had an alluring and unbothered vibe that I was incredibly drawn to. He wasn't afraid to go against the mainstream, and he was really entrenched in cool underground music circles. He truly didn't care what people thought of him, and I deeply respected that.

With the Older Man, I felt safe and seen as the artist I was deep down but didn't have the balls to be out loud. We discussed spiritual concepts, religious frameworks, music, economics, family structure, therapy, and the African diaspora (a subject he had studied and was beyond familiar with). He'd play bossa nova in the background while whipping up meals from scratch, all cooked from ingredients he'd grabbed during a Sunday afternoon trip to the local farmer's market. Discussions were sometimes more like lectures where he talked and I listened—but he had a lot to say and I had a lot to learn. He taught me how to cook without recipes or measurements, and how to make something delicious out of a few kitchen and pantry staples. Most importantly, he never said no to me. If I wanted a sixth drink, if I wanted to chain-smoke cigarettes or be high all day, if I flirted with someone in front of him, if I wanted to make out with all my girlfriends in one night—everything was okay. This radical acceptance was completely foreign to me, and I wasn't sure it was a good thing.

We kept things fluid until we decided to close the relationship container and really try settling into a monogamous partnership. One of our first dates was to the Lake Shrine that had been set up by Paramahansa Yogananda, author of *Autobiography of a Yogi* and founder of the Self-Realization Fellowship. It was gracefully tucked into nature and just a few blocks from the ocean. Once I walked inside the golden lotus archway, I found myself transported to a whole other world. We strolled among the unbelievable diversity of flowers and peaceful waterfalls, our eyes lingering on everything from the white swans that swam along the lake to the statues honoring ascended masters from the five major world religions.

Eventually, we wandered into the Dutch-style windmill, which had a chapel inside. It was silent as the desert in there. We sat next to each other in meditation for what felt like an hour, tuning into one another's energy without saying a word. It moved me, but somehow, it seemed to move him even more. Like my father, he was a sensitive soul who would often show his emotions and was comfortable shedding tears in front of others. Since he was older and wiser than me, I wanted to prove that I was just as deep and capable of sitting in the silence, but in reality, I was restless. Eyes closed, I felt him relaxing into the moment, almost concentrating his energy to calm mine, his breathing getting deeper and slower. I followed his lead and matched my pace with his. I didn't realize meditation could be so sexy.

In many ways, this guy balanced out the inauthenticity I was still trying to convince myself I was okay with in my career. He was both easygoing and difficult and loved to get into long-winded debates that I tended to tap out on, but he refused to apologize for being all shades of who he was. I knew My Manager hated him for a multitude of reasons, not least because "it didn't look right" and she felt he had a Svengali-like presence in my life. But he encouraged me to take a stance and change directions musically, to completely surrender to my eccentric self—whoever that might be at any given moment. Not many people around me seemed to understand that I needed what he provided: total opposition to the mainstream. He hated pop music—but he liked me even more. I felt so special in the crosshairs of that dichotomy.

One night, a few months into our newfangled monogamy, he came over to my place and sat down next to me on my turquoise-colored couch with a very soft yet serious energy. He took a deep breath (it seemed like he'd been rehearsing this all day) and admitted to me that he'd been hooking up with someone from his past even after we decided to go exclusive. Recently, though, he'd tried to cut things off with her, so now she was trying to blackmail him, threatening that she'd reach out to a friend of mine and tell him everything.

Essentially, my boyfriend was trying, in his own way, to soften the blow by telling me first. But that didn't make the pain any easier to bear. It felt like all the blood was sucked out of my body in that moment. When I'd been cheated on in the past, I'd immediately lash out verbally and sometimes physically, but this time, I stayed still and rooted myself down deeper into the couch. This betrayal hit different. I thought we'd done everything the right way—to *avoid* something like this happening. I clicked into dissociation and asked him—in the most monotonous voice possible—to leave. It must have been scary to be on the other side of this chillingly calm nonreaction. But I was really fucking done. I had no energy to fight anything or anyone anymore.

After the breakup, he gave me the physical space I asked for, but sent emails and poetic, heartfelt handwritten letters, letting me know how much he regretted everything and how he would do whatever it took to get me back. He took full accountability, saying that he'd learned his lessons and understood the spiritual ramifications, and he even outlined how he would put in endless work to regain my trust, *blah blah blah.*

That was great and all, but I didn't have time for that shit anymore. I was about to go out on tour to promote the three songs I'd just released and would need to focus on trying to make people (mostly myself) love them. And here he was, telling me he'd be in Arizona for a work thing the same time I was? *Fuck.* I went back and forth, but ultimately, I just couldn't resist the opportunity to see what he would do if I gave him a shot. Plus, I felt desperate for dopamine and distraction.

So I sent him the address of where I was staying.

My Manager told me I was ruining my life by associating with someone like him, and even though I knew I'd end up hooking up with him again, I believed her. What did he have to show for his big ol' age? He kept vampire hours, staying up in his room watching movies and television and smoking weed until 5:00 A.M. and then sleeping in until 1:00 P.M. every day. He kind of reminded me of Dad in "Joel the Mole" mode. And *HE* fucking cheated. On *ME*!?! My ego raged.

Mom never judged people based on labels or status or material offerings, but My Manager did. "Perception is reality," she'd say. As much as I resented that phrase, I agreed. The entertainment industry was a total facade—and whoever had the best facade won. Having the Older Man play such a big role in my comeback story just did not "look right." I hated that I allowed myself to think about someone I loved in these terms, but it also helped keep my walls up high and reinforced so that I couldn't take him seriously ever again.

Still, I felt the craving for physical and emotional validation. That's why I'd given him my address in Arizona. Somehow, I managed to keep his visit a secret from everyone I was traveling with.

Then, after midnight, I snuck him into my hotel room. I told myself that I'd discard his ass after I got my rocks off and felt adequately soothed by his love and regret.

In bed together, in the throes of the moment, I told him I had already been with someone else (I hadn't, but I was planning on it). A better lover with a bigger dick (nope, maybe just my vibrator). He responded the way I hoped he would: sad and upset, but because it was him, there was also a healthy dose of understanding and acceptance woven in, too. Ultimately, I just needed him to know how utterly disposable he was after being unfaithful to me. Of course, the truth was that as much as I didn't want to admit it, I still loved him. And no matter how angry I was, I couldn't disentangle my feelings for him from what had happened.

In the morning, I watched from bed as he packed up his duffel bag. As he walked toward the door and reached for the handle, I got the call I always expected but never wanted to get.

Dad was dead.

CHAPTER 15

JOEL

THE NEXT FEW MOMENTS WERE A BLUR, AND YET THEY SOMEHOW STAND OUT AS VIVIDLY as if they happened yesterday.

It's November 14, 2015.

I'm wrapped in the bedsheets as the Older Man stands at the door and we exchange our final words.

I notice Mom calling, but I hit ignore. After she calls me three times in a row, I pick up the phone.

She is hysterical on the other side of the line and can barely choke out the words.

"Joanna . . . Jo . . . I'm so sorry. Your father died this morning. I'm . . . so . . . sorry. I'm so, so, so sorry . . ."

"No. No. No no no no no . . ."

I scream.

The sounds that proceed to tumble out of my mouth are primordial, raw utterances that a human can only produce when they are faced with unfathomable grief and loss and sheer overwhelm.

The Older Man drops his bags and runs over to rock me tight in his arms, crying with me, letting me completely lose it as he wraps his body around mine.

Just a week prior, when I was in Minneapolis for the opening night of my most recent tour, I had spoken to Dad's doctor, who called me and expressed concern that Dad was potentially getting drugs from other doctors.

"Yeah, he probably is," I said. "He's a good talker. Apparently, he's done that for decades now. I just don't know how he still gets away with it."

I was grateful that this doctor was responsible and wanted me to know that he was not providing my father with painkillers he didn't need, but it didn't change the fact that Dad was resourceful as hell and would do whatever it took to get what he wanted.

He'd recently had open-heart surgery, something we weren't sure he would survive. Before he went into the OR, he told me he was scared and didn't want to die. He still wanted to see the world. To spend time under the stars in the desert, like he had in his twenties. To walk me down the aisle. He wanted to stay clean. To sing with me onstage one day. And be a grandfather.

Under this doctor's care, he miraculously survived. He'd made a full recovery, and once again, I believed in my heart that this could be the start of a new chapter.

Now that dream had died along with him.

He was gone. I pictured his big body, taking his last few breaths, cold and alone in his apartment. All I wanted was to teleport to Nashua and hug him—just one last time. A lifetime of joy and pain and memories whizzed across my mind just like when we hydroplaned across the highway. I burrowed under the bedsheets and wailed into the pillows. The Older Man comforted and cried with me, then helped me make the phone calls that needed to be made. Even to My Manager, who was just down the hall at the same hotel.

Nothing mattered.

I didn't care how I or anything about my life looked.

As a little girl, I'd always loved bath time. When I'd visit Dad on the weekends, we would sing together in the bathroom and he'd read me stories using all his character voices while I splashed around and played with my amphibious toys. Eventually, when I became aware of my private parts, he told me I should probably bathe alone because I was becoming a young lady. But I didn't want him to leave—ever. As a compromise, he would sing to me from outside the bathroom door. I just loved knowing he was right there. My favorite playmate and protector. Being in the bath always made me feel renewed, refreshed, loved. Time in there was sacred, and I was truly safe.

Now, in this hotel bathroom in Arizona, I stared at the water pouring out of the spout and falling into the tub. I oscillated between grief, fear, and profound anger. My lover was on his knees next to me, feeling the water and trying to get the temperature just right for me.

"Show me your phone," I blurted out, slumped in the corner of the bathroom. "Let me see if you've been texting that bitch since I saw you. I wanna see your camera roll. Your emails. Snapchat. WhatsApp. I don't believe a FUCKING WORD you say."

He wouldn't show me.

I slapped him across the face and instantly regretted it.

It only made me feel worse, not better.

"FUCK YOU," I spit out through my teeth.

I pushed him into the wall, and he put his hands up to cover his face as I tried to make all five foot four of myself as menacing as possible to his six foot three.

Fuck this asshole. *Fuck* my father. *Fuck* all men.

Someone would bear the brunt of my anguish—and the closest person to me was this man who had hurt me so deeply. Exhausted from the one-sided fight, I crawled from the floor to the bathtub he had filled for me and sobbed until I lost my voice.

That night, after hours of emotional madness and making preliminary arrangements for Dad's body, I wanted a fucking *drink*. My Punching Bag and I walked to the strip mall next door, and my new guitar player ran up to me with flowers and a big hug.

I thought I'd been numb before?

No.

THIS was numb.

We sat at the bar, and I ordered a whiskey on ice. My lips impatiently connected to the glass, and as the brown liquor warmed my mouth and cascaded down my throat, I felt a wave of reassurance. I think my ex was shell-shocked by the intensity of the past eighteen hours, so when he got up to go to the bathroom, I—of course—took the opportunity to catch him slippin'. Yet again. He'd naively left his phone on the bar. And lo and behold, he *was* texting another woman. Nope, not a colleague. Not his sister or his mom.

I fucked around and found out.

This asshole was making plans to see another woman as soon he got to New York.

On the night Dad died.

"Can I have a shot of Jameson please?"

Seconds dripped as I swallowed in a single gulp.

"How about another?"

When he came back from the bathroom, I started to make a scene at the bar. He knew I must have seen his phone and started explaining and apologizing profusely. So naturally, I got the bartender and the poor unsuspecting patrons involved.

"Can you fucking *IMAGINE* what a dirty piece of shit you must be to be texting another woman when your girlfriend's father just died? And this motherfucker tried to act like he wanted me back? HA!! What is life????"

We walked outside, and I proceeded to go wild on him in the parking lot, using all my strength to try to push him to the ground. This rage was certainly not just for him. It was for Dad, too. These men had hurt me in ways I couldn't even put into words.

But the worst part of all?

I had *let* them.

Over and over again.

It was the definition of insanity: doing the same thing and expecting a different result. And I blamed myself. For being so naive. For not being able to protect my squishy, sensitive, inconveniently open heart. But that being said, another voice raged inside me, screaming.

FUCK.

YOU.

BOTH.

Two days after Dad passed, I kept my obligation to sing the National Anthem at a NASCAR rally. Dad had always been very patriotic and proud of his time in the navy. My Manager, Katie, the Older Man, and Carlene all rallied around to love and support me as I fought my way through the day. The lack of judgment for my emotional state and appearance felt amazing. I was fully free to be as raw and devastated on the outside as I felt inside.

As broken as I was in the wake of Dad's passing, I knew I couldn't just sit there and lick my wounds—no matter how painful it was. So I continued the tour. In my mind, there wasn't another option. I had *just* restarted my official recording career and it felt like there was too much riding on this moment. No matter how much grief I was going through, I didn't want to let my fans down or add the financial implications or unreliable reputation that would come along with canceling to the weight I was already carrying.

In the end, getting up onstage every night and getting to sing my heart out in front of people who cared was therapeutic. I had written a memorial for Dad on Instagram, and my fans came out to see me perform, holding up handmade signs in support and sharing their own stories of loss, tragedy, and addiction. It connected us in a whole deeper way. They would finish the lyrics when I started to cry onstage. The song "Save My Soul"—which was about addiction—always got me in the end. I was singing to that hungry ghost inside me, inside Dad. The broken spirit that could never get enough. I, too, often felt powerless and resigned to its insatiable appetite.

This time was such a blur. But what I remember most were the meet and greets. The long, knowing hugs and the genuine human connection. We ALL will experience loss in our lifetime. No one is exempt from that—it's the one universal truth: no one makes it outta here alive. My fans were literally holding me up when I felt like I could fall at any second. But I knew I had to push through. Still, I cried my mascara off almost every night, as my emotions overrode the SSRI meds I was on.

Thankfully, people on my team were incredibly supportive, too. My Manager and Katie had this loving routine of checking to make sure no one was hiding out in my hotel rooms on the road (there have been a couple scary stalker situations over the years), and a few nights after Dad's transition, they wheeled my bags to my room as we headed on to the next stop on tour. They offered to stay with me, to cuddle, to cry, to eat all the food I wanted, to drink with me, to scream with me, to pray with me. Anything I needed. But I just wanted to be alone and sleep. The hotel was old and felt a little haunted. And somehow, when I walked into my suite, alone, the entire room was bathed in the smell of Dad's signature cologne, Obsession. It was inexplicable. I had never smelled him so strongly unless he was right next to me.

I cried deeply and even chuckled. Was this how our relationship was going to be now? With him always lingering around, dropping sensory hints and reminders as to his everlasting presence in my life? I pictured him now having a bird's eye view of me and all his sisters, wherever we were in the world. He could be ubiquitous now that he had transcended the body he'd been trapped in for years. I tried to intellectualize this, but my heart hurt.

At the same time, I felt so grateful for the love and support that held me in my grief. I rarely asked people for help, and I was so touched by how everyone didn't hesitate for a second to lend a hand.

It moved me to tears when my tour bus driver volunteered to drive us all to New Hampshire so I could speak at Dad's funeral and go through his things. Dad didn't have much in his apartment—just some stacks of DVDs, coin collections, a couple guitars, harmonicas, the djembe I had recently gotten him, toy model cars. But he'd also kept every single newspaper and magazine clipping of me from over the years. And then I found a letter in his handwriting, one that was to be read upon his death. He knew deep down he wasn't gonna make it to my wedding or to meet his grandchildren. Not with the way he treated his body. My tears mixed with the ink from his cursive as they fell down on the paper in my shaking hands.

We all talked about all the good times at his funeral. We wanted to remember his essence and how he could light up a room with a smile. My speech focused on his humor, creativity, his unforgettable soulful voice, and how, at his best, Dad was fucking *awesome*. I wish he could've known how awesome he was.

"I missed you even while you were here," I wrote. "I will miss you infinitely more now that you're gone. Thank you for holding on as long as you did. I know you tried your best. You are free now. I will love you always, Dad. I can feel you with me. Rest now. In PEACE. I miss your voice. I wish more people could have heard it. I promise I will keep singing for you."

Joel Maurice Levesque
January 8, 1955 – November 14, 2015

My eyes were heavy and dry from staring out at the ocean for five days straight.

The tour had just ended, and I'd rented a room in a random woman's house in Malibu on Airbnb. It had a beautiful view of the water, and all I wanted to do was be alone and cry, letting the waves mirror the ebb and flow of this weird-ass life. This was my first self-guided solo retreat. I was ready to surrender to the energy of Mother Earth as I slipped into solitude and journaled, prayed, read spiritual books, watched the rain drip down to kiss the ocean, and hiked the trails nestled into nearby mountains whenever it stopped pouring.

Dad was free, and I could hear him in the sounds of nature, feel his embrace in the wind. All the imperfect parts of him had turned to dust, and now he was part of a higher consciousness.

Meanwhile, I was still here on Earth and *pissed* at the cards I had been dealt. All that spiritual shit I was trying to believe was easier said than consistently practiced. I yelled at the waves and cursed him out as if he were literally waiting for me in the wind.

Dad always used to chastise me for swearing.

"You're so smart and have such an expansive vocabulary, Joanna, don't cheapen yourself by using profanity."

OH, YEAH?

WELL, *FUCK THAT*, DAD.

Deep down, I knew he was probably right, but I brushed off his advice as flawed—just like he was.

Amid the agony of grief and a war between spirituality and self-righteousness, I grappled with the undertone of relief I felt now that I no longer had to worry about him. I kept thinking about something he'd said to me a few years prior, back to a time when he had arrived to pick me up and was visibly high. His words echoed across the silence.

"Addiction is like Arnold Schwarzenegger pumping iron in your backyard. He's waiting for you. You got it honest on both sides, from your mother and me. You're just like us. Don't you dare throw stones in this glass house and judge me."

He'd been right about that, too.

Just like them, I had grown to love the way substances ripped me right out of my mind.

I was reckless and broken now, too.

After spending a few days in Malibu, I felt called to visit Sedona, Arizona—even though I'd never been there before and didn't know anyone who had visited, either. Dad used to speak of his time in "the American Southwest" as a highlight of his life. Before he had me, he and his best friend had rented a camper and driven across deserts. They even did peyote with First Nation tribes.

I'd only seen pictures of the otherworldly beauty out there, but I wanted to find myself in the middle of a vortex. I was searching for something, *anything* that would anchor me, hold me down. So I booked a room in another older woman's cozy home.

I did my best to focus on the red rocks in the distance, the red soil in my sneakers.

The desert equaled freedom. Away from everyone I knew, I was free to process my grief and cultivate my eccentricities without judgment. Free to be terrified. Free to scream out loud, as loud as I wanted. To dream, if I so dared. I saw the most radiant moons in the blackest skies. More stars than cars. Electric sunrises that woke me up early since I slept with the blinds open. Unobstructed views that started to calm the insane chatter of my restless mind. The desert felt infinite. It's a place without expectations, a place where you can literally "come as you are."

On December 20, 2015, I spent my twenty-fifth birthday journaling by a stream, and New Year's Eve at a local community center where, instead of getting fucked up as the ball dropped as usual, I tried kirtan chanting among strangers. I stuffed my emotions down with organic vegan treats until I was in a food coma and sat by the creek with my head in my phone, texting loved ones who wanted to be there for me. My friend Zelda had lost her dad the year before, and she knew intimately the kind of pain I was going through. I was thankful for the few friends who had experienced the same kind of heartbreak I was trying to process—fellow members in a club that no one ever really wants to be a part of.

When I got back to LA, I realized that I'd tucked the last CD that Dad was listening to in his car before he died into my carry-on. It was Crosby, Stills, Nash, & Young's classic album *Déjà Vu*, and I hadn't heard it before. I put the first song on in my car and ugly-cried, knowing this was his message to me from across the Universe:

> *"One morning, I woke up*
> *And I knew (that you were gone) . . .*
> *We have no choice*
> *But to carry on . . ."*

CHAPTER 16

MAD LOVE

THE TERM *MAD LOVE*—WHICH ENDED UP BEING THE NAME OF MY THIRD ALBUM— means a couple different things to me, but it's all rooted in this big inexplicable connection I feel for my people. Like what me and my fans have. My beautiful, one-of-a-kind *fans* who've stood by my side through all seasons of life, even when they didn't know what was going on with me behind the scenes. Fans like Sabrina, Dawnielle, Kyle, Timothy, James, Jacob, Marleen, Tatiyana, Amber, Jimmy, Kevin, and Doug, who has been working with us internally since 2018. He's a priceless gem of a tour photographer that Katie had found via my fanbase. These beautiful humans shared their unbelievable stories with me online, in letters, in person. Sometimes I related but oftentimes I was just struck by how you never know what someone is going through based on how they look. We grew up together and formed a tribe of misfits that bonded over music. There was also another aspect to the phrase that tied back to Dad and the Levesque side of my family, who

219

always said, "I love you madly." I really wanted to pay tribute to him somehow with my next release.

Toward the end of the recording process, after Dad's death, I was in a session with Justin Tranter, Hayley Warner, and Jussi. We were all bonding over this shared childhood feeling of "otherness," talking about how music had been our most trusted confidant in those dark times. Jussi came up with an emotional piano progression while Justin and Hayley helped to sum up my feelings into song:

> *"Everyone rises, everyone falls*
> *Everyone spends some nights alone*
> *Rich or for poor, I'm always yours*
> *You never left me on my own*
>
> *Tell me who, who would I be without you?*
> *No matter how much we lose*
> *Every time, I bet my life on you"*

I never say the word in the lyrics, but it was obvious that the name of the song should be "Music." That's who I was singing to. That's what I felt in my soul. There's a reason that the first tattoo I ever got, at the age of seventeen, was a treble clef on my ring finger.

Music was my first love—and I mean *music*, pure music, without the weight of everyone else's opinions and an industry cosign—in many ways, it would always be my deepest love.

As much as "Music" spoke to my soul, I was still part of an industry (and running my own business, basically), and I knew we needed something sticky to push as a single. After what I had just gone through and the spiritual and therapeutic journey I was on, a plunky, sassy bop called "Fuck Apologies" felt pretty out of line with where I was at the time. But once again, the label and M.M. (and the comanager we'd recently brought onboard to keep she and I from killing one another) were telling me this was my best possible option. There was simply no other song they liked enough to put money behind.

"Fuck Apologies" had the biggest, stickiest hook, and in retrospect, it *was* the best song to lead with. I just wasn't totally in sync and in love with the concept.

"What you want from me?
I would say I'm sorry if I really meant it . . .
I'm not perfect, I got pride
That's not what it is this time
So fuck apologies,
I would say I'm sorry if I really meant it"

If my fans only knew.

By the summer of 2016, I felt like a sad little turtle constantly retreating inside its shell. I was *constantly* apologizing to my managers for being myself. For not "getting it."

So how could I sell the unfuckwithable energy of this song?

Overall, it still felt like a win for me since I liked it more than "When Love Hurts," and Atlantic had Wiz Khalifa on the track and in the video. So I convinced myself that this might just be the hit we'd been looking for. My feelings just didn't matter to me as much as results did. Dad's death had made it incredibly clear that I *had* to make a way and a future for myself. There never was and never would be any type of inheritance or even financial assistance coming from anyone else—and, to put it bluntly, living, touring, and being an artist in general is expensive as *fuck*.

I also knew I was in good company at the label as far as the other talent was concerned. Bruno Mars and I were both signed to Atlantic and had been working out of the same studio compound. He'd rented out a wing there so that he and his crew could work on a new sound and craft his next album. We'd met a couple times over the past few years, including one time when I was hanging out with Somalian-Canadian artist K'Naan and we stopped by Bruno's old studio in Hollywood, and another time at the House of Blues. He was always so cool and embracing. And after seeing him perform live at the Hollywood Bowl, I counted myself among his biggest fans. The way he synthesized all his inspirations into modern musical masterpieces was *just* what I always dreamed of figuring out how to do. I knew Aaron wasn't involved in his creative process anymore, but I assumed they were still cool.

One day, I was early for my session, waiting for the producer to arrive, when I bumped into Bruno walking out of the kitchen area. He seemed genuinely tickled to see me there, and I didn't feel quite as awkward around him as I did around other artists. He was a massive star but still had this beautiful down-to-earth quality. We walked outside together, coffee mugs full to the brim, and he invited me to join him and Craig Kallman, the president of Atlantic, at a table under a fig tree in the courtyard.

I tensed up. Did he really mean that? Or was he just offering that to be polite? No *way* he really wanted me there. What could I possibly add? With all my self-editing and not trusting myself? If he didn't know already, I felt like he would soon figure out that I was fraudulent.

My Manager didn't like me talking to label people without her present or me being able to recount every single bit of the exchange so we could pick it apart for hidden meanings and analyze it after the fact. I rarely spoke to my own *lawyer* without her on the phone. I'd only take us farther away from where we needed to be, so she was the mouthpiece protecting me from myself. Surely Craig didn't want me there. I'd heard that Atlantic was trying to convince Bruno to go back and write a bigger single for his album, anyway. Maybe this was *that* conversation. I was so self-conscious about saying the wrong thing around my favorite artist and the CEO of the company that I took myself out of the equation altogether.

"Oh my God, thank you! But no, no, no . . . you guys do your thing. I'll just let you be!"

I couldn't even keep eye contact with them as I walked back to Studio B and wondered if I had just cut my own legs off. Bruno was literally offering me a seat at the table. What could have come from just seeing what happened? Why did I run from all these opportunities before I even got a real taste of what they could become?

I'd entrusted my managers—first Mom, now M.M.—to make the final decisions for me since I was obviously incapable of making the right ones on my own. First, because I was a child, and then, because I just innately wasn't strategic in the way I lived my life. I believed what I was told, that indulging my nonmainstream tastes would not propel me forward. And I had dreamed of forward motion for so damn long. I could not fail again. It was clear that My Manager loved me and wanted what she thought was best for me. But in therapy, I later learned that I had started operating in a state called "learned helplessness," which occurs after a person repeatedly experiences stressful situations and comes to believe in their bones that they are unable to change things, so they stop trying—even when opportunities for change present themselves. Think: flight, fright, fawn, or freeze. This was freeze.

Now in my midtwenties, I was tired of fighting my own team and having to defend what I liked artistically only for the conversations with M.M. to descend into intense arguments about how all the ways I saw myself as an artist—if I still wanted big success— were wrong. We were each frustrated with the other and exasperated by continually having to defend ourselves. Even though I never truly stopped caring, it was easier on our relationship when I stopped trying. After going back and forth for days about one asinine point or another (such as, I wanted a more creative single cover, but she thought me looking slim and intense and "eye of the tiger-ish" were the more important aspects), I'd finally hit a wall. It all just felt so *unbearably stupid*. I'd break down in tears, earnestly begging, "Please!!!! Just tell me what to do and I'll do it. Tell me what to do to be successful. I don't need to even like it anymore." We were on such different pages about everything, and I felt so weighed down by her judgment and emotional distance. I just couldn't handle it.

It seemed like *everything* about me was up for debate: I was too left of center, too jazzy, too R&B, too thick, too random, too open with my life stories in the studio, too specific in my lyrics, too tense in meetings. My Manager promised me she would never lead me astray and that if she ever felt there was someone else who could do a better job at managing me than her, she would graciously step aside. She'd staked her whole career on my success and had pulled me out of dark times more than once with her pep talks and consistency. I felt I owed her for sticking by me like that when no other adults in my career had. Most importantly, over the years, she *had* become the constant maternal figure in my life, and I was convinced that no one other than her could ever know and truly love and manage me with my best interests at heart.

Fundamentally, our drastically different worldviews became more evident the deeper I got into therapy. After Dad died, M.M.

gave me ample time and support while I went through my grieving process, but when I came out of it I wasn't ready to step up to bat and claim victory in the way that she'd hoped. She said that my fans, and audiences at large, would really want to cheer me on and celebrate the hard-won freedom I finally had from my former label—but I was still super depressed. "Bad bitchery" just did not feel authentic, and I was not up for being an actress.

I was fragmented between following my heart and trying to be whoever I needed to be in order to, once again, touch the career heights I'd reached as a young teenager. My fans didn't know how much I lived and died by the approval and validation of others, especially M.M. She called me a "tortured soul" and a "reluctant popstar" and maybe she was right.

I felt like I should tell people the truth: I had no *idea* what I was doing or who I was.

With *Mad Love* on the horizon and the first single out in the world, it was clear that I needed to be visible and on the road. Demi Lovato and Nick Jonas's tour offered me the opening slot on their coheadlining ticket—but my ego just couldn't handle it. Demi was a sweetheart and always gave me so much praise and respect, and I loved that I'd grown up alongside Nick and his brothers back in the *TRL* days. But my team agreed that it would be best for not just "optics" but also my fragile sanity to not put myself in that position.

Fifth Harmony, however, was the biggest girl group at the time, with a massive following around the world. I wanted to show Atlantic that I was playing the game and doing my part to promote the single and album, so I agreed to be the "special guest" on their 7/27 Tour, knowing it could introduce me to a whole new audience. Even though I was honestly embarrassed to be opening up for a new group like them this far into my career, I tried not to give that thought too much energy. I focused on my excitement to be playing for larger audiences again, swallowed my pride, and committed to the bigger picture. It helped that I reveled in being a big sister to the 5H girls, and I loved connecting with every single person in those crowds.

Performing with my band night after night, I worked hard to prove—sometimes just to myself—that even if singing a few songs made me feel silly and unreal, I was a *real* musician. I was super inspired by the act that went on first in the lineup, Victoria Monét. At the time, she was known and respected in the industry mostly as a songwriter for other artists, but she'd recently been putting out her own music. Her dancing and live singing blew me away. She went out there and gave superstar energy every day while the sun was highest in the sky and sweat dripped down her body to the stage, all as the crowd trickled in. We'd pass each other on our way in or out of the gym sometimes before the shows, and I loved her gentle, humble spirit. It felt like there was an unspoken acknowledgment between us: "This isn't glamorous, but I'm gonna make sure that audience remembers me tonight." Maybe I was projecting, but I wondered how she felt about being so talented and hardworking and still fighting for her spot. I'll never forget how kind she was. Meanwhile, I wrestled internally with my ego to make it stay in check.

Fifth Harmony had dancers *AND* a band *AND* an intricate stage setup—and none of that was remotely close to being within any budget I'd ever had. What I could rely on, however, was my connection with other human beings through music and the gifts God entrusted me with. I knew I had grown through spirituality and therapy when I was able to find silver linings and lessons in every moment. But these girls were packing amphitheaters and arenas, and that fact wasn't lost on me. I felt the pressure every single show. And after "No Apologies" failed to live up to the potential Atlantic thought it had, I was losing faith that I could ever do the same.

When *Mad Love* came out, it performed well, all things considered, and debuted at number 6 on the Billboard album charts. Although it wasn't the rocket ship commercial comeback we'd all hoped for, my fans supported it in a major way and it got decent reviews in the media. I was also so busy promoting it, I didn't have the bandwidth to spiral into a depression. I was happy that this third album—which had had so many false starts and stops and incarnations over the years—had finally come out, but I'd ended up making so many concessions about songs, music videos, single covers, etc., that I promised myself I would not compromise that way artistically again. It just wasn't worth it, especially since it never quite yielded the results that I was promised. I could no longer stand to look myself in the mirror knowing I was doing shit that didn't really feel like me. Not at the ripe old age of twenty-five, anyway.

I was starting to come into my own in other ways, too. Over the span of several months, I gradually fell into a relationship and then madly in love with someone who'd been one of my best friends for years. One night in New York, we were drinking and laughing like we always did. Conversation free-flowed from spirituality to history to sex, and we sang and harmonized to the soulful trance-inducing set the DJ was spinning. After a few tequila sodas, he gently took my hand and led me to a rooftop party where we danced, sweated, and let ourselves be free under the magic of the city. We moved our bodies together in ways I would've never expected. Over the years, I'd grown to trust him implicitly, so I didn't feel embarrassed or afraid as we locked eyes a little too long. Fueled by liquid courage, I leaned in close to his ear and asked, "Why have we never made out?"

He flashed that pure smile and said, "I honestly don't know."

In seconds, it was on and *poppin'*. It felt like we were inside the cinematic disco of George Benson and Rod Temperton's euphoric hit "Give Me the Night":

"Because there's music in the air and lots of lovin'
everywhere, so give me the night."

We'd both been in relationships over the course of our friend-ship, but now we were single—and at the same time, too. I had no idea whether it would be a one-time thing or something more, but I knew either way, it would be all right. Once we crossed the line of becoming intimate with one another, I saw him in a *whole* other light. We already knew all about each other's heartbreaks and hangups, strengths and inadequacies. First, we tried to take our time and go slow. After all, I was still figuring out how to untan-gle myself from the Older Man, who'd been by my side when Dad passed. But after I finally cut that off for the umpteenth time, my new boo and I dove in headfirst, spending as much time as possi-ble together. Hiking, driving to the beach, listening to obscure vinyls on his vintage record player, staying up all night talking about anything and everything. We laughed 'til it hurt, tears roll-ing down our cheeks, feeling like we'd done a thousand crunches.

He flew from LA to Massachusetts to hang with me for my birthday, and I showed him all around my hometown, holding nothing back about the mixed memories it held. By that point, I rarely shared my stories with people because I didn't think any-one genuinely cared. But when he asked questions, I could see in his eyes and feel in my soul that he genuinely wanted to know the answers. He was a California kid through and through, and I knew he always would be, but I was still searching for a place to feel truly at home. I soon realized that I felt more at home in his presence than I ever had anywhere else. We made a habit of staying up 'til sunrise, choosing an album to listen to on repeat as we tested the limits of our flexibility and stamina, generally keeping the whole neighborhood up. Nothing was off-limits in the ways we would explore and care for each other.

We both prided ourselves on hard work and having our own lives and careers, but we still chose to spend all of our free time together, either in nature or in conversation or in shared artistic creation—anything that soothed our hearts and nurtured our inner children. Both of us felt tossed around by the music industry and the people we'd trusted to guide us. We were sensitive, intuitive people, and because of this, we were also able to hold a mirror up to the other person whenever they needed a reality check. When he changed his diet to veganism for health reasons, I supported it wholeheartedly and eventually joined him on the journey. We threw parties, integrating our friend groups, and we could read each other's minds from across the room in just about any situation. We knew when it was time to wrap up and call it a night, retiring to his bedroom to decompress with one another. I also really respected his opinions, as he had seen and done it all from a young age.

Despite how in sync we were, I was the first one to admit that I couldn't really commit to being in a serious relationship. Looking back now, I think I loved him so much that I was afraid to find out just how bad he could hurt me. So I did it first. He had a female cousin who I *thought* I was close friends with, but when she found out we were together, she chewed his ear off. She was aghast and doubled down that I was a "trash bag," "a slut," "a hot mess," and in no way good enough to be his girl or a part of their family. I never even confronted her about it when I found out because I agreed with her: I wasn't ready or worthy. I identified wholeheartedly with my brokenness. But he stood by my side and even stopped talking to her. Yet in moments of insecurity, fear, and/or selfishness, I'd still get very drunk and flirt with other people. I always regretted it as soon as I sobered up. In truth, I was deeply in love with him and terrified sick that I would inevitably ruin it.

M.M. warned me that I was once again playing myself and endangering my persona as an "edgy pop/R&B girl" by being associated with someone who didn't look or act the part of "cool, edgy, successful dude." So if I was going to be in a relationship, I should keep it secret and not post anything online. I was triggered, thinking back to the fiasco of my first relationship and how I was told I was ruining my career. M.M. leaned in hard to the old industry attitude that "female artists don't have boyfriends or babies." But it made me angry that we were being distilled down into such little boxes. This guidance didn't sit right in my core, and I had to stop letting her negative comments about other people just roll off my shoulders. Being with him was beautiful and even gave me some of my mojo back. Now, I'd fight back and ask her to explain just what she meant when she said certain things.

"Jo, you know *damn* well it would change the game for us if you were with someone on The Weeknd's level. It would give you the instant career boost to put you in the stratosphere of fame your talent and star quality deserves."

She'd always bring up examples of women whose trajectory completely changed for better or for worse based on who their partners were. On the one hand, there were women like Beyoncé, who chose a husband that matched her star power; on the other hand, there were the kind of women who chose partners who weren't "on their level" that would negatively impact their image.

I was insulted by the insinuation that my talent and our hard work wouldn't be enough or that I needed to be publicly associated with *anyone*. Isn't being with someone who brings out the best in you and makes you happy the goal? If not, then why even bother?

I wasn't totally opposed to the idea of a PR relationship, though—as long as no one got hurt. My team said they wanted to try to make something happen, but then I got cold feet and pulled out. I confided in my boyfriend that I hated the fact that I came so close to doing damn near anything to help my career. How gross. What the fuck was I thinking??? He was outwardly supportive of whatever I felt was best for my life but questioned why I was always being told that I was the one who needed to change. He wondered if I was being misguided, if I'd just internalized M.M.'s worldview instead of figuring out my own.

"If you keep taking a back seat to everyone else's vision for you, what *are* you going to stand up for and when?"

Confronted. Mirror in face. See yourself, Jo.

After that, I subconsciously started doing things to push him away or at least provoke some kind of a reaction. He showed time and time again how much he cared with acts of service, quality time, and good ol' tough love, but now I *needed* him to *want* to lock me down. Even though I showed absolutely no signs of being ready. He didn't fully integrate me into his close-knit family life, either, which I took as another sign that he didn't think I was worthy. Sure, I was actively being a hot mess on the regular, drinking too much and picking fights, but he was always first and foremost my friend, accepting the different sides of my personality, always encouraging me to live up to a higher version of myself.

Still, he never applied pressure, and I was so used to pressure that I confused its absence with thinking he didn't really love me like I loved him. In retrospect, I think he was letting life unfold, supporting me as I flailed around like a T-shirt in a tornado, seeing where the chips would fall before trying to put a title on the bond we had. He let things just be easy between us, and I didn't really know how to handle it.

In the first few months of 2017, I set out on my own headlining tour for *Mad Love*. During the morning of one of the California shows, I woke up with a high fever. It was the last resort but: steroids and a Z-Pak to the rescue. I didn't love using 'roids—they can make you bloated, eat away at the lining of your gut and throw off your delicate microbiome, and cause weight gain, *especially* with how many times I've ended up using them over the years— but I just didn't see another way. And honestly? Those things are too good. Singing becomes easy again, and they make me feel like I'm *invincible*. Low-key, I wish I could take them all the time.

Anyways, I invited a bunch of other artists and creatives, including a couple successful single male friends, to my LA show, and they all stood near each other, watching me perform. My actual man thought I was maybe messing around with one of them, but I wasn't. I just really got off on feeling desired and admired, and there was a big part of me that also needed him to see that I was *wanted*. Also, it was never quite as simple as he made it out to be; these were people from the same industries I was in, and since I perpetually felt like an outlier, I was just happy that they wanted to be there in the first place. My boyfriend's concerns ended up being for nothing; we went home together and celebrated the beginning of a successful tour kick-off with some of our mutual friends.

The next day, I woke up in his bed and did the usual thing I do in the morning to see where my voice is at. I located the sound in my diaphragm and brought it up into my nasal cavity with a "hmmm." This time, though, I could not produce any sound whatsoever. The 'roids were not gonna cut it anymore. I cried in his arms as he soothed me and helped me come up with a game plan. I could already feel the pit in my stomach knowing that I'd have to tell My Manager. There was no way I could talk, let alone sing, so there was really no choice but to postpone tour dates. In the past few years, more than one vocal coach had told me that I was singing in a way that wasn't sustainable. Too much intensity and force, not enough air and proper technique. As a kid, singing harder and louder was always what got a response from people. But now, it was unbecoming and dangerous. Essentially, I had to relearn how to sing, or I wasn't going to be able to make it as a touring artist.

Eric Vetro, one of my favorite vocal coaches, suggested getting on an anti-inflammatory diet, implementing periods of vocal rest between shows a lá Celine Dion, and not ever speaking over loud music or being in smoky environments. My ENT (ear, nose, and throat) specialist, Dr. Schnitman, also prescribed more steroids and strict and total vocal rest. I had been getting stereoscopes of my cords (they look like the inside of a vagina, btw—just sayin') from him since I was thirteen so we could track how my prenodules had been developing. He told me some singers can fuck around and be perfectly okay vocally, but that my instrument was sensitive and I had to figure out what works for me and just *DO IT.* In other words: experiment with cutting out alcohol completely while touring and also cutting down on dairy (AND spices, AND sugar, AND acids, AND caffeine, AND . . .) to eliminate mucus production.

My Manager was always in the doctors' rooms with me asking questions as well, seeing how she could help keep me on track. I don't think I'd gone a full month without alcohol since I turned eighteen, and I honestly didn't know if I could follow through with it. Before she even had to recommend it, I knew it would be best to stay with M.M. at her house because she didn't think that I could be completely silent over at my boyfriend's. She didn't trust me, and I didn't really trust myself, either.

Fourteen days of total vocal rest—no speaking or whispering whatsoever—and living under her roof again in my midtwenties had me feeling a bit crazy. But when the tour resumed, I was vocally renewed. It may be annoying, but it's true: for singers who need their vocal cords to repair themselves, there really is nothing like shutting it *ALL* the way down and going radio silent. Now when I went to sing, though, my voice had to pass through an additional layer: the fear of causing further damage to my cords and permanently ruining my gift. When I was younger, I truly believed my voice was limitless, and it showed up as such. But now, I'd psyche myself out and avoid the notes I used to hit with ease. "Don't even try it, bitch," a voice inside me said.

I'd shown myself in various ways that I just wasn't someone I could trust. All the back-and-forth and second-guessing felt like I was constantly at war within. I'd stand my ground for what felt right and then eventually bend or fully back down when someone I trusted more than myself questioned it. It felt like my sense of security and safety was always in flux, and this manifested in the way I sang now: I could *feel* the tightness in my chest, the restriction in my voice box. It wasn't free. It wasn't fun. It was *sad*. So intensely afraid of doing the wrong thing, I seized up.

Instead of being excited to perform in front of people again, even sound checks in empty venues without the lights and the good vibes of an audience made me anxious as hell. My mouth would dry up when I saw M.M. by the soundboard, shaking her head at all the modifications I made to certain melodies and notes. Was she actually doing that? Or was I just projecting my insecurities onto her?

For a while now, I'd been thinking about the fact that I was praised for being good before I developed habits that could make me great. I was strangely young and isolated when I reached the top of a mountain most artists are never able to summit their whole lives, and I'd never had anyone to really mentor me or show me the ropes. Obviously I'm no doctor, but I can only imagine the impact of fame on a developing brain. A cocktail of adulation and attention mixed with pressure and chaos. Mom was understandably afraid to let other adults close to me before I turned eighteen, so I was in a protective bubble away from people who could have hurt me—or helped. I was allowed to take the easy way out with schoolwork, and I wasn't made to stay in any dance or voice or acting lessons I didn't want to be in. I kind of ran the show from a young age. There wasn't much discipline or routine to be found. Now, as an adult, I wish someone had given me some structure. Said "no." Or at least taught me how to function in society. How to clean or fold laundry. I didn't know where to turn to do my taxes (a business manager had been in place for over ten years now), and I couldn't even mail a letter myself— someone had always sent off the fan mail responses I'd written out. How was I supposed to instinctively know how to form good habits at *this* point? I felt like it was too late, and I was angry at my parents for not teaching me for whatever reason. But I knew that holding anyone but me accountable was unfair and a waste of energy. So I doubled down on blaming myself.

Conversations about my weight and looks were still par for the course, too, so to prevent unflattering pictures from materializing, I stayed in a constant state of sucking my stomach in. This was fine for looking slim from a side angle but not so good for proper breathing technique for a singer. I found myself not taking full, deep breaths onstage and sometimes feeling faint while singing because I simply wasn't getting enough oxygen. No one had ever explicitly *told* me to do this; I'd just observed it as a thing to do and picked it up as a by-product of my own insecurities.

The rest of that tour was a total mindfuck. I couldn't get over the feeling that My Manager was disappointed with me in every single way, but maybe it was just me projecting my disappointment with myself. I fainted walking through the airport in Chicago and woke up surrounded by security and doctors. Exhaustion? Stress? It was probably a mix of everything. It wouldn't make news. No one cared.

M.M. and I couldn't stop fighting, and it was weighing heavily on us both. I felt she was condescending in the way she spoke to me and others. But wait . . . maybe I was just misunderstanding her? I always questioned myself and ended up apologizing, saying I knew she had my best interests at heart.

To this day, I really believe she did want the best for me. Unfortunately, intention and impact aren't always the same. I bristled against her management style, feeling mortified when I perceived her to be micromanaging people on my team and at the label. I just didn't think that it was the way to get the best out of people. In the mornings, we'd be coming out of our respective rooms at the hotel and I felt like she would dart her eyes over my room service tray by the door and shake her head in judgment over whatever it was that I'd had to eat the night before. If I ordered chicken fingers and french fries, that meant that I wasn't taking my career seriously. Part of me felt this was all incredibly ridiculous, but another part internalized it as more evidence of my failure. So I continued to eat my shame in a cycle of deprivation and bingeing. I'd eat very healthfully and mindfully throughout the day, and then I'd unhinge myself as soon as I was alone in my room. At a dinner meeting, I'd order a nice big salad, maybe some additional protein, a Diet Coke, and then share a dessert with my dinner mates. Then I would get back to my hotel room and lay out the assortment of salty and sweet snacks I'd bought at the airport.

Sometimes, I wished I had the willpower and discipline to be anorexic. Binge eating was counterproductive to my entire life structure, and yet, at the end of the night, I felt like a bottomless pit and wanted to gobble up everything in sight like Ms. Pac-Man, trying desperately to fill the void I felt from not being good enough.

I couldn't figure out how to get comfortable or feel free in my skin and in my life, and I felt like it had to have something to do with M.M. After ten years of working together in this capacity, we had exhausted every option we could think of to try to see eye-to-eye. I was being told that the people I loved making music with weren't good enough, but all I wanted was to defend them and prove her wrong. And no matter what picture or video clip we went with, I resented it being nitpicked down to the tiniest detail. We were becoming more like oil and water with each passing day. Every time it started to be calm between us again, it was so short-lived, never more than a week at best. It felt like she was open-minded—until my opinion wasn't the same as hers. She said I was incapable of delivering commercial music. I said the way she spoke to me was toxic.

As the older person, I wanted *her* to be the one to give up. To say, "Look, I've done all I can do at this point, and we need to go our separate ways." But I think we both felt like we *HAD* to make it work, or else all the years we put in and the sacrifices and compromises we made would be for nothing. We continued to squeeze a square into a circle, wanting to believe that success would somehow magically fix the tension between us. I know we both loved each other like family—and I will *always* love her. But with every month that passed, every comment from her seemed that much more belittling, that much more condescending, that much more crippling. And yet, like Mom had predicted years before, she *was* like a mother to me. She split or fully copped the bill for a lot, believed in me when I didn't believe in myself, did my dirty laundry without me asking, stood up for me when other people tried to short me off a set list. She loved me *fiercely*. We were also both fire signs to the extreme, and at a certain point, we burned each other down.

After *Mad Love* had come and gone, M.M. advised that I ask to be released from my contract with Atlantic so I could move over to Interscope and work with Aaron again. We negotiated my release, and I hoped and allowed myself to believe this would be the fresh start I needed, we needed.

Quietly, for the second time, I headed back to Interscope.

CHAPTER 17

HEARTBREAK

ONE MONTH INTO RECORDING MY NEW ALBUM AT INTERSCOPE, THE PHONE CALL CAME. This time, at least, I had been prepped and was ready with my response. We'd already caught wind of the rumors on *Hits Daily Double* and *Variety*. Once again, it was Aaron and his golden rocket ship.

"Look, I'm upset and concerned for myself . . . 'cause you know the only reason I left Atlantic and moved over to Interscope was to work with you . . . ," I explained. "And look, I really understand that we all do what we need to do and that this is an incredible opportunity for you, Aaron. But I won't lie and say I'm not scared for what it means for me."

I had just signed with Interscope in mid-August of 2017 and created my own imprint, Clover Records, under a joint venture. (The sighting of a rare four-leaf clover represents faith, hope, luck, and love, all things that have guided me on my path.) Essentially, Clover and Interscope would enter into an agreement where they could help distribute, market, and promote my projects. It felt like a big win for me. If I'd learned anything from my years in the industry, it was how essential ownership was. Now I would have more responsibility, be able to sign and develop artists, and stand more of a chance to make a bigger profit and also to see more of how funds were appropriated and budgets were spent. But before we even got settled, we quickly started hearing that Aaron was being courted by Warner Records to become the chairman of the company.

By October, it was official.

My Manager advised me to sit down with John Janick, the president of Interscope, and ask to be released from my contract—again. Aaron's new role at Warner was basically the biggest position any executive can get, the one everybody dreams of.

"He wants you to follow him over there again. Now he has *real* power and can put you on top in a way he wouldn't have been able to until now." Yeah, *right*. Part of what she was saying made sense, but part of me was disturbed at the idea of hitching myself to this dude's wagon for *another* go-around. 'Cause truly . . . what the *fuck*. Was he really going to prioritize little old me when he had a whole new label at his fingertips? Why would he? *My* jaded ass?

I understand shiny object phenomenon—we all crave newness and excitement—and the music industry craves it to the *n*th degree. Just because you might want something going *into* a new role doesn't mean it's going to happen once you're finally there. Plus, when you join a new company, even as a president, and start looking at the inner workings of a system, you're bound to go, "Wow, this is way harder and more complicated and political than I ever realized."

Aaron and I had also slowly but surely been growing apart over the past couple years. My disillusionment had crystallized. Even with the eternal optimism of a Sagittarius sun and an Aquarius moon, I felt like I might have a mental breakdown if I went along for another round of getting my hopes up—having a solid body of work, getting excited about a cohesive direction, and plan—only to have it crumble again under a new Frankenstein'd regime. So instead of feeling more comfortable around him, I became really nervous every time I was in his presence.

"Aaron really believes in you. The way he talks about you so passionately . . . after all these years—that's the kind of support all artists *wish* they had." It made me feel fortunate when I heard things like that from other people in the industry. But I was too shell-shocked to believe it. Years ago, Aaron had chosen me to shine his light on, and now, people assumed he'd want to take me to the top with him. But did he really? Or did he just feel bad for stringing me along and wasting my time? I braced myself for the next disappointment, and I could not find an ounce of chill. The effects of yoga and meditation could barely last me the first few minutes of a meeting, so I would now take a Xanax before I saw him or My Manager (who I saw a lot more often).

I used to be funny—spur of the moment—someone it seemed like people generally liked to be around. Now my tone was serious, closed off. I gave off an air that I'd seen it all, and no one better fuck with me. Nothing was light or fun; I was all business and no trust.

I'd tried to protect myself from getting let down by relinquishing control to other people who I still felt knew better than me. But where had that really gotten me in the long run?

I don't know really know how to say this because several paragraphs ago, I told you how much I loved this boyfriend of mine, but I cheated on him.

Point fucking blank.

I can't even blame it on a blackout. To make it worse, since I'm being real here, I knew it was going to happen before it happened. As if holding on to the longest grudge ever toward Freddy, my high school sweetheart, I cheated with one of his former frenemies, another professional athlete. This guy had kept tabs on me for years, checking in every few months, taking me or me and friends out to dinners, but we'd always kept things platonic. On one trip to New York, though, he suggested I extend my stay to watch his game and go out afterward. *Hmmm.*

He invited me up to sit in the box with his family and managers, and, deep down, I was thrilled. I didn't feel good enough to spend time with my then-boyfriend's successful family. So I let the idea float through my mind that if this other guy actually thought I was worthy of showing off, especially as we had been slowly getting to know each other after all these years, well—maybe seeing where it went *wasn't* such a bad idea.

After a long night of playing boyfriend/girlfriend at 1 Oak with his teammates and agents and conveniently omitting certain details when my boyfriend asked what I was up to that night, me and the athlete took it there. The sex was drunk, intense, and dark. It wasn't validating. Before we got down to it, we made it okay in our minds by telling each other we were "on a break" from our partners. Maybe we convinced ourselves in the moment that it was true.

Over the next few months, I wrestled with whether or not to tell my man what had happened. When I brought it up in therapy, Dr. Janice asked if I would ever do it again.

"Fuck no!"

"Well, then, Joanna, look . . . perhaps it's even more selfish to tell him and break his heart, just so you can assuage your guilt." Instead, she suggested that I could just deal with it internally, do the work to make sure I was dealing with all my validation issues, and spare him the turmoil.

But I wasn't hearing that. Ultimately, my boyfriend was also my best friend. Things weren't perfect in our relationship, but he was pure-hearted and didn't deserve to be lied to like this. The closer we got over time, the more I realized that I could have lived in a cardboard box with him and still found joy in just being together. He was the most solid man I'd ever met, and I felt more calm in his presence than I did with anyone else in my life—ever. And yet I'd never quite felt worthy of his goodness, and now, this act of betrayal made it so obvious.

The guilt was seeping out of my pores. He kept saying I was acting weird, but I chalked it up to hormones, stress.

Ultimately, I knew I couldn't keep something like this looming over us.

The only chance I had at redemption was to come clean.

During this period, the athlete flew into LA for a game and asked if he could see me again. My immediate gut instinct was: NO, BITCH. RUN. Ignore. BLOCK. But then the little devil on my shoulder opened up my brain to remember our evening together as a fun, playful, sexy moment and planted seeds that sprouted to say: "Well, you've already done it once—what's a second time going to change?" I was scarily able to dissociate from the reality of breaking my best friend's heart and focus on how good it was going to feel to extend the fantasy just a little bit longer. Maybe the chance of feeling the high of his desire and attention—existing in a surreality where there are no consequences to our actions—before everything came crashing down was too enticing to pass up. If the first time was selfish, then the second time was diabolical. I was feeding my addiction and biding my time before telling my man that I was theworstpersonintheworld. The sabotage switch flipped, and I responded to the athlete. I mean, at this point what was I if not a sucker for self-betrayal and overindulgence? Somehow, I convinced myself it didn't matter. I didn't consult a single friend about what I should do. It was glaringly obvious how unacceptable this was. But all around, I felt so bad and I just wanted to feel *good*.

He sent a driver, and I met him at his hotel like some kind of escort. The car ride was over an hour long, and I stayed glued to my phone the whole time, scrolling through Instagram to keep my mind as far as I could from the wrongness of it all.

When we pulled up to Nobu, I was fully in my head. Had I really turned into the kind of woman who puts on a little dress and uncomfortable heels and goes to clichéd, overrated, and overpriced restaurants to see if the man in front of her will indeed swoop in and stand in as her latest distraction from reality? I popped .5 mg of Xanax. By now, I knew this wasn't something long term; it *wasn't* going to turn into a relationship. One time should have been *more* than enough because it should have never fucking happened in the first place. But sometimes, I just have to touch the stove a few hundred times before I get the message that it's burning my skin off.

I threw back another lychee martini at the table, trying to override my instinct to run. The vodka removed my inhibitions and seductively reminded me, whispering in my ear, that I could have my cake and his cake (and *his* cake) and eat them *all*.

I hated myself. There was a man who truly loved me back in LA, and yet there I was acting like an insatiable whore.

A few weeks later, I couldn't stand it anymore.

I confessed to my boyfriend that I had been with someone else.

In the passenger seat of his car, as we drove through the hills to a mutual friend's house, I found the words spilling from my lips, dribbling out and clinking around us like marbles. He acted like he wasn't surprised, and we kept driving in silence. It scared me that he was able to maintain such a calm demeanor until we pulled up to our destination. Then he instructed me to get my stuff and get out of his car. I'd never heard him yell before.

"Was it just once?"

The look in his eyes pierced through my heart.

I glanced down at the upholstery of his truck, hoping to find some miraculous way to spin this conversation into not-the-worst-thing-ever.

"I'm so, so, *so* sorry. It happened twice."

"ARE YOU FUCKING KIDDING ME????"

I wished I was. Maybe he could have gotten over one time.

"I *knew* you were lying to me the whole time you were in New York. I just *knew* it. How could you do this to us? Why would you lie? To *ME*? You didn't have to!! We don't lie to each other, Jo!!!!"

His voice broke, and I wished there was something I could do to make him look at me the way he used to. The way he was looking at me in that moment—I'd *never* felt dirtier or more disappointing. I wanted to hold him and stroke his face and show him the insides of my heart and promise that everything was going to be okay from here on out. But the truth was that *nothing* was okay. And it never would be again.

"It's my fault. I knew deep down that you weren't ready and I ignored that. We should have never been together. People told me it was going to end this way. I can only blame myself."

It killed me to hear him say that.

Especially when I knew, without question, that the only person on the planet to blame for the agonizing pain we both felt in that moment was me.

Leah LaBelle was an angel-goddess walking among us. She floated into every room with grace and ease and reached for the microphone with long, elegant, ring-adorned fingers that gave way to the sickest nail art. Her impersonations of Kristen Wiig's *SNL* characters were utter perfection and had both of us doubled over with laughter, holding our stomachs, crossing our legs so we wouldn't pee our pants. She'd wear these colorful head scarves, chunky gold jewelry, vintage Chanel, and animal prints that would've made anyone else look like an old lady, but somehow, she rocked it like an off-duty supermodel. This was one of the coolest chicks I'd ever met in my whole life. When we first connected on Massachusetts Ave. in Boston back in 2009, her confidence rocked me. I wasn't even sure if she liked me at first, but I think that's mostly because I was taken aback to see someone so beautiful, talented, and self-assured. She knew she was dope and she *owned* it.

It wasn't just style and natural beauty, either. Leah had SOUL, an undeniable gift for singing and performing. When we both moved to LA after Boston (she'd gone to Berklee College of Music), we continued to cross paths time and time again, always happy to run into each other at a party before going off into a corner to chat, until we realized that we had genuinely become good friends.

She also had the most amazing group of people in her life. As soon as we got to LA, we introduced the friends in our circles, exploring all the things we had in common and finding ways to make our new location feel as much like home as possible. She was the kind of friend who would write these legendary essay-length texts, celebrating your accomplishments and hyping you up for a future that she fully believed was inevitably yours. Eventually, we got so close that people sometimes thought we were sisters—in part because of our pale, freckled complexions, coupled with our shared passion for R&B and hip-hop. We were also the only children of single moms who had been professional singers in their own right before we came along.

She was one of the first people in my life who I'd ever seen truly practice and prioritize the act of self-care. One time, when we went on a girl's trip to Vegas, I noticed the way she cared for herself while we were pregaming with Hennessy, singing along to

Usher songs, getting ready for the night. Dead-ass, I had never seen someone perform such a lengthy and loving routine on their body and face. She'd even massage the bottoms of her feet with Kiehl's Soy Milk & Honey Body Butter and apply a thin layer of oil on top of it before washing her hands and starting the process all over again. I was low-key in awe of her as I went into the other room for a few minutes, only to return to the bathroom mirror and realize that she was still not done with her multistep process. Now she was moisturizing her face and neck, using gentle upward strokes on her décolletage. I was trying not to stare and come off like a fucking creep, but I couldn't help but watch and wonder: "Is *this* how someone who loves and respects themselves treats their body?" She got underneath her breasts, behind her ears, in between her thighs—all without reservation or shame. I was always in such a rush when it came to prepping my skin, and it was truly educational to me, seeing someone take such generous time and enjoyment with their body. When I got back to LA, I immediately purchased all the products she'd used and began taking time with myself that I'd never taken before.

By 2011, Leah had put up a bunch of incredible covers that were going crazy on YouTube, and she was being courted by pros like Pharrell, Jermaine Dupri, and Bryan-Michael Cox. She needed representation to navigate it all, so I recommended My Manager and they began working together. Honestly, at that time I was a little worried that M.M. wouldn't give me the same kind of focus if she was working with another artist, but I also believed that it would be positive for all parties (and hopefully, for our relationship) if some pressure was taken off the necessity of my success.

Leah was naturally tall and model-esque, so her weight wasn't up for discussion, but dating outside of her race still was. Both of us had been told the same thing (by people involved in our professional lives who were of various races): unless we were with a man of a certain financial or social status, dating Black men was going to be harmful to our careers. So if that's what we were gonna do, it would be smart to keep that part of our lives hidden. We spent many nights drinking wine at each other's apartments, tears spilling into our glasses, talking about how awful and damaging going along with this concept was. Both of our best friends were Black women, and when we asked them what they thought we should do, they agreed that perhaps keeping who we were dating private was just the easiest option.

"The entertainment industry has enough hurdles," they'd say.

Is that how we were supposed to live, though? Dodging the truth as much as possible instead of actually standing up for something, for someone we loved?

In 2013, we went out on tour together at a time when we were both essentially being shelved and didn't know what else to do but get out there and perform live. She brought her best friend, Aysia, out on the road with us to help out with everything from merch to costuming to tour management. I admired the way she could cuddle with her in a completely sisterly, nonsexual way, whereas I felt uncomfortable holding someone's hand for too long. She showed such fierce loyalty in her friendships, the kind most people only dream of. I felt lucky to be in her orbit, to watch how she put just as much time and effort into nurturing these relationships as she did working on her craft. She was truly one in a million.

Leah had fallen in love with an NBA player, Rasual Butler, a good guy and (in my experience) a rare breed of pro athlete who had been there, done that, and was now ready for something of substance. He became like a brother to all her girls, and Leah became like a best friend and confidant to his teenage daughter. It was too good and too real to let anyone's opinion hold much weight over how it might affect their careers. She followed her heart and eventually threw caution to the wind, refusing to hide their relationship from anyone.

When Katie (who was now comanaging me at my request) rang my cell in the early morning on January 31, 2018, I knew something had to be wrong. For as long as we've known each other, we've shared an endless text thread filled with irreverent banter and ping-ponging of ideas, and we have an unspoken call-only-if-completely-necessary policy. I love this about our relationship. We really know each other. And this means I also know that early mornings in general are just not her style.

"Hey, um . . . I don't know if you've heard this . . . and I don't want to startle anyone cuz I don't know if its real . . . but . . . *TMZ* is reporting that Rasual died in a car accident, and they said someone was in the passenger seat . . ."

No. No. *No.*

I couldn't believe the pain Leah was about to go through. Losing her partner. Finding out there was another woman in his life. That's where my mind went. How would we support her through this? Because it *couldn't* be Leah. It just wasn't possible. My sister couldn't be dead. There must've been someone else with Rasual in the car.

We blew up Leah's phone but received nothing in reply. Then our friend Tavares called and told us what had happened. He'd been bowling with them both the night before, and he hadn't heard from her like he normally would after she made it home safely.

Leah and Rasual had been together in that car. And at 2:00 A.M., Rasual accidentally crashed into a railing at a shopping plaza on Ventura Blvd., going 90 mph. They both died on impact.

She had lives to touch. Songs to make. Trips to take. We had plans to raise our future kids together and protect them from all the pitfalls we'd learned and grown from. Those dreams were now suspended in time. We wouldn't get the chance to grow old together.

She'd be forever young.

Losing someone your age, who you assume you'll have around for the rest of your life, fundamentally changes you. How is this person who was sharing takeout pasta with you on your couch a couple weeks ago just . . . gone? It was a harsh reminder that aging is a privilege and life rarely goes the way we think it will. We are mortal and fragile and tomorrow is never promised, no matter how much we deserve it.

Her funeral was the most surreal, beautiful display of love and admiration from a group of friends I've ever seen. When people spoke about her, they mentioned her gifts and beauty, but what really stuck with everyone—and what was talked about most—was how she LOVED. She loved deeply and fully and without any hesitation or restraint or apology.

Love was her true legacy.

I struggled to accept the fact that she would no longer be on this Earth in her physical form. We all did. But we, her people, knew we needed to do something to immortalize her voice, her spirit, her soul. So we all came together to put out her first official EP, *Love to the Moon*, which included some of her favorite songs that she'd made over the years.

The one that always gets me is the very last track, which comes from the voice note recording of an original song her friend had written for her called "Orange Skies." A woman approached me in the bathroom, where I had gone to catch my breath after I sang at the service. She hugged me like an old friend, saying she'd been working with Leah and had kept an unheard voice note that she wanted to share with her family. Listening the next day, I cried my eyes out once again, feeling like the Universe had somehow found a way to let my friend say goodbye:

"When I'm gone, promise that you'll smile
And remember we had this little while
'Cause life is lost, but did you know
That we really won, baby, 'cause we had each other
Just close your eyes and visualize me, yeah
Look up to the skies and visualize me there
When the sun sets
Look to the orange skies
When you lay your head, don't you cry
Cause love doesn't have to come to everyone
We were fortunate to have it come to us
Say goodbye, say goodbye, say goodbye
When I'm gone, look to the orange skies . . ."

CHAPTER 18

NEW OWNERSHIP

BY 2018, MUSIC STREAMING HAD COME IN AND CHANGED THE GAME, JUST LIKE WHEN Napster had the industry's panties in a bunch in the early 2000s. But this time, it was much more for real. Labels had to make individual deals with the digital streaming platforms like Apple and Spotify to have their artists' music available amid this changing landscape. CEOs scrambled to understand the math behind this new model yet somehow found a way to keep the numbers from artists and creators. The labels I had been distributed by in the past had massive rosters of other artists, so they prioritized getting those deals done ASAP. But not Blackground.

"Where are your first two albums, girl?"

"Why did you take your old stuff off Spotify?"

"Why can't I find 'Too Little, Too Late' on Apple?"

It seemed like whenever I checked my social media, questions like this flooded my mentions and DMs. None of the masters that Blackground owned (including my first two albums) could be found anywhere music was available to stream. I heard through the grapevine that Barry was holding out to make his own plat-form and app, just like what Jay-Z did with Tidal. News flash, buddy, no one's gonna pay for that shit.

So here I was, having spent the last decade feeling virtually helpless about my own career, stung with embarrassment every single time I saw one of those tweets come through. Didn't Black-ground want to make money off what they contractually owned? Why did I constantly feel like I was between a rock and a hard place with that company? A handful of my songs that they owned the master recording rights to still streamed consistently well, and once again, I was baffled by the logic—or lack of it. I couldn't believe they thought so little of me that they wouldn't even bother to do the work to complete the deal.

But it *wasn't* just me. My labelmates Tank, Toni Braxton, Tim-baland, and Magoo suffered the same fate. And worst of all? It happened to Aaliyah's music, too—and she was Barry's *niece*. This all made no sense.

Fuck that.

I had been consistently crying to My Manager, telling her that we HAD to do *something*. Aaliyah's family and fans had been fighting for her memory to be preserved properly, and I realized it would be up to me if I didn't want my own contributions to be snuffed out.

It was time to take back control of the narrative and stand up for my own legacy.

Streaming wasn't the only thing that jump-started this shift in me. Deep down, I also knew that my team and I needed to reas-sess the way we operated. I was sick of feeling and acting like a victim of circumstances. After Aaron moved over to Warner Records to become president, M.M. said it was best that I follow him there since he had consistently been my loudest and most powerful supporter. I loved and respected Aaron, and I was grateful he went so hard for me . . . but was it smart to move labels for him twice? The ink was barely dry on this newest contract. What if something happened and he moved *again*? Or what if some more appealing, less jaded artist came along and he suddenly forgot all about me? Fear dug its talons into my neck.

My Manager told me to text him and keep him engaged but, of course, she wanted to look at everything before I sent it over. Every time I needed to talk to him, I had to rehearse over and over what I was going to say and anticipate all the ways it could go. God forbid he called without warning—I didn't want to do anything that could potentially rock the boat. My mind would race and jump to getting dropped, losing all support, and ruining everything I'd tried to hold on to with these labels. I was so scared that history would repeat itself. That I would have once again latched myself to Aaron's ever-moving musical chair, only to be assed-out with no place to sit when the music stopped and some shiny new PYT was chillin' in my seat.

When I inevitably signed a new contract with Warner, M.M. said it would probably be the last major deal I got, so I should do everything I could to make it work.

Let's just say I did *not* appreciate the sentiment.

Look, maybe it would be. But uhhh . . . what exactly was it about this deal that I should feel so jazzed about? The points were not *that* sweet, sweetie. *The advance was not advancing.* From my vantage point, I'd been dragged around for years, holding on to Aaron's coattails and looking like a spineless moron. And here she was, telling me this was my best-case scenario. More than anything, the insinuation that I wasn't a hard worker, that I hadn't done everything everyone had asked me to do to push my career forward pissed me the fuck off.

But the truth was that the light had extinguished from my eyes and M.M. saw it. My vibration was low and being around me was hard. I had cried to her countless times confessing how I wanted to be a different kind of artist. I wanted to put out the bodies of work she had told me were too left-of-center or not digestible enough. My heart wanted to take more chances, collaborate with different kinds of artists, inhabit different kinds of spaces, and break away from mainstream convention. Yet I never had the courage to step out and do it because I didn't want to do it alone. I didn't *want* to do it without her or without a label; it was all I had ever *known*. However, in trying to fit into what other people thought I should be, I could never quite do what was expected of me. And after trying *so* hard for *so* long, the likelihood that that was going to change wasn't very high. I was steadily losing trust in myself, in the process, and in her with each passing day.

By this point, I was twenty-seven years old, but I felt like a child. Actually stepping into adult shoes and learning how to stand on my own opinions and make concrete decisions for myself was proving to be easier said than done. I intellectualized the reasons why giving this opportunity with Warner everything I had was the smart thing to do. I would commit myself to the major-label way one last time, fitting myself into the system, playing the role of edgy pop/R&B star as best as I possibly could. People still believed in me, and I didn't want them to feel their investment was in vain. My Manager and I had been through SO much together; we had come too far and seen too much over the years to give up on this before we really got to enjoy the fruits of our labor. If I could pull this off and we could be successful, everything in the past would have been worth it.

Things with Aaron were a bit complicated, even after I switched over to Warner (and brought Clover Music along with me). He was excited and communicative, which was a great sign, but it was also harder to actually pin him down. It made sense since he was trying to balance being the CEO of an entire major label for the first time in his career on top of trying to A&R my project. I empathized with him but couldn't help but wonder if I'd be able to get the attention I needed for this to work.

Fortunately, he was open to going in a less straightforward pop direction as long as we could balance it out with something more "commercial." We got creatively inspired and on the same page, agreeing that I would make a full-on R&B project first and then quickly follow up with a more rhythmic pop album. *Bang BANG.* I was happy to be in a good flow with him and itching to get started, but he wanted me to pause for a bit while he organized the new company he had just inherited.

It was here where our priorities were really starting to diverge. I had been on other people's time frames for too long. And I knew that if we couldn't put out new music until he could focus more on me, then my team and I had to find our own solution and figure out how to work with the cards we'd been dealt. I remembered how entrepreneurial, optimistic, and creative I had been as a little girl, before I ever got started in the industry, and I hoped that spirit was still somewhere underneath all the scar tissue.

One day, M.M. called me up with a sparkle in her voice and put this crazy idea out there, inspired by a revelation from my old contract.

"You know, Jo . . . you can legally cover your own songs now. Enough time has passed."

"Okaaayyy . . . ?" I was lost.

"So," she went on, "we could have your producer friends like Jordan reproduce the tracks from your old albums and make 'em sound close to the OG versions, and then we'll go back in and record new vocals. I think it's genius, Jo! It could start a mini revolution."

No artist I knew of had done this before, though that's not to say artists hadn't been actively regaining control over their creations from the jump. Back in the 1990s, Prince famously shook shit up when he changed his name to an unpronounceable symbol, raging against the industry machine and publicly fighting his label for the rights to his masters. But this wasn't exactly the same thing. I had long been down to changing my name back, but that wouldn't satisfy the issue in front of us. I wasn't sure if it would be a waste of time to record updated versions of old music, as opposed to putting new, fresh music out there. Would it look like I was stuck in the past? Like I was obsessed with my teenage golden era? When I voiced my concerns, M.M. understood but gently reassured me that it would be empowering for everyone— me most of all.

I loved that we were now conspiring to do something nontraditional and make artisanal limoncello out of lemons. This could turn a source of pain into a story of creativity and resilience. Me and M.M. felt like partners again. And more than anything, I had digested enough spiritual texts to know it was time to put the concepts I said I believed in into practice. Fear of taking a risk that might upset my label or make me look silly had kept me clinging to false stability and nonaction long enough. One of my favorite spiritual thought leaders, the late Wayne Dyer, said "If you change the way you look at things, the things you look at change." I needed a new frame to look at my career with. It was time to *do* something, start dreaming again.

We were set on rerecording and rereleasing new versions of this music, but the label didn't think it would be worth their investment. Fine! M.M. and I would fund it ourselves and put it out through Clover directly. There'd be less profit sharing with nonbelievers and more ownership this way. It was starting to get easier to see silver linings and open windows.

Katie booked studio time and I paid my producer friends to re-create the tracks from the ground up to sound as close to the originals as possible. My favorite engineer, Ryan, and I locked ourselves in the studio for about two weeks while we dissected my first two albums. Memories from long-forgotten recesses of my mind came flooding back when I took the time to connect to the moments those songs came from. As we opened up Pro Tools each day, every harmony, vocal stack, reverb, and delay setting was considered. The choices I made as a preteen and young teenager were so different from the ones I'd make now, as an adult. But I smiled and enjoyed spending time playing inside the songs I'd made as the free and fearless child I once was.

Strangely, I identified with the lyrical content of those first two albums more as a grown woman than I did as a kid and thought my current, more mature voice lent itself to the subject matter better. Not just the songs about love but also the ones about a life philosophy. *The High Road* had pretty much become a mantra for how I wanted to show up, corny as that sounds:

> *"I'm gonna keep walking though it may seem far*
> *I'm gonna keep reaching when life gets too hard*
> *Not gonna let you bring me down*
> *I'll take the high road."*

My fans have told me these songs feel like a cozy childhood blanket to them, but up until rerecording the two albums, I hadn't listened to them front to back for over a decade. Tapping into the nostalgia of my younger years was bittersweet. Between Vincent and Barry and Mom and the confusion I found myself in in the midst of trying to re-create the success I'd had as a teenager, it was just easier to disassociate. But there was something about hearing my new voice on these old songs.

On December 21, 2018—the day after my twenty-eighth birthday—I released the new versions of *JoJo* and *The High Road* online as well as two of my more recent singles, "Demonstrate" and "Disaster." For the album artwork, I commissioned one of Leah's best friends, Cristina Martinez, to interpret the original covers in her signature style. Clover Music's first release was me taking my power back and tapping into young Joanna's scrappy never-scared energy. I'm happy that in even more recent times, someone as massive and powerful as Taylor Swift has shed light on the nuances of ownership in recorded music. It's an important conversation. While I chose to rerecord my first two albums under very different circumstances, I applaud her for doing the same thing a few years later due to her own situation with her "Taylor's Version."

Over the years, I kept hearing about this guy named PJ Morton. He was the son of a legendary preacher, part of Maroon 5, and now a bona fide solo star who'd steadily built up his own musical empire in New Orleans. I had mad respect for his journey and obvious talent as an artist and businessman. We'd been following each other on social media for a while and would like and comment on one another's stuff but had never met IRL. He was just coming off a Grammy win for his cover of the Bee Gees's "How Deep Is Your Love" with one of my favorite artists, Yebba, when I got a message from him. He asked for my email so he could send over this song he thought I'd be great on.

It also just so happened he was in LA that week, so I went to his show and got to experience his musical genius up close. A few days later, I got into my car (the *best* place to listen to music) and opened up the song waiting for me in my inbox. It was intimate— just him and a Wurlitzer electric piano—and damn, it sounded like *warm butter*. The chords, the message, the simplicity. This song was *real* R&B. An instant classic in my opinion. I immediately hit him back and apologized for not listening sooner.

He laughed. "I thought you just weren't feeling it!!"

When I told M.M. I wanted to work on it with him, she knew I was now in a place where I was going to do it regardless of what she or anyone thought. She agreed that it was a good song, but she was a bit worried it might signal a move in the direction of contemporary R&B.

See, up until this point, the music industry had always been super focused on genre, reliant on putting things into easily digestible and understandable boxes. A part of that was probably for radio, which followed a particular format, but it was also a marketing strategy since they always wanted to know which audiences were being targeted with the "product" being sold. Listen, I *really* wish I didn't know or think about this shit. Over the years, it's clouded my judgment and made me think more than feel. But in my heart, I just didn't care that some people around me considered R&B more "niche" and "regional"—not international like pop could be. If it's good, people will like it! Besides, artists who refused to be reduced to little containers had always been making waves in their own way. It just took some more creativity, audacity, and courage to step out on what they really believed in.

Anyways, when it came time to record, PJ wanted to make sure that we were really singing it together—not just comping in separate vocals from different locales—so he brought me out to his studio compound in New Orleans. He and his team had been putting the finishing touches on another project, and seeing him in there was like watching a master at work. He was at the helm of every part of the process—from writing, arranging, and recording to programming and producing, mixing, and mastering. It was great to see up close all that he was able to make happen while not having to live in Los Angeles. He was an independent artist creating his own world and his own rules. And I felt honored to work with someone like him.

One year later, we found out that "Say So" had been nominated for a Grammy: R&B Song of the Year. Since PJ had written the song by himself, the award would technically just have his name on it, but he made it very clear to me that this was *our* song. He didn't need to say that, but he did. Getting calls from friends, family, and colleagues when the nominations came out felt so surreal and emotional. Back when I was thirteen, I'd made myself a promise when I was nominated for a VMA that I wouldn't go to the Grammys until I'd received a nomination there, too. I didn't think it would take another sixteen years for that dream to come true, but now that it had, I decided I was going to celebrate my unique journey and bask in it.

Meanwhile, my ex hadn't spoken to me for damn near two years. He'd cut me all the way off—and I understood why. I sent him a couple of long apology emails and song demos that I'd written about him, constantly putting my regret down to paper, but I never expected a response.

On the morning of my first session with Lido (who would eventually become one of my favorite producers and people), I woke up from a vivid dream about running into my ex. I walked into the studio buzzing, *needing* to get this feeling out of my chest and onto some chords.

> *"I've been trying to move on*
> *And it's obvious that I can't*
> *It was my fault we're broken*
> *But I can't let go of hopin'*
> *So, I leave my door wide open*

All my friends keep telling me
I just need to f*ck someone new
Whenever I do, I'm gonna think of you
So, if it seems like somebody took your spot
Well, that's just not true . . .
Whenever I do, I'm gonna think of you"

No matter how much time had passed, forgiving myself for what I had done and who I had been and how much hurt I'd caused . . . all that just seemed impossible. All I could do was reflect on the mess I had created, feeling so undeserving of such a good man.

For about a year, I stayed abstinent, which might not sound like a long time to you. But keep in mind that I had been jumping in and out of relationships ever since I started dating at fourteen, using them as a distraction from all of my problems—whether they were with my career, my parents, or my anxiety. Looking back, there were *far* more constructive ways I could have spent all that time. However, I was trapped in what Janice called "love addiction," and sex became intertwined with that. I used to think it was permissible, even fun and cute in my early twenties. And if it served as inspo for a song? Even better. But now, approaching my thirties, I considered myself a bad person who repeatedly engaged in flat out toxic behavior. Quite frankly, I was sick of my shit.

So naturally, as fate would have it, I spotted my ex across the room at a mutual friend's album release party in Hollywood.

Tears welled up as I made my way over and asked if we could talk. I had no idea if he ever read those emails. As I rambled on about what I'm sure came out as a very incoherent apology, his energy stayed calm and grounded. I knew he was probably frustrated and thought I was being selfish for trying to alleviate my guilt, but he showed me kindness and grace. Even as I went on about how terrible I'd been, I couldn't help but appreciate how good it felt to finally be next to him again.

He expressed that he had healed and moved on; he didn't hate me but instead would always love me, and he wanted me to forgive myself and be able to let go. I was awestruck by his maturity. And truly happy for him.

I exhaled. There was nothing more to say. I wished I could stretch the moment out further, but it was clear that we both needed to return to the party. So he went back inside, and I gripped the balcony banister for a few minutes, looking out at the neon lights and asking myself the age old question: "What the fuck?"

In 2019, I rented an Airbnb and invited some of my favorite producers and writers to come out there to make music with me. Walking through the house was a dream come true—all these beautiful, special, talented people under one roof who all brought their own flair and perspective to making songs. No judgment, no worries, just playing with music. I felt like if we all went to school together, we would have sat at the same table at lunch. There was also a pool outside that overlooked a ravine, and before sessions, we would sit out there for a few minutes of guided meditation to get our energy on the same wave before getting started.

One of my best friends, Nat Dunn, a creative/artist/writer/executive, quickly became a staple of the camp. She always helped bring me back to center whenever I veered off and started doubting myself. A majority of the time, when I walked into writing sessions back at the studios in Hollywood, I started out excited and optimistic, like "Hell yeah, we can make *anything* today and anything has the potential to be incredible." Especially if they put me into a room with a new cowriter or a new producer, I'd feel like the execs had faith in our ability to write something dope that day. But that confidence was always pretty shaky. If someone said something off, or if I caught two people giving each other a not-great look, I started questioning if everyone could see right through me. Could see how fragile and uncertain I was at leading the charge. My chest would start tightening, squeezing my stomach up into my throat. When that anxiety started building, it was paralyzing and I went inward. Not only was I unable to express creative thoughts; I'd cease to *even* have them. It was like the string that connected me to this archive of ideas inside my soul was severed, and all of a sudden, I'd be falling, falling, falling into a sea of nothingness. Embarrassed and incompetent. Feeling like everyone else knew more than I did and I should just keep quiet and defer to them.

Another songwriter friend at the writing retreat, Rose Gold, asked what I thought people expected from me. I said I had no fucking idea. And I meant it. But when I really sat with that question, I started wondering if the problem rested in other people's sky-high expectations . . . or my own. For years, I'd been living with a deep judgment of myself that I lacked the courage, conviction, and consistency to stand up to whoever I thought opposed me and to be the artist I wanted to be, to put the music I really believed in out into the world. I would take steps forward and then retreat backward. And I just wasn't sure when I'd ever be able to fully let go of that crippling doubt.

A couple times in the past, I'd made the mistake of reading some nasty comments that former fans (and straight-up haters) were writing online. I'm not sure if they thought they were being helpful and constructive, or if they were just being dickheads. In the end, it didn't really matter; what hurt most is that I agreed with some of their assessments—but it did inspire the lyrics to a song I called "Joanna," where I projected all of my darkest thoughts about myself onto an archetype of a "stan" character.

"We go back a long time
I've been riding with you since day one
Oh I, remember we were just kids
You were singing, winning, so young and innocent
But these days
You don't really sound the same
Do you still have the same range
That you did when you were 14, girl?
I don't really know

You should date somebody famous
That'll probably put you on the A-list
That'll probably get you on them playlists
Stop you being so damn underrated, oh
What is goin' on, Joanna?
What is goin' on, Joanna?

You peaked
Sorry to get deep, but
Heard your story before, it's not unique
You're sounding resentful, take a seat
It must be something that you did
Did you go and have somebody's kid?
Your shit don't even go that hard
Why can't you just play your part?
Speaking of which, where did your acting career go?
You were supposed to be somebody
You were supposed to make more money
Make us proud
Nobody likes you in Massachusetts
You should just hurry and drop your new shit
Hurry and drop your new shit"

In the midst of working on my fourth album, I found myself out in Canada with Doc McKinney at House of Balloons studio (where they'd recorded The Weeknd's first project by the same name). I'd been singing professionally for two decades by then, but all of a sudden, that inner saboteur came roaring back in and I started questioning everything. It used to be my greatest joy in the whole world, but being in the booth didn't feel fun or liberating anymore.

A big part of the problem was that my voice *had* changed since I'd recorded my most popular songs. Not only does every singer go through natural vocal thickenings as they get older; I'd also run my cords through the *ringer*: I had prenodes from singing recklessly without proper training, I went through periods of smoking and drinking like a fiend, I'd taken steroids for vocal swelling to make it through tours, and I'd been on various forms of birth control over the years that had majorly fucked with my hormones. I mentally *struggled* to embrace this richer, deeper tone.

I did take after take after take, never quite satisfied with what I heard playing back to me. I kept trying to make myself sound brighter, younger. But all I could hear on the playback was the sound of my own numbness and dissociation. I'd stopped trying to hit big notes or do intricate runs because I no longer believed I could.

Who did people want me to be? "Marvin's Room" JoJo or "Too Little, Too Late" JoJo? I really hated myself for even thinking about myself this way. Like a product for mass consumption. I was *not* a marketing person, and yet I now processed shit like one. Another artist told me that the way I spoke about what I wanted for my music sounded like an A&R. *EW.* Seeing as we both hated the industry at this point, it wasn't a compliment.

It didn't help that I'd been working with three different A&R guys at Warner, each with different ideas of what they thought my music should be. On top of that, there was M.M.'s opinion. I was still waiting for someone to shake me out of this never-ending cycle and say, "You know this is your shit, right? No one truly cares OR knows what they're doing, so *you* have to decide. Choose your own adventure, bitch."

Even with all that overthinking, there were so many moments where I felt completely free to try out new things with Doc, Dylan, Merna, and the rest of the crew up in Canada. Aaron gave us a week or so to experiment and then wanted to hear what we had been coming up with. Every day, we'd start out at the piano or guitar or bass and come up with a new groove. Of all the songs we worked on, "Sabotage" was the one that felt most like the beginning of a new sound for me. Funky. Dark. Soulful. One I could really sink my teeth into. When I heard that sticky bass line, I instantly started singing the lyrics from "You Used to Love Me" by Faith Evans ("I remember . . . the way . . . you used . . . to love . . . me . . .") and felt inspired to write something that felt like that. We started unpacking my regrets from all of these new angles, squeezing out all the remaining juice we could. It wasn't just regrets about love; it was also questioning why I continued to betray *myself*. By letting other people's opinions be what I trusted over my own instincts, I was delaying the inevitable. If I didn't stop sabotaging my own happiness, I would just keep repeating the same destructive behaviors and hurting people I love in the process. Thank God for the people in my life who stuck around to patiently have the same conversations for years—the ones who reminded me that I was worthy and this heavy feeling wouldn't last forever. Thank God for the music that held me down in the meantime.

Around the making of this fourth album, I needed to have some hard talks with myself. It all stemmed from the fact that I was slowly—but surely—beginning to accept two very different but equally important truths. The first was that when it came to my career and the new, more authentic direction I wanted to go in, I knew I was playing the long game. I accepted that it might take me longer than I wanted to deprogram and decondition my default ways of thinking and acting, but I just needed to keep my head down, stay focused, and put in the work. The second was that my relationship with My Manager was no longer sustainable or healthy, and if I wanted to be true to my vision, I had to let go of the baggage that came with hers.

For years, we'd tried bringing in different comanagers to act as buffers between us because we simply couldn't communicate without getting into fights. Every issue was a five-alarm fire. At the root of a lot of my frustration was that it really hurt to write and cut as many songs as I did and know that she didn't think any of them were good enough. Whenever we'd talk about the music other artists were putting out, it seemed like we were listening to two completely different tracks. And to be honest, I didn't think that what they were putting out was better than the songs I'd been working on—including the ones we'd left on the cutting room floor. After ten years of trying to make bigger waves than the ones I was making, the only thing it seemed like we were really achieving at this point was making each other's blood boil.

The dissolution of this relationship was heartbreaking—more so than most of my romantic relationships in the past. As much as I was like the daughter she'd never had, she'd become a mother to me when I desperately needed stability and consistency. But the way we thought about music and life was just fundamentally different. And it wasn't serving either of us anymore.

All of this rising tension inevitably led to a massive blowout in the Warner Records garage before a meeting. Katie was there, too, caught in the middle as always, doing everything she could to defuse and get to the heart of what was really going on. She never picked sides and always tried to use humor to make things lighter. But there was no lightening anything this time. If I remember correctly, this particular fight came about because we couldn't agree on which version of the song "Small Things" I was going to play for Aaron. It was a song we all liked that he had found for me, and I was trying to make it sound even better. I'd recently recut the vocals and added some 808 percussion sounds that hadn't previously been there, so I thought we should play this updated version.

"You're just wrong," she brushed me off, telling me I should stick with the original.

You've got to be fucking kidding me.

I breathed deeply through my nose and exhaled quietly so as not to be outwardly dramatic. But I was *BEYOND* tired of arguments that revolved around the most minuscule details, and I couldn't back down. She stormed out of the car, saying she wasn't coming to the meeting if I didn't play her version. Fuck this shit. I threw up my hands, exasperated. *FINE.* We'll play your version. I don't care enough to die on this hill. She had already made us late for the meeting, and I didn't want to be even later.

As we sat down with Aaron and the other A&Rs in his office, I started to play all the songs we'd brought up for consideration, including "Small Things." I truly don't even remember which version I played. Again: there were only *minor* differences in these versions. And yet she stayed silent the whole time, only opening her mouth to greet Aaron and answer his questions with one-word responses. I was appalled at the pettiness and wanted to jump across the room and smack the smug look off her face. That's how bad it had gotten.

Once I'd cooled down later that afternoon, I called her and apologized for the part I played in it all. I expressed my frustration about how unnecessary and hurtful that whole thing was. We were too grown and loved each other too much to have it devolve into childish tantrums like that. I didn't think every single thing was supposed to feel *this* hard. It didn't take long before it became clear that, once again, we were just going around in circles. She didn't seem ready to make up. And I wasn't emotionally available to argue anymore.

Vibrating with anger and confusion after the whole incident, I called my ex and asked if I could come over. Somehow, we'd gotten close again. As in, he opened a window and I threw my entire body through it. I knew that he was the only one who would understand how I was feeling and know how to set me straight.

When I walked into his place, I asked about his day and tried to act like everything was fine, but he could tell something was off. We were still acutely attuned to shifts in one another. There was no point in keeping up a facade, so I wrapped myself in a blanket and collapsed onto the couch, letting all the tension of the day out of my body as I explained everything that had happened. He turned away from his computer and gave me a serious look.

"Jo, I'm honestly really tired of hearing the same story with you guys over and over again. This is insane. You should not be in tears after every interaction with your manager. You're supposed to feel like you can trust her, not like you have to suppress your opinions and shrink yourself," he said. "And you *definitely* should not be made to feel like, after all this time, you don't know what you're doing. She *doesn't* know better than you. *Only you* know what's right for you. You have more experience in this industry than most people ever get. If you're not happy, stop acting like a victim and make a change."

I sat in silence.

This was the wake-up call I'd been waiting for. I'd already taken the first step by getting out of my contract with Blackground, but there was still so much I relied on external forces for.

Everyone around me—especially M.M.—had guided me since I was a teenager, and the thought of no longer having that to fall back on made me feel inept and embarrassed. And *scared*.

What the hell would it actually look and feel like if I took ownership over not just my music but my whole *life*? I needed to do something drastic if I wanted anything to change, and letting her go was the most drastic thing I could think of.

We both knew it was coming and were probably waiting for the other to build up the guts to pull the plug. We didn't speak for a while after the Warner meeting, but after the dust settled, I held my breath and called her up. Voice shaking and feeling like I was going to pass out, I asked if she would meet me for coffee that weekend. Since most of our conversations now ended up in a fight, I thought it'd be more effective to get all my thoughts out in letter form and read it to her in person. On a chill Sunday in Brentwood. In public. Besides, I'm better at communicating when I can lay it out in black and white; I'm less likely to freeze, backpedal, anxiously trip over my words, or close my heart in fear of rejection. I wanted to make sure my immense love for her was front and center in this break-up letter. I didn't want either of us to walk away feeling all the years and sacrifices were for nothing.

As I put my almond milk cappuccino down and started reading out loud to her, the words came out as clearly as they could. I think watching it finally come to an end at that little café was a relief to her, too. She had tried so hard to manage, mother, and save me from myself. But I no longer needed saving or parenting. We had given it our all over the past ten years, but if we wanted to try to salvage any type of relationship going forward, we needed to walk away and move on.

CHAPTER 19

JUMPING WITHOUT A NET

IN FEBRUARY 2020, I WENT TO THE GRAMMYS FOR THE FIRST TIME. I WORE A SPARKLY blue strapless dress that reminded me of the night sky in Sedona, complete with a high slit up the leg and a diamond thigh-choker for just a touch of sluttiness to balance out the class. My twin cousins got me glammed up, and I felt more beautiful than ever. I'd been running on the beach in the morning; preparing raw and vegan meals; and fasting for clarity, inspiration, and willpower. My body was totally streamlined, I was noticing daily God winks (my and Mom's term for synchronicities), and I felt connected to the way things were unfolding. As much as I would have loved to celebrate this moment with M.M., I accepted that that chapter was now closed. I had jumped trains. I must have been the happiest person on the red carpet that day. I had a real reason to be there and I couldn't stop smiling.

For the first time ever, I felt a sense of peace—like everything I'd gone through up to that point was worth it just to be here, basking in this moment. I genuinely loved and embraced my entire story, knowing the narrative arc of it all would inspire others to never give up on their dreams. Being nominated was a win on its own.

Since I didn't have a dedicated on-camera seat for the actual award ceremony, though, I decided to head home after the red carpet. My publicist said they got one for me, but it was kinda far back. I couldn't help but hear M.M.'s voice in my head, saying that "perception is reality" and unless I had the "right" seat, I'd be better off watching from home. Plus, the R&B categories weren't even televised, and there was no way our song was going to win, not with the competition being as stacked as it was.

On the car ride back to my condo, I scrolled through social media, flipping back and forth between hot takes from the media coverage that day. The narrative was clear: I was happier and healthier than ever. In my prime. It felt like redemption just to *be* there.

When I was about halfway home, I got a FaceTime from PJ followed by an onslaught of calls and texts.

"Where are you, Jo?!??!?!??! Can you hear me? WE WON!!!!!"

The tears, the disbelief. The Motha. Fucking. Validation. The frantically calling my family and friends and silently wishing Dad could have been one of the calls. The beating myself up for leaving prematurely when I could have experienced this moment in person and not from the back seat of a Cadillac sedan.

Why was I always assuming I knew how things were gonna go (aka not in my favor) before they had a chance to happen?

When was I going to stop counting myself out of the game before it even began?

By 2020, a seismic existential shift had already been in the works and I could see the effects rippling across multiple areas of my life. I'd started thinking a lot about relationships—with myself and others—and felt this renewed sense of compassion, believing that everyone was doing the best they could with what they had at any given time.

I started to empathize with Mom on a level I'd never been able to before and looked at her struggles in a new light, recognizing my own tendencies to go down similar depressive and anxious ways of thinking. As hard as I'd always been on her, she'd done the best she could to protect and raise me in a completely foreign landscape, an industry that capitalized on our naivete. She did a remarkable job. What would I have done in her shoes? How scared would I have felt?

By this point, she'd maintained her sobriety for several years and was deep in the thick of her own healing journey. We were both so focused on becoming better versions of ourselves, reading many of the same books and thinking about the same concepts. She liked that I was taking more of an interest in the Twelve Steps and would send me her daily passages. I was proud of her for making a choice (to get sober) and sticking with it, which was something I still struggled to do.

She hated New England winters and was itching for a change so she ended up moving into the place I had recently bought in LA. It wasn't massive, but it was big enough for us to live together and not constantly be in each other's faces. She promised that she'd start looking for work and eventually help me with paying down the mortgage. Dr. Janice didn't think it was the best idea, but the little girl in me felt grateful to get a second chance at living with Mom again.

While Mom focused on getting her footing, I decided to officially ask Katie to be my new manager. For the past seventeen years, she'd been the glue that held so much of my life together and was consistently a precious gem of a human. I admired the way she didn't treat anything like the end of the world, was rooted firmly in her faith in God, and made everyone she met feel seen and respected. She'd walk into a room and say, "Who's ready to party?!" which was hilarious coming from someone as responsible and nonpartying as her. But she turned even stressful days into good vibes. She'd been doing the legwork of my day-to-day business for well over a decade, and through the ups and downs, we managed to maintain a loving, trusting, sister-like relationship—there are actually no words that properly convey just how lucky I am to have her by my side. I was so excited for the chance to partner with her and watch up close as she spread her wings and stepped into the role that her hard work warranted.

But I also wasn't sure if she'd want to continue on with me. I knew what a loyal person she was, but I didn't want to rest on that or take advantage. We'd spent such a big chunk of our lives together. I would have understood if she wanted to start fresh or join a management company that offered more stability and less emotional investment. Envisioning a life without Katie made me feel a little nauseous, but I was prepared to accept whatever was best for us both. One night over tapas and wine, we laid out all our questions, concerns, and needs on the table. We got right down to the heart of it all. We wanted to do things differently and prioritize happiness and peace in our vision of success, growing from what we'd learned over the years, both individually and together.

The timing couldn't have been better since we were putting the finishing touches on my fourth album. *Good to Know* seemed like a fitting title for where I was in my life in that moment. I'd finally started really recognizing the ways that ego, addiction, and fear drove me to repeat the same patterns. And if I really wanted to change, knowing where the roots of my problems were was a pretty good place to start.

A lot of that self-awareness was coming out in my lyrics, too. My friend Nat and I had just written a song called "Don't Talk Me Down" with Lido at Rick Rubin's studio in Malibu. It was just as much a reflection on my long-winded on/off dramatic and codependent affair with The Older Man as it was about breaking up with M.M.:

> *"Intuition's such a funny thing.*
> *There's some things you really can't explain with words,*
>   *I've learned.*
> *Opposites attract, but do they last?*
> *Light us up to burn out just as fast, that's lust. That's us.*
> *And it's not what you want but it's what you need.*
> *You're just so good at convincing me.*
> *Changing my mind when I finally believe we're done.*
> *Don't talk me down.*
> *Don't fill my head with doubt.*
> *Don't call me late at night knowing what I'm like.*
> *Can't trust myself.*
> *When you walk out, don't turn around.*
> *Don't talk me down."*

A lot of the other songs on this album centered around breaking down this "Broken Girl Who Does Bad Things" narrative I'd been carrying around over the years, the one that kept reinforcing all my bad habits.

One of my favorite songwriters, Sebastian Kole, wrote a really cool song for me at a writing camp in Bali. He works in a way I'd never seen before. Normally, when collaborating with other writers, we come up with melodies and lyrics together. But Sebastian will ask some questions and then leave the studio, go walk around, smoke some herb, and drink a Dr. Pepper, and in a matter of minutes, he'll come back with a verse and chorus fully flushed out. The man is a fucking *savant*. He must have some psychic ability because I'm telling you, he READ ME. We'd only spent a few minutes talking before he randomly excused himself from the room to go on his solo writing journey. DAMN, the way he somehow saw into my soul and reflected it back to me was *SO* confronting:

> *"Feed me love, sex, and drugs.*
> *Bring me more, it ain't enough.*
> *Tell me I'm pretty, yeah, I need that.*
> *I think I'm too sober*
> *Where the weed at?*
> *Pay me attention.*
> *Give me any and everything to forget all that I'm missing.*

It reminded me so much of what Gabor Maté talked about when he described the "hungry ghost."

The lyrics startled me and I *loved* it.

So I put that in as the very opening of the deluxe album.

Good to Know leaned more consistently toward R&B than any of my previous albums had since maybe the first one. And that was very much the intention, knowing that we'd follow it up with another album that was more of a crossover record.

I'd been hoping to release "Think About You" as a single since I loved it most and felt it would really connect with my fans. But when we brought it up to the label, we were told we'd "get to it." I honestly wanted to do my whole album with Lido, carving out a cohesive sound and banking on that being good enough. But I reminded myself that I said I'd give things one last shot doing it the label's way. They wanted me to keep trying out other producers and cowriters and striving to make a hit. So I hoped for the best, tried to believe in a future where this didn't all fall apart for one reason or another, and showed good faith toward the people who held the purse strings.

We went out with Aaron and some executives from the label to celebrate the upcoming release of "Man" as the first single by going out to a fancy dinner. No time like the present to get over my shit, let go of the past, and believe in the future. We had a solid two-album plan, I had Katie by my side as copilot with me as captain, and it felt entirely full circle to finally put something out with Aaron after all these years.

On March 19, 2020, we released "Man"—the exact same day the government issued a mandatory statewide stay-at-home order. We were officially in the thick of a global pandemic. Life as everyone knew it changed instantly, and all progress came to a screeching halt.

Mom and I sat next to each other on the green velvet couch in my living room glued to our phones in silence, closely following the news, watching the unbelievable situations people were facing, many of them alone. But we got to be in it together—not three thousand miles apart like usual. I felt so lucky we could be shoulder to shoulder and keep eyes on each other—aiming to keep our collective spirits up. We even established a little routine. She'd make the coffee strong in the morning, and I'd prep our healthy vegan meals and treats. She'd read us passages from her A.A. book aloud, and I'd decide which virtual workout we should try that evening. I ordered a treadmill to put in the basement, and we encouraged each other to stay consistent with it for our mental and physical health. We blasted musical theater soundtracks and gospel music through the speakers, walked Agapé around the neighborhood, and watched Netflix shows on my projector together. It was more quality time than we had spent in years, and it felt so good that somehow, we were both in such a positive place at the same time.

I'll be the first to admit that Instagram was a saving grace during the lockdown. Amid all the uncertainty of a pandemic, I was determined to focus on what I could control. Every day at noon, like clockwork, I went live and talked and sang and just hung out with folks online. It felt *AMAZING* to connect with people from all around the world who were so cool and interesting and kind. I wondered why I hadn't done it before.

Sometimes, Mom would join in, too, and listen intently as singers came on to either share their talent by themselves or duet with me. She once decided to make a public service announcement about the kind of man she wanted for me. Someone who had his own life going for him, who was honest, kind, real. It was embarrassing but adorable. Part of me was mad that it might make me look like I was lonely or that I couldn't find a good man by myself, but the other part felt grateful to be so loved. I'd be singing a song someone requested in the chat, and she'd text me from the other room that I wasn't breathing deeply enough. Annoying, yes, but she *was* right. And she cared enough to tell me the truth. She helped with my Savage X Fenty shoots from home and all the other stuff I was doing from within those four walls. She watched Agapé while I spent weeks with my friends and producers Jordan, Austin Brown, and Brian London, creating a Christmas album in the middle of the summer. When I'd come home from a long day of writing and recording, I asked her to come listen to versions of new songs in the car. She hadn't really loved my music for a while, and I knew it, so I felt tense about playing her stuff. But it was disarming, even healing to see the tears well up in her eyes, knowing that she was incapable of faking that reaction.

Over the years, she (mostly) stopped giving me her opinion to spare us arguing (just like I had with M.M.) but she certainly said enough to convey that she wished I hadn't sold out to what the labels—or management—wanted from me. She seemed relieved that I was in the process of waking up. We cried as she told me she loved hearing me sing from my earnest heart and could tell I was having fun again, trying new things and expanding outside of music, remembering who I was before our lives changed. Fearless. I think she was happy to be included in this part of my world again, too. Mom was my rock again during those early pandemic days, and I was so grateful that we got to be in the thick of it together. She was even brave enough to play guinea pig and try out all my new vegan recipes before I shared them with anyone else. By now she had several years of sobriety under her belt, and I really admired her for the humbleness and integrity it took to keep showing up, *sober*, one day at a time.

Promoting a single and album felt silly AF in the grander scheme of things. But being able to relate with people about love, relationships, and regret was timely. The album debuted at number 1 on the Billboard R&B chart, and knowing I'd be confined at home until further notice, I said yes to every virtual interview or performance that came my way. Not gonna lie, it was most pleasing to my inner teacher's pet when Warner praised me as the example of how they wanted their artists to push things forward during a time of such uncertainty.

But the truth was that I was doing it as much for the music as I was for my mental health. Staying busy was all I really knew. For God's sake, most of my adult life had been spent feeling like I needed to play catch-up to everyone else, and if I slowed down for too long, I'd be slipping even further behind. This internal engine sometimes motivated me to create and continue and made me feel like whatever I was doing, wherever I was at was not enough. When the world shut down, I told myself I would do the opposite. I was testing my mental toughness and would not accept a failing grade. This was the longest period I had spent in one place in years, and I tried to see it as an opportunity to learn how not to crumble but to grow stronger in embracing uncertainty and flowing with the randomness. Even though all plans for the album were up in the air, I would get it out into the world as best I could and do the most with promotion, creation, cooking, yoga, running, mixology, reading, and online community building to do my part and not fall victim to an aimless mind.

By the summer of 2020, the events including and surrounding the murder of George Floyd deeply affected me and my friends. We downloaded untraceable apps to share information, opinions, and articles. We listened and held space for people's visceral anger. According to the news, the whole country was burning. A bunch of us in the chat decided we would ignore the stay-at-home order and join some protests as a unit. The old systems needed to fall in order to make space for new ones.

As our protest group grew and grew, there was one new guy who caught my attention. He was kind and present with everyone and led with this big smile and even bigger, brighter energy that kept me noticing him even in the sea of people. With his loud-ass sneakers and his patterned windbreaker co-ord that "swished" together when he walked, I initially chalked him up to just being a kinda corny but very nice new acquaintance and left it at that. He wasn't really my type, anyway.

I silently questioned whether he could possibly be as nice as he presented. It seemed like he was always "on." No one could possibly be *that* upbeat, could they? We mostly spent time together in groups in the beginning, either in his backyard or at our other friend's house where people were allowed entry upon a negative COVID test. He instantly hit it off with my childhood bestie LeMicah, and they learned that the new guy's uncle had played percussion in LeMicah's granddad's group, the O'Jays, way back in the day. It was too cute to see these grown men jumping up and down, sharing stories from childhood when they realized they had met as kids over twenty years ago.

Slowly, my disbelief in his authenticity started to dissipate. One day, he was talking about his past mistakes and I opened up about cheating. It was something that I fundamentally refused to be involved with again and something I still struggled to forgive myself for. We admitted to each other that we'd both hurt people that we'd loved in the past and vowed never to put ourselves in positions to do that ever again. He made me feel safe and understood, and it really felt like he didn't want or need anything in return. And he was always thoughtful, noticing and acknowledging the little things. He would never hesitate to make someone a plate, offer a seat, lend an ear or a dollar, or see if there was any way he could help. When my quarantine performance of Diane Warren's song "The Change" debuted on *The Late Show with Stephen Colbert*, he surprised me by sending a big unicorn balloon and chocolates to my door. Excuse me? I had *never* celebrated things like that before. I thought it was a little silly but also incredibly sweet. He knew that Leah's friends referred to her as our unicorn, and a handful of us cherished the blown-glass unicorns that her mother had gifted to us after she passed. The fact that he remembered a detail like that blew me away.

Was this the man Mom had made the public service announcement about on IG? At the very least, he was someone I wanted to be around and be more like.

In the spirit of full transparency, I told the new guy that I was hung up on my ex and deep down still wanted to make it work. He understood. But he also said I deserved to be seen for who I was now, not for who I'd been in the past.

So he invited me over for a night of cooking and watching a movie. In my mind, it was absolutely not a date—I wasn't ready for romance—but he pulled out all the stops. Days before I came over, he asked about dietary restrictions and wanted to know my spirit of choice. When I got there, he had candles lit and music on, and he had made these craft cocktails to start and had a wine pairing to go with the flavors we'd be having over the course of the evening. This nondate was the date-iest date I'd been on in years. I forgot a key ingredient of the dish I'd agreed to make, and he got up and grabbed it from the store for me without a second thought. My dish *paled* in comparison to the deliciously creative three-course vegan meal that he whipped up for us from scratch. Full-bellied and a little buzzed, we sat at a distance on the couch and debated music and movies while good naturedly ragging on each other. It was wholesome and fun, but I still didn't really feel like there was anything more than friendship brewing. Before I went home, he packed me a to-go container with leftovers for Mom and gave me "friendly flowers." It was a bit much, but it was really fucking nice.

In those early days, I found plenty of reasons to keep this guy squarely in the friend zone. He was unlike anyone I had met before though, constantly doing or planning something new and exciting and jaw-droppingly thoughtful. I'd be brutally honest when he asked how I felt about him or wanted my opinion on things— even when I knew he wouldn't like what I had to say. But I had nothing to lose and was curious to see how he'd handle my raw, unedited truth. He stayed open and curious to learn more about where I was coming from. He explained he'd been waiting on the right woman to come in and care enough to help him level up his life, à la that Beyoncé song "Upgrade U."

He wasn't shy about expressing from the jump that he wanted to be a husband and father, while continuing to build his career.

At this point, I was twenty-nine, about to turn thirty, and finally admitting to myself and others how incredible stability sounded. *Home.* I felt such a longing for it, deep in my bones. Before I knew it, he was starting to break down the walls I'd built up over the years as I felt myself slow down and soften—and really care about him.

Early on, both of our moms happened to be in town, and he asked if he could take us all to dinner.

"No pressure," he said. "I just think they'd have a lot in common, being single moms from the East Coast with only children who started in this industry really young."

Sure, why not?

Everything just flowed, one milestone to the next. His mother, a well-respected family law attorney who'd had him later in life, was brilliant and deep. And Mom was definitely impressed with both of them.

"Jo, who knows? He might be the real deal. Why don't you just take a chance and see how it goes?"

It was all happening so fast, and we both wondered if this dude was too good to be true.

Adventurous home-cooked meals. Handwritten poetry. Surprising me on a work trip.

Was I being love bombed?!

Or was this how real love without baggage was supposed to feel?

If I were to take this seriously, I'd have to fully close the door on my previous relationship, which had opened again at the end of the previous year. After all the pain I had put my ex through, I didn't want to add more. We had finally revived our friendship and I was still in love with him, but he clearly didn't want the same things I did, at least not with me. I craved romantic partnership and dreamed of creating a family—whether that included children or just me and my man. Prioritizing love and a life outside of a career. All the things we tried to work through and the dreams we had for our lives . . . at a certain point, I had to let them go and believe him when he said he couldn't get over what I had done. Dr. Janice had a heart-to-heart with me, saying I was wasting time wishing he would take another chance on us.

I had to own it.

On December 20, 2020, I celebrated my thirtieth birthday by skydiving with LeMicah. Friends offered to throw a party or organize a dinner, but I just wasn't feeling it. My soul was heavy, and I needed some wide-open spaces. LeMicah and I don't require any social battery to hang out; he's one of the only pals I've known since before I was famous, and we were both looking for something to shake us up. So, on a total whim, he booked it. We jumped. We survived. We hugged. Then we ate tacos and went our separate ways. The two men my heart was involved with reached out, and I felt guilty for my embarrassment of riches in the form of love. Soberly sitting in the discomfort of my own company was how I thought I needed to start the new decade. Sex and snuggles would only delude and delay whatever was going to unfold.

I rented a lovely little one-bedroom cottage in Santa Barbara, and after two days of walking around the town with Agapé, phone off, journal in pocket for whenever inspiration struck, and begging God for clarity on what to do next—I asked Mom if she would drive from LA and come hold me. She was the big spoon. The next day, we hiked. We watched movies. We sat by the fire. We watched as fan dedications came through social media, and I cried at the genuineness of their comments. What an honor to be so loved. I wanted to get "right" for them and come back to the world a more whole, less broken package. This healing shit was surely not a straight path, and it was taking too *GAHT. DAMN. LONG.*

Here I was, unmistakably grown for REAL now, finally on the verge of trying someone new. If it didn't work, it would mean that walking away from a meaningful friendship with my ex, possibly making him feel slighted yet again—all that would have been in vain. But I was even more scared of letting whatever this newness was slip through my fingers, without ever really knowing what it could turn out to be. I got back to LA, and the new guy threw a big surprise party for me. One I didn't want but felt I should be grateful for.

So I jumped. And I prayed a net would somehow materialize.

CHAPTER 20

UNMASKED

CAN'T SAY I'D EVER ENVISIONED MYSELF IN A THIRTY-POUND BEJEWELED BLACK SWAN costume, red latex gloves lined with fringe running up my arms, singing cover songs through a mesh shield while Robin Thicke, Ken Jeong, Jenny McCarthy, and Nicole Scherzinger judged me. But there the fuck I was when I signed up to be a contestant on *The Masked Singer* in March 2021.

What will people think?

What if I get voted off right away?

OKAY, BITCH, GET OVER IT. If that happens, THEN WHAT???? ARE YOU GONNA DIE? WHY THE FUCK DO YOU CARE? Literally no one else does!!!! Just DO YOU!!!!

I had gotten into a practice of observing and questioning my thoughts as they arose, so my internal dialogue was often argumentative and always fully unhinged.

At the time, there was no end in sight to the pandemic (business was *not* back as usual), and this was an opportunity to work—which was *always* good for my restless mind (and bank accounts).

It sounded fun to get paid to sing other people's songs and put my own spin on them. But driving onto that set every day, rehearsing with masks (and more masks), and keeping distant, knowing that I was doing the kind of show M.M. had said I should never do, it was hard. I wrestled with how people might perceive it. I didn't want to be looked at as a has-been.

You already know.

I ate my feelings and put on a damn good show.

Who knows if I would have said yes to the show if I hadn't faithfully started watching it with my brand-new boyfriend. I've never been much of a reality TV gal (besides a brief stint of addiction to *Housewives* drama in my twenties), but we had gotten really into the lightheartedness and talent focus of *The Masked Singer* and watched it faithfully every week. A show concept that would have made me cringe and die a few years before was now something I thought was just good, clean fun. We got our popcorn and wine and yelled out our guesses about who was under the costumes, complimented and critiqued the musical arrangements, and started to be invested in the arc of the "characters." When I signed on, I tried to remain neutral and walk in with an open mind and heart.

Just go out there and have fun, Jo. Just use this as a platform to play with music like you did as a little girl.

Rehearsals were smooth sailing and fun, but the *second* I stepped out onto that stage and saw the judges in front of me, I got the worst stage fright I'd *ever* experienced. Thankfully, I had a comically massive mask to hide the tears that sometimes dribbled their way down my cheeks as I waited for the judges' response or dissociated while Nick Cannon asked me preplanned questions through the blur of mesh.

One week, during my cover of Kings of Leon's "Use Somebody," I couldn't help but feel the weight of the lyrics on my heart. I wondered, "Is this what my career has come to? I'm sub-jecting myself to being judged by these singers I know and respect as they pretend not to know it's me behind the mask and throw around different names for the viewers at home to guess along with. And for what? Money? Time in the spotlight? What am I doing here?"

The voices in my head that harshly whispered how ashamed I should be—I had to tell them to shut the fuck up. I questioned their origin and who they belonged to, replacing them with a new, more maturing narrative. "Just go out there and sing, Joanna. Like the old days. Stop taking yourself so seriously. You've been told everything is the end of the world. NOTHING, other than the end of the world, is the end of the world."

Fortunately, when my thoughts inevitably regressed, Katie was there on set to talk me off emotional ledges, and my new man and Mom helped to lift my spirits with ice cream or a movie or going for walks around the neighborhood with Agapé.

One thing the show really helped me with, though, was reig-niting some of the vocal fire that I'd been missing in recent years. The show's vocal coach, Eric Dawkins (who I'd known since child-hood from The Underdogs), helped me prepare for each perfor-mance and always encouraged me to go for the interesting choice, the run or the note that would feel satisfying in my bones as a vocalist. Since all the contestants were kept separated and not allowed to hear each other sing, I was only competing with who I was the day before. My boyfriend was super supportive and even recommended a song for me to add to my list for the show, Michael Bolton's "How Am I Supposed to Live Without You." It ended up being the song I sang for the finale, and it was my favorite to sing across the whole season. It shocked me, but I knew right away why he suggested it. The lyrics hit too hard. Although I was moving on by then and choosing to start a new relationship with a clean slate, he knew a big part of me was still in love with the man who came before him.

Meanwhile, Mom had been spiraling bit by bit over the past few months and was slowly sinking back into her own depression. It wasn't looking like she was going to take the necessary steps to get out of the dark place she was in, so I offered to pay for therapy or treatment or whatever she wanted. As much as I wished I could save her from this despair, I also wanted to heed the advice that family and other people who loved me had been shouting for years: focus on saving myself and unsubscribe from the pattern. I really wanted her to get well again and back on her own feet, but I was also scared of getting back on the emotional roller coaster with her—and that made me feel like a bad daughter.

Perhaps the desert would be as healing for her as it was for me. We took a weeklong trip to Sedona together and then talked about how it might be best for her to stay there longer and get some extra treatment. She was despondent. Nothing brightened her spirits, not even her usual antidepression tools of rigorous exercise, sunlight, and clean nutrition. I just didn't know how to help anymore. Her mind had been going to the darkest places, and the air around us was thick with tension. When she would say that she didn't want to be on this planet anymore, I had to choose a different way of hearing it—one that didn't tell me I was responsible for making her happy. Dr. Janice had said many times that if something happened to her, it would not be my fault. When our relationship was codependent like this, it wasn't healthy for *either* of us. As selfish as I felt, I finally had a partner who helped me see that I needed to focus on creating a life of my *own* that made me want to stay in it. I couldn't control anyone else.

With momentum gaining thanks to *The Masked Singer*, Aaron sent me a new song called "Creature of Habit" to mull over. I didn't love it initially—there were other songs that I loved and felt would be much stronger to put out—but he thought this one could be a hit for me. So, after I gracefully declined a few times, he circled back around and asked me to reconsider. He knew more about playlisting and algorithms than I did. Maybe he could see some blind spots that I couldn't.

Fuck it, I'll put my voice on it.

Then, naturally, it became the only song the label wanted to put out, and—what do you know—it didn't perform the way he promised it would. We shot a video and everything. I sold it as much as I could, bringing on some of my favorite visual creatives to make it as palatable as possible. But deep down, I was relieved. Cuz I didn't know how to fit myself into this song. I didn't like choppy verse melodies, the formulaic production, or really anything about the song except for my ad-libs at the end where I let loose. If the song did well, I would have had to sing it over and over again for audiences while they sang it back to me, thinking this is what I represented. Yet I was *still* willing to betray my taste "one last time." When would I get off this hamster wheel? It felt like God's protection. It also ended up being the very last time I would ever cut a song I didn't like. I'd been detached from my own discography for so long, and I hated not feeling ownership over the songs I was putting out. My boyfriend asked me why I would ever record something I didn't fully believe in—which is the same question everyone who loved me and didn't make money off me always eventually asked.

I didn't have a good enough answer.

There were so many questions and thoughts running through my mind—why I kept repeating the same cycles, Mom not being around anymore, the shame of not living up to my potential, crippling self-doubt, the uncertainty of life, corrupt systems and politics, fears about finances, memories of my ex, questions of whether this new guy was for real . . . but endless ruminating never got me anywhere. So I decided to throw my emotions into a new project. Aaron said that if I trusted him on "Creature of Habit," that he'd support me as I made whatever EP I wanted before the next full-length album. He thought it was a "brilliant idea." It made me feel so optimistic. Maybe all the compromises hadn't been in vain, and it was now safe to bet on my own instincts. I explained that I'd always wanted to make a concept record, and it came together naturally as I started to write about what it felt like to live inside an anxious mind. The EP took shape as a cozy, rich, sonic landscape, crafted by JordanXL, D'Mile, and Nikki Flores, and chronicled a season of broken heartedness and blues. Two months before its release, an A&R from the label called Katie and said they weren't sure if they'd be able to fully support it. After reminding them what Aaron had said, they came back weeks later and agreed to cover the recording costs but not much else. They weren't going to really get behind the EP, and it was clear they didn't really understand or believe in what I was doing. I was pissed at myself for getting my hopes up yet again. But this time I didn't intellectualize my way out of doing something I believed in. I had spent too much time thinking and not enough time feeling. This was a project I felt I had to make. On my own terms.

Trying Not to Think About It was the only title that made sense to me.

The songs I sang from here on out had to be *my* story. My body always ended up disagreeing in one way or another whenever I tried to relinquish control and give in to what other people thought I should be doing. I'd grown up thinking adults always had the answers. And guess what? Now I was the adult, and I still didn't have a fucking clue and neither did anyone around me, it seemed. So why not at least do something I felt good about and then fall on my own sword if it came to it?

Thanks to years of therapy and a discomfiting amount of self-reflection, I've learned that one of the most effective ways I can work with my own tendency toward anxiety (an invisible asshole I've personified and named "Burlinda") is to slow down, limit overstimulation and distraction, and let my nervous system (and that little voice inside me) tell me what it needs and what to do. There are moments when Burlinda jumps on my back and I can only see life through her grubby hands as she tries to cover my eyes. She's a manifestation of the overactive ego, harshly judging me and others, screaming that I "should" be something/somewhere different. I think she thrives a bit on the addictive tendencies in me, too. One of the best ways to shake her off and get out of my head without a mind-altering substance is to focus on engaging my five senses (through dance, yoga, breathwork, and working out or some other physical activity). Only then can I say, "I've got the wheel now. You can take a seat in the back, sweetie."

I wrote a song about this toxic internal relationship and included it on the EP:

"I wish that I could shut you off, keep you muted.
I wish I knew the difference between your voice and mine.
I'm always putting out the fires that you started
And every time I look around, it just looks bad on me.
You only show up when it's inconvenient.
Always talking loud. Fill my head with lies.
Keeping me home keeping me from leaving.
You love just to take my time. Why you hate me?
Hate me . . . all you do is suffocate me. Can't breathe.
And if I could choose it'd be me without you.

You drain me, drain me
All you do is try to change me lately.
And if I could choose, it'd be me without you."

Trying to untether from the mindset that kept me feeling small, ashamed, regretful, and never enough has—without question or comparison—been the longest, most back-and-forth breakup of my life. It's been heartbreaking to realize how many of my decisions and subsequent results have been motivated by anxiety and, ultimately, fear. As a kid, I'd get so entangled in the worldviews of the adults around me that I confused them with my own. And I'd wanted acceptance so badly that when I got a taste of stardom and then fell from those heights at such a young age, I never stopped climbing to get back up to the top. I've craved external validation for so long, but it just wasn't enough to scratch the itch anymore. Releasing this project out into the world represented a new beginning for me. It meant that I wasn't hiding behind a facade or worrying about how my next hit would stack up on the charts. And I was finally putting those outdated habits to rest.

I pictured a listener taking in *Trying Not to Think About It* while lying on their bed and staring up at the ceiling, AirPods in, tuning out the world.

"Today would be a good day as any to get on up get on out of bed. Step outside and be surprised at what you're finding. You deserve a day outside your head."

I hoped that somehow, putting that EP out and making it available for someone who needed it just as much as—if not more than—me might make us both feel less alone.

As travel bans lifted and the world started inching back toward a new normal, my team and I could finally tour again. Being back out on the road was a little freaky because if I, or any of our touring party, got COVID, we would need to shut everything down, and it would all fall on me financially. Touring at any level is supremely expensive, and there are a lot of risks as well as rewards. As an adult, I never took tour support from a label since it was all recoupable. In other words, you can stand to make more if you *don't* take money for touring. *EVERYTHING* you're given by a label is recoupable.

The plan was always to build up my touring base over the course of each album, playing small venues and working my way up steadily, growing each tour. Even though I hadn't had a big hit on pop radio in over a decade, I was now playing the biggest headlining shows of my career and selling out fast—without any promo outside my own social media—signaling to promoters that next time, we could size up the venues and get bigger guarantees. My fans were showing up and showing OUT all around the country and around the world. I couldn't believe it. And all I wanted was to be able to put on better and better shows for them.

After the tour, my man and I went to Puerto Rico to celebrate my thirty-first trip around the sun. We had been dating just under a year, but leading up to the vacay, we were getting on each other's nerves. Some girlfriends told me that that was normal and to get ready . . . 'cause he was about to pop the question. On my actual birthday, he arranged for me to get my hair done and have a spa day; he ordered balloons, champagne, flowers, and chocolates, too.

Oh my God. It's happening.

The day was beautiful, and I softened into the glow of the evening, realizing that he was just stressed trying to get everything perfect for me. I felt feminine and relaxed, something I had long craved to be comfortable enough to feel. When we arrived at dinner, I understood why he'd been so nervous—just as he got down on one knee and asked if I would marry him. I think I blacked out a little bit. The whole thing felt surreal, like we were being filmed or something. After I said yes, our moms and a few of our closest friends all came running out of the next room, cheering us on and capturing the moment on their iPhones and professional cameras. He had gotten a stunning custom ring made with a massive diamond set in between smaller diamonds and the first letter of our names on either side. I thought karma might keep me from finding a good man in this lifetime, but here he was, loving the shit out of me.

We'd quickly become best friends and realized we both were ready for someone to share life with and were equally willing to put in the work to make our relationship last. Fancy gifts or expensive dinners didn't matter to me; I loved the day-to-day of being together. Like spending time with family, playing games, watching virtual church service on Sundays, helping each other around the house and with fitness and nutrition goals, binge-watching shows. And inhabiting a present and building a future we didn't feel the need to escape from. I no longer gave a flying fuck what my personal life looked like to anyone else in the whole wide world. This was *my* man. Even though it was fast. "Let's Get Married" by Jagged Edge blasted through the speakers in our hotel suite as we kicked off our shoes and popped champagne, dancing and singing along in celebration with our loved ones: "We ain't getting no younger, we might as well do it."

As December dipped into January, we enjoyed the next level of our commitment, and I took the stability I felt as a green light to dive back into student mode: taking acting lessons, getting deeper into yoga, and doing individual and couples therapy. It was as if having the solid ground of our relationship made me feel more confident to go out into the world and expand. I suggested that some of our friends and family come together to take one of those virtual financial planning classes. We would be the ones to break the generational pattern around financial illiteracy. Of course I invited Mom, who was now back in Massachusetts, living with her on-again partner. She was in a better place emotionally but said it was too late for her to learn a new way to look at finances. I had to accept that she felt that way. But it wasn't too late for me.

Shortly after getting engaged, I gradually moved into my man's place a few towns over while LeMicah rented out my condo. We were pretty deep in our Bible bag at the time, and it only felt right to let my fiancé lead and be the head of the household (even though I didn't love his crib). It was a rental with low ceilings, very little natural light, and an outdated kitchen and bathroom. He had a friend living in the guest room, who I loved, but I felt cramped sharing such a small space with. I told myself to stop being so bougie and just suck it up—it was only temporary!—but sometimes it made me feel like "what am I actually doing here" and irked my fragile sense of pride and thoughts about where I "should" be. In the meantime, I tried to keep the extent of these thoughts to myself as we did all the little things to turn his house into our home.

Plus, Agapé just loved her new front and backyard to run around in. We had people over often, and my man was the most gracious host. I genuinely relished playing the role of wifey and tidying up, fixing plates, making drinks. There was always a fire going, hot tub bubbling, a surplus of yummies on the table, and a great playlist vibing in the background. Barbecues, pool parties, basketball games. He really prioritized the importance of family and was thrilled when my little cousin and his girlfriend came to stay with us from Mass. He even encouraged me to make the effort to get to Dad's side's family reunion in upstate NY.

I loved all his family and friends and mentors and neighbors, too. It was fun to share responsibilities, even if it was something as simple as doing laundry or taking a neighborhood walk around the block and picking up the furbaby's poop. Agapé had a permanent dad now. He loved her like he'd been with me the day I got her from that shelter ten years earlier. I realized in those first few months just how meaningful all of this was to me, so much more than any career accolade. Love and trust that you can cultivate and spring out into the world from. A steady home base to come back to.

During this time, Aaron and I had been playing phone tag. The end was in sight and I could feel it. He had originally loved the idea of me putting out a concept EP in between albums, but had changed his mind. I said I was okay with the lack of support but still stood behind my work. The man was running a publicly traded company, with numbers to hit and people to report to. I also knew I wasn't his biggest moneymaker or priority. My pragmatism didn't make it sting any less, though.

When we finally connected, I was in between tour dates and felt confident enough to say the thing that scared me. This time, I let my internal guidance system lead. I told Aaron that I wanted to be in partnership with a label that saw me as an artist still worth investing in. Also, there were too many cooks in the kitchen and it was really confusing trying to get anything done in a cohesive manner. Couldn't I just have ONE fully dedicated A&R? My jaw clenched and my heart was pounding as I tried not to waver or get embarrassed. So much had happened over the years that I think we'd exhausted the good feelings and optimism that once existed in our dynamic. He said that he would be down to move forward in making another album with me, but that if I wanted more from Warner, he couldn't commit to that. And ultimately, I respected the honesty. It made it easier to have a very hard conversation with myself and get real.

When I was twelve, I had fallen for the trap that record-label people could be my family. And I feel like I was sweet-talked into that same feeling again in my twenties. I respect Aaron and appreciate the belief he had in me. But I learned the hard way, over and over again, that in the music business, people are going to put themselves first, even when they mean well.

It fucking stung. I was scared and angry. If I wanted to bet on what felt right in my heart and look for something different, I could choose to do that—but I would also be choosing to be label-less for the first time since I was a child.

So I chose to walk away.

BREATHE IN.

HOLD.

NOW LET IT ALL GO.

I'd never been great at free-falling, but then again, it wasn't something I had a lot of experience with. I'd jumped from relationship to relationship and label to label for the past two decades and had been so focused on preserving or advancing myself that it was actually a welcomed relief to just let go of my own career for a moment and be more present to support my partner in his endeavors.

When I was visiting him on the East Coast, he surprised me with tickets to see *Tina* on Broadway. We had the honor of witnessing Adrienne Warren up there, giving her absolute EVERYTHING as the legendary Tina Turner, and I was a wreck from the audience. I couldn't remember the last time a story and performance had moved me so deeply. Over the course of her career, Tina overcame adversity, abuse, racism, agism, and so much more, and reliving that journey through Adrienne's performance was one of the most inspiring things I had ever seen. Even when it went against the odds, Tina *never* stopped fighting for herself and her family. Career-wise, physically, spiritually.

My fiancé and I went to see musicals whenever we could. He took me to see the opening of *Moulin Rouge! The Musical* when the touring company came to Los Angeles's Pantages Theatre, and we took Connie and Dale with us to see my girl Angelica Ross star as Roxie Hart in *Chicago* in New York City. I was far from ready to even think about making a new album and didn't know what I wanted to put out into the world as "JoJo" anyway. I didn't even really like being called JoJo that much anymore.

I was also deep into planning our wedding by then. We were crunching numbers, hiring a planner, looking at vendors. I've never been the kind of girl who dreamed of her big day and what her dress was gonna look like. Maybe because I've already been blessed with many moments of getting dressed up and many days and events that are all about me. Plus, I was uncomfortable thinking about spending so much money and getting pretty grossed out by the wedding industry in general. My biggest dream was to make sure we had a strong, stable, fun partnership and a home we loved and felt proud to return to. I would've much preferred saving to buy our dream house, but I knew how important it was to him to have a big wedding where all of our friends and family could be there and celebrate us. We respected each other's positions, but I realized someone was going to have to compromise, and I begrudgingly accepted that it would be me. Turns out that wedding planning is among the *least* romantic things you could do with your partner.

I didn't realize it in the moment but, apparently, distance was growing between us. Enough for another woman to take up space. While he was in another city, he got particularly close with someone he was working with.

Look, we all make stupid choices sometimes. God knows I do. So I was initially able to give him the benefit of the doubt and suspend my disbelief about certain things. Because I'd made a conscious decision to really, truly trust this man and not let my past color the present. But then things started to unfold in a way where it was clear I wasn't getting the full story. Like I was being gaslit. Turns out, I was—and when I went to visit him, that girl had the balls to be in my face, pretending to want to be my friend. It was fake as shit. I wasn't born yesterday.

Still, I tried to play it cool. When he came back to LA and sat down with me at last, I was glad he wanted to be honest. But it never really felt like the full scope of the truth was revealed. The whole incident just highlighted all these other red flags and gut feelings I'd been ignoring. All the shit I'd swept under the rug because he was just such a "good guy."

It felt like a thick layer of ice had started freezing its way around my heart, blocking any and every way he'd ever been able to get through to me. And those rose-colored glasses I'd been wearing, the ones that blinded me from all that other shit? They straight-up shattered.

I took the ring off and flew to Sedona to stay with an eccentric older lady friend, where I dry-heaved into my pillow and took long baths and stared numbly at the red rocks and frantically searched Zillow for a new place to rent in LA. I didn't even really care where it was; I just needed to find a small sliver of that god-forsaken town that didn't host emotional land mines and memories attached to an ex I might run into.

I told ALL my friends and family what had happened. That was the only thing that could make it real in my mind and hold me accountable so I wouldn't go back to him. I impulsively posted "Took the ring off my left hand and moved it to my right" followed by the definition of a narcissist on my IG story. Oops. No one could believe it at first—well, except for Nene and LeMicah and Katie. Then I called *his* friends. I couldn't stand how it seemed he couldn't keep our business between us, and now I was about to give him a taste of his own medicine. I was in such a state of utter shock and needed to hear the story over and over to even believe it myself. I was looking for any kernel of information that might reveal something I'd missed.

Should I have seen this coming?

Did I bring this on?

Our *whole deal* was we refused to bring the ways we'd acted in the past into this relationship. We promised to be 100 percent genuine. No half-truths. No excuses of "I was drunk" or "I can't quite remember." No making the other person feel or look crazy.

Even though things were all bent out of shape (and low key got even weirder . . .), we did try to make it work. He came to me, humbly, with every approach from every imaginable angle to prove his love and commitment. So many different tactics and tones that I wondered who the real him even was. But I, too, had been in that desperate position before. Truthfully, my heart just couldn't handle the rug getting pulled out from under me again. In his frustration, he'd remind me of the ways I'd hurt people I loved before and that I shouldn't be a hypocrite. Touché. I said yes to the additional couples counseling after my friends helped me move out and set me up in a new condo. Yes to meeting up at a neutral park location to play with Agapé and talk it out. Yes to the "completion ceremony" in the desert where he watched the sun set hoping the past could die and we could use it as compost to fertilize something new.

But no.

I couldn't get over it, and, frankly, I didn't want to.

I understood to a lesser degree what exes in my past might have felt when they were wanting to forgive me but struggling to forget how I'd hurt them. But it wasn't long before a new, uglier feeling started to take root.

Before I knew it, my body was *pulsating* with electric self-righteousness. It was like the survivalist inside flipped a switch and guided me down an alternative path to keep from descending into the personal hell of feeling bad for myself. Sure, there were several days when I ordered UberEats and kept the curtains drawn while I scrolled Instagram, trolling myself and looking at pictures of past lovers who all seemed to be doing fine without me. Then I ate myself into a deep pizza-and-ice-cream–fueled slumber, and when I woke up the next morning, I felt like crap and knew I had a choice to make.

And this shit was *not* going to break me.

Knowing I needed to turn my attention to something new instead, I cut my losses and threw myself into full-on preparation for a role I didn't even know I had yet, but one I hoped would be just around the corner.

CHAPTER 21

THE SPARKLING DIAMOND

I'D PLANTED A SEED WITH KATIE AFTER SEEING *TINA* ON BROADWAY, ASKING HER TO PUT feelers out and see what opportunities might possibly be out there for me in the theater world. Hanging out with the performers after the show, seeing the awe and wonder in the audience's eyes as they watched the story unfurling itself onstage, the glamorous set designs and costumes, walking through these gorgeous historic venues, the heart-skipping emotion of it all—theater just made me feel *so* alive. I didn't want to stop putting out my own new music, but when I tried to sing pop, it felt like I still needed to exercise some kind of demon I'd picked up along the way.

Something told me to go back to the beginning again. To relearn how to feel. And how to sing. Not with the instrument I had as a little girl but the one I had now. I'd go to voice lessons with Nick Cooper and sob, trying so hard to let my nervous system relax, to unfurrow my brow, soften my shoulders down, and let go of perfectionism. Sometimes, even opening my throat to let the sound out was a challenge.

Nick calmly told me I had to stop fighting. Stop *trying* so damn hard. I had to *surrender.* "Okay, but HOW do I *do* that? There's nothing I want more than to just let go of whatever I'm still holding on to."

Time.

And practice.

And total commitment to not running from the fear but running toward it. He spoke life into me as he uplifted and affirmed my gifts and my spirit. When I needed calm conversation he offered it. When I needed discipline he demanded it. He served as the mentor that I wished I had as a little girl. I always knew that the mind, body, and soul were connected, but I didn't realize how much my mind had affected my voice. The disillusionment and disconnection I was carrying around came through in my performance. And his spiritual approach to the voice was right on time. And like with other lessons I was taking in dance, yoga, and Pilates, his encouragement and belief in me kept me coming back to those voice classes. I could feel something changing.

So when *Moulin Rouge! The Musical* flew me to Manhattan to meet with casting and producers at the end of 2022, I convinced myself I already *had* the job. Little Joanna was back online. Somewhere in the midst of all the practicing for the lead role as the irresistible courtesan Satine, I became delulu enough to fully believe in my soul that not only could I do it, I would *eat.* I learned the scenes they sent me inside and out. Satine came to life not just in my voice and body but in my head and heart as well. They only asked me to learn one song, but I learned the whole soundtrack, the tigress within me alive and purring once more. Whether or not I got it, I was really proud that I had the guts to fully put myself out there in a whole new arena, looking those casting folks squarely in the eyes and leaving it all on the stage.

About a month after the audition, I had all but accepted that I didn't get it. I was out on a walk with Agapé, deciding whether or not to override my inner guidance and keep trying with my ex, when I looked down at my phone. I picked up the call and heard the excitement of Katie, Randy Jackson (yeah, dawg, we ran into each other in Ireland, and he was comanaging me now), and my agents before it even started to sink in.

I had booked the lead role in a Broadway show.

I was moving to New York City.

I had been *praying* for something to make it abundantly clear which direction I should head in next. The tree-lined street in Burbank turned technicolor, and I knew right then that I would not be taking any ex along into this next chapter. I was going to do this alone.

Before moving to New York in March 2023, I had one more music gig on the books: a performance in Brazil at the GRLS! festival. I hadn't performed in that country since I was seventeen, but nearly fifteen years later, I was now headlining a night in São Paulo alongside a Brazilian artist. Brazilian fans take the number 1 spot for most passionate online. They are active in every IG live, every YouTube comment section, always asking their favorite artists when they plan to visit Brazil. And I had waited so long to be able to give them an answer. Finally, the moment was here, and my team and I worked for months to make it happen and make it *special*. My stylist and I collaborated on a loud, custom stage look, paying homage to the Brazilian flag. My pal Alfredo Flores filmed original screen content for me to use, for the first time in my career. And my musical director, Wow Jones, created a set list and soundscape especially for the São Paulo audience. We were going to figure out how to elevate and make things work whether I put the entire paycheck on the show—*period*. In preparation, I spent more time singing and rehearsing, allowing myself to feel the discomfort and fear in my body when I went to hit certain notes or moved in ways that were out of my comfort zone.

As I walked onto the stage and looked out into a sea of smiling faces the day of the show, I hadn't felt such an immediate and organic connection to an audience in a long time. Some signs I could see people holding made me tear up, signs like: "I've been waiting to see you for 18 years!!!!!" and "JoJo, you saved my life." If only they knew about all the times their support and encouragement and caring had saved mine. It was surreal to know that we were connected, thousands of miles away, through music. English might not have been their first language, but the love I felt from them didn't need translation. It was beyond words.

When it came time to prepare for *Moulin Rouge* and move to New York, it wasn't about the money or career strategy. Honestly, it was about choosing what might help me grow and help mend my broken heart.

Agapé and I moved into a beautiful furnished one-bedroom apartment on West Fifty-Sixth Street, just a couple blocks from Central Park. All I needed to bring were a couple suitcases and her doggy bed. Mom took the train in from Boston to visit us and we explored my new neighborhood and shopped for healthy groceries. The simplicity was freeing and the schedule offered a routine that I think my inner child really needed. It felt good to my nervous system to *know* what was going on. This was something I could understand. Every day for three weeks, Agapé and I would walk from Fifty-Sixth to the rehearsal studio on Forty-Second. I'd put my winter jacket down on the hardwood floor for her to use as a bed, and she'd keep an eye on me while I learned the show with the associate director, Matty, and his team. I'd asked for a copy of the full script ahead of time so I could mark it up, highlight my lines, and make notations on the sheet music. At my request, my script binder had my real name, "Joanna Levesque," on the front.

It's crazy how you can be a whole adult, but on the first day of something new and exciting, you get the same nerves as when you were the new kid walking into a new school. I put my little faux-leather backpack (containing a colorful lunch and study supplies, of course) on the floor next to the table with the director team as I attempted to mask the imposter syndrome I felt.

Maybe I've bitten off more than I can chew and will be exposed. Maybe I'll get laughed out of the city and the industry before I even step foot onto the stage. Maybe the leading man won't think I'm . . .

But before I could really get on with overthinking it, the work had already started.

Every day was a nine-to-five crash course in breaking down the scenes, deciding what point of view I would bring to Satine, learning which marks to hit, countless costume and wig fittings, running scenes with understudies and swings, and then working with the cast, who would come by for a few hours before they took the stage that night. The *Rouge* was a well-oiled machine that had won an epic TEN Tony Awards and was already running eight shows a week. They had a standard to uphold. I reminded myself of that whenever I started to doubt my abilities. There are some shows that famously "stunt" cast, but this one hadn't done that. It was too demanding a role and too expensive a production. I'd record myself and Derek, our leading man, singing the songs and then listen to the voice notes on the way back to my apartment.

Slowly but surely, it was coming together and making sense. I was there for a *reason*. The performers and the people behind the scenes who made everything run smoothly were sharp but kind, hardworking but fun, individual but not trying to be cool. Theater kids all grown up. I wondered if I hadn't had the most unreal teenage experience ever if I would have moved to New York and found my people sooner.

The Al Hirschfeld Theatre was on West Forty-Fifth Street, and after a stage blocking, I'd run the eleven blocks back to my apartment, smiling like a maniac and singing the musical score out loud and not giving a shit because everyone in New York City is in their own world and doesn't give a rat's ass about you. I even found the time in those first three weeks of rehearsal to go on a few Raya dates. Nene had encouraged me to download the bougie dating app while I was in a new city and just see what was out there. I used it as a way to see and eat my way through Midtown and the surrounding neighborhoods with a neurosurgeon, a high school teacher, a creative director, and a personal trainer. It was fun, light, and a good way to practice not putting all my eggs in one basket. And because I was feeling so alive thanks to the work I was doing, that burst of confidence radiated out from me across the table as I shared a meal with a total stranger of the opposite sex.

At the end of the night, I'd go home to walk Agapé and chat with the doorman about the weather or some Boston versus New York rivalry, and I'd have that unavoidable thought that every woman in her early thirties has had while being single and living in New York City: I was having my very own Carrie Bradshaw moment. But even more than that, I reveled in the fact that my life had changed *SO MUCH* in just a matter of months—and *I* was the one who made it happen.

Corseted down, sitting on a velvet bar high above the stage, and strapped into a harness, I could hear what sounded like a show going well thundering beneath my feet. I was getting ready to descend from the ceiling of the theater for my entrance on my very first night on Broadway: April 11, 2023. The show was sold out and the air in the theater was thick like my thighs. I had changed the way I spoke and the way I sang to become Satine, and when the rhinestones from my first costume hit the lights, I'd *become* the Sparkling Diamond. But I still feared I might crack from all the jitters. Maybe even pass out from the lurking whispers of disbelief still burrowed deep within my body.

As my mind attempted to avoid the negative grooves it was used to traveling, I convinced myself that I wasn't me anymore. I was Satine. What would her thoughts be?

"Darling, I've come down from this very ceiling thousands of times. I am the main event here at the Moulin Rouge. They've all been waiting for me. Performing is who I am and what I've worked my whole life to be great at. I know men like the back of my hand. It's all very simple, really. They want me, so I put on a show. I always take care of myself and my people. I am beautiful. I am elegant. I am the Sparkling Diamond, naturally. My whole life has prepared me for this very moment and I don't even have to try."

Letting this kind of internal conversation flow, I could barely hear the music coming from the sixteen-musician orchestra in the pit underneath the stage over all of the applause. I looked over at the balcony and then the mezzanine as I began singing,

"Diamonds are forever . . ."

And we were off to the races. I made it through the first number. The first wardrobe change. The first kiss. The first act. The second act. The curtain call.

And I couldn't fucking *believe* it.

Applause. All those smiling faces. Standing ovation. But more importantly, and something I was even less familiar with, the internal satisfaction of believing and *knowing* I did a good job and should be proud of myself.

When I got offstage, my family flooded into my dressing room while Katie, Connie, Dale, and some of my other team and friends were waiting to celebrate just down the hall. I looked for the opinion on Mom's face, but she was just in tears. In shambles. I can't remember her exact words, but she made it clear that she was totally blown away. She said she could feel the joy radiating off of me and that's what made her happiest. Even though I still had things I wanted to improve on, she said she didn't see the flaws and couldn't have been prouder of me. A cry came from deep within me as I melted into her embrace.

Over the next few weeks, I learned what I needed to do to not just make it through seven shows a week as a leading lady—but thrive in it. I took vocal rest seriously on Sundays and Mondays (my off days) and prioritized consistent physical exercise and recovery so the movement of the show would feel easier. Since I had twelve costume changes—some side of stage, some backstage, and some even onstage—I didn't have much time to pee. So staying adequately hydrated but not too full of water was a delicate line to walk. There were also two wig changes in those two and a half hours (which is more complicated than it sounds), but my main dresser AJ and my wig stylist Akilah made sure that every single switch went off without a hitch. Having all this designated support backstage and knowing what our routine was every show allowed me to focus on what I needed to do—I was less tense and probably more fun to be around than I'd been on a job in years. Even when things did go left—cuz, shit happens!—we were always ready to think on our feet and laugh along the way.

It takes a village to keep a Broadway production of that magnitude running smoothly. Associate directors, choreographers, physical therapists, conductors, pit musicians, wig artisans, vocal coaches, wardrobe departments, security, box office, cleaning crew, carpenters, audio department, lighting department, stage managers, company managers. As many shows as I had seen over the years, I truly had no idea how much was going on backstage—especially for a spectacle like *Moulin Rouge.*

I loved our two-show days best of all, as physically and vocally challenging as they were. This was truly a team sport. Being with the rest of the cast and crew when we were all running on fumes was kind of hilarious, and no person was more or less important than the next. I was so proud that our show was one that you could come back to time and time again, just to keep your eye on one ensemble member the whole night. Everyone gave their absolute best every show and added their own unique flavor to the company and production. If I didn't get to see close-up how the sausage was made, I'd tell you it was magic.

Derek Klena, who played the role of Christian, became such a great friend to me and held my hand during the whole process. When I flubbed the curtain call bows the first night, we laughed it off and tried again the next night. He would come and hang out in my dressing room as I did my makeup and Akilah was putting my wig on, and he would answer all my Broadway newcomer questions. (How much and how often should I tip my dresser and wig stylist? What do you eat in between shows? Do you think I should wear a mask while signing autographs at stage door? Have you had any ghost encounters at this obviously haunted-ass theater?!) At his encouragement, I was hyped to get to follow in the footsteps of the other cast members and host a SNOB (Saturday Night on Broadway) in my dressing room—a tradition where the whole company gathered around to unwind with food and drinks after Saturday's second show.

One night, Derek had gotten sick after the matinee and the alternate and swing were also out, so they called back the OBC (Original Broadway Cast) Christian, Aaron Tveit, to cover the part. Thankfully, he agreed; otherwise, they would've had to cancel the show. We'd never sung together before and only met briefly in passing when I was still learning the role. But, upon getting the unpredictable update from our company manager a little after getting out of the first show, I raced back to the theater so I could squeeze in a little time with Aaron before hitting the stage. We plucked through some songs with the conductor in their room on the fourth floor, chose which notes to hold straight and which to bend together, agreed on which side we were going to tilt our heads when we kissed, and went for it that night. One of the most exhilarating parts about live theater is never knowing when you might need to pivot—and it was just that kind of unforeseeable improv that always kept me on my toes.

The downside of that old, iconic, possibly mold-infested petri dish of a theater was that it was a breeding ground for illness. People were dropping like flies left and right. Whether it was a cold or COVID, shit was always going around. I added another prescription allergy medication to my routine and was on a course of antibiotics and steroids more than once. About three months in, I kept it between my ENT doctor and me that I was feeling under the weather . . . but when I went for the final high note in my first number, I knew I was going to injure my voice and maybe even fall offstage if I kept going. The scene proceeded in front of me as I went through the motions of talking with the cast upstage, obscured by the moving set. I told them I didn't think I was going to make it through the show. Everyone assured me this had happened to all of them before and that this was exactly what the entire Broadway system of swings and alternates is there for. They calmly alerted the stage manager.

I was in such a state of shock and didn't want to look unprofessional or let people down who had spent their hard-earned money and came specifically to see me. I knew some of them had probably even traveled here from out of town. The thought of disappointing *anyone* in the audience was low-key paralyzing. But my castmates calmly assured me there was no other way. It would have only prolonged my getting better and coming back if I kept trying to push through.

Within fifteen minutes, Tasia, who usually played a showgirl named Arabia, was whisked offstage, put through hair and makeup, and corseted up as Satine. I called an Uber and went home in tears. But the show went on. And as much as it sucked, it honestly felt good to know that nothing *actually* rested fully on my shoulders. I genuinely loved being a part of something bigger than myself.

Getting to fall in love every night onstage, slipping into the most exquisite garments my body has ever been adorned with, and singing a mashup of seventy-plus songs from throughout the decades was something I looked forward to all the way up until my one-hundredth performance when I took my final bow. I laughed more than I had in years and found the fun and the freedom in repetition. I didn't even take my usual half .5 mg of Xanax before I went onstage. I racked my brain but couldn't think of a time in recent history—other than falling in love—when I've been happier. Don't let my glowing memories of it mischaracterize the reality, it was *really hard*. But it was so fulfilling, and I reveled in the structure, stability, and community. Throughout the run, I was also at my highest weight (I decided to take a break from dieting or restricting whatsoever and just see what my body did) and yet still felt worthy.

Strong.

Capable.

Beautiful, even.

At the stage door where I'd sign autographs every night, there were little girls waiting patiently in line with their parents to tell me that they wanted to be on Broadway one day. I'd ask them what their favorite show and dream role were before telling them that I couldn't wait to see them shine up there onstage someday. I was sure they had never heard of "JoJo," and if so, there was definitely a colorful bow and a "Siwa" involved, but I didn't care. The fact that they were born years after my last radio hit didn't make me feel old or less-than. It felt like a relief. I was being appreciated for my talent, not for chart positioning or the ability to squeeze myself into a size zero. They couldn't wait to tell me how much they loved the show and would excitedly squeal about how my performance that night had inspired them.

I couldn't overlook the similarities between Satine and I. She had grown up as a bohemian, raised by a crew of people who tried to protect her but also profited from her. Later in life, she fell in love with Christian, a pure soul who caught her off guard, but she felt inclined to make the more pragmatic choice of being with The Duke, who offered her the stability she'd always craved. But, even in that, her heart still longed for Christian.

In the final scene, while she's performing a play within a play, Satine lays her agonizing self-conflict out there: "Who are you, Marie? In the mirror, I see only my sins reflected. A lifetime of degradation. And that one chance for love . . . I threw away. I broke his heart. And for what?"

I didn't inherit Dad's gift of crying on cue, but tears would often happen naturally.

I let them come.

The company asked to extend my contract for quite a while longer, and I thought deeply about whether I should stay right where

I was. Burrow into the routine. Being a part of this world was giving me life. I dove headfirst into this chapter, and I loved having the city as my playground, frequenting the haunts of the theater district, partaking in community events like Broadway Bares and Broadway Barks. For the first time in a long time, I felt accepted and embraced just as I was.

But at the same time, I knew there was something inside of me that had been reawakened and needed to be channeled into new music. All the experiences I had acquired in the past five months— feeling like I could maybe do it, like I was too scared to physically do it, like I was born to do it, like I'm so glad I *did* it—I knew I would likely go through again with whatever creative endeavor I started up next. And now, without a label to direct me, it would be on me and the team of my choosing to determine what was good enough. What I wanted my narrative to be and what it would look and feel like. What I wanted this next chapter to be about.

After taking my final bow at Al Hirschfeld, I spent an extra week in New York resting and eating and exploring my way around the city. I spun the block on a couple of those Raya dates but quickly remembered that dating was awkward as *hell* and, honestly, I needed some time alone to heal and grow if I wanted to do things differently. Before I even knew it, it was time to pack up my suitcases and head back to the West Coast.

Touching down in LA was a mixed bag. Part of me was happy to be back in the place I'd called home the longest, but NYC had allowed me to escape the triggers and memories of the past thirteen years. And I'd fallen so in love with being back on the East Coast, closer to my family, moving at a different pace.

At the same time, my engagement ring had been burning a hole in the bottom of my purse. It felt so heavy, this ancient relic of nostalgia and what could have been but wasn't. I had first felt very entitled to hold on to it, maybe sell it or turn it into another piece of jewelry. Something petty. But I knew that wasn't what I was being called to do. It was time to think about the long-term effects and karma of that. Grow up, girl. It was time to be *her*, the woman I knew I was capable of being.

I reached out to my ex-fiancé and told him I'd like to grab a matcha if he was open to it. I packed the ring up in its original box and met him at a neutral place in between our two homes. He had come to see me in NYC, but it didn't go as he'd probably hoped it would, and I realized he wasn't sure what this new exchange was going to be like. But as awkward as it could've been, it actually wasn't that hard to keep things loving and high-vibe. I wasn't mad. I was grateful. The series of events that unfolded sent me on the ride of my life, one that was strangely just what I needed when I needed it the most. We talked it out and accepted that this was goodbye. And I had never meant it more. Historically, I had left doors open and recycled old relationships out of comfort and habit, but this was different. And I walked away, post-matcha and ringless, feeling empowered.

I was alone again, yes, but it was on *my* terms, and I no longer felt suffocated by what LA signified for me. I wanted to take this forward-moving energy and make new music with it. So I reached out to some of my favorite collaborators—Lil' Eddie, Neff-U, and Sebastian Kole—and asked if they'd be down to help me flesh out these ideas I'd recently been flooded with. These were some of the people who, throughout my career, really saw and understood me more deeply than most. I wanted to create something special with *them*.

As soon as I walked into Neff-U's studio, it was as if we had all taken the *Limitless* pill. I was barely sleeping or eating; I was almost bursting out of my skin with ideas and inspiration. That's what passion and excitement can feel like. Natural drugs. I recognized it as that same vibration I'd clocked as a little girl. A gift

I was given and something I needed to follow. Just like little Joanna when she was ready to sing for anybody who would listen or take whatever stage she could scrounge up. The excitement within me came from the purest, most uncontainable place.

Melodies and lyrics rushed out like a waterfall—it was a total flow state and something I feel blessed to experience on the special occasions that I do. I honestly thought I might have snapped and lost my mind. It felt so foreign, the ease of this process, like all the resistance and doubt and disbelief that usually stood in my way had somehow been brushed aside. Maybe Jesus took the wheel or something. For some months now, I had been experiencing synchronicities that I couldn't ignore. Leaning into them and sharing how it all made me feel was what I knew I had to do for this new project:

"I don't know what's coming over me.
Took a look into the mirror, found clarity.
The moment I got rid of everything
I realized that I was my worst enemy
I had to break it and rearrange it
And turn into a beautiful mosaic
I saw a problem
I had to change it
I left my sadness in fragments
PORCELAIN.
PORCELAIN.
Shattered pieces on the floor like porcelain, porcelain.
Had to shed a couple layers just to feel my skin.
Porcelain.
I let it happen 'cause I'm tired of forcin' it.
Porcelain.
And now I'm stronger than I've ever been."

OUTRO

MY LAPTOP HAS BEEN MY BEST FRIEND THESE PAST EIGHTEEN MONTHS. IT KEPT ME company on flights, in the back of cabs, on Amtrak trains and ferry rides where I opened up a document called "WORKING LIFE STORY" and word-vomited as the world whizzed by. I overthought my way into periods of procrastination and then hyper concentration writing and rewriting section after section. Who the hell did I think I was doing this without a ghostwriter?

Now, as I get ready to turn this in to my editor, I'm sitting at a vineyard on Waiheke Island in New Zealand with my right hand hovering over the keyboard and my left hand stroking the stem of a half-full glass of white wine. My crew and I have a day off on this Australia/New Zealand festival tour, and although it's raining a bit, I decided to check out a winery and take in the sunset before hitting "send" and closing my computer for a few weeks.

What a ridiculously amazing life I have gotten to live. Twenty years into my career, I feel more grateful than ever—but I also realize I have *a lot* more growing to do, across many different parts of my life. Sometimes I still question whether my choices come from the wisdom of my heart or the influences of the past echoing in my head. My triggers buzz around me like flies, thick in the summer heat, humming right along the surface of my skin. It's gotten easier to resist dropping whatever I'm doing in the moment and either swat at them or soften into them, but I still notice as they start to cluster.

When I was in London back in November, I had breakfast with an old friend who played my love interest in a music video. He's been sober for some time now, and before I got into town, I texted him over WhatsApp and told him I'd kinda like to go to an A.A. meeting with him. So there we were, sitting across from one another at a table, talking about it. He couldn't help but furrow his brow and tilt his head, trying to figure out why I would want to step into those halls if I didn't have an unmanageable problem.

"I've always seen you as someone who has a great head on their shoulders. You're good to people, you work hard. You're not a twat. You're not the 'typical product' of child stardom we think of. Or even of being an only child—you guys are usually cunts. When's the last time you drank too much? Do you ever drink too much? Or is it drugs? Sex? What's your thing?"

I knew what he was really asking. Basically, he was wondering if I was bad *enough*. I laughed as I looked down at my muesli and then rattled off what has become my standard explanation: "I don't discriminate. I like all those things. It's validation. It's love. It's stuffing the grubby mouth of this hungry ghost inside me with whatever it can find to feel good . . . have you heard the way Dr. Gabor Maté talks about it?"

"Yeah, yeah. Of course. But why *now*?" he pressed. "Why do you feel like you need to go to a meeting *now*?"

"Well." I took a deep breath and thought about it for a moment before responding. "I'm just sick of this shit. The way its been. The way I've been. I'm in search of community. Maybe even comfort—just not in the ways I used to get it. The tricky thing is there's never been a solid rock bottom for me. I *could* go on repeating the same patterns for the rest of my life. Just coasting on the edge, feeling like I'm one step away from checking into a mental health facility so someone can wipe my system clean and teach me a new way of being. But I *can't*, though. I refuse. I'm *over* this shit."

Sometimes you just need witnesses. People who understand. You don't always need to hit rock bottom to know that you need a reset—if for nothing else than your own sanity.

Gone are the days when I was content to just coast along that edge.

Gone are the days when substances, self-doubt, and the fear of failure keep me from living the life I want to live, the way I want to live it.

People always say, "Life begins at the end of your comfort zone," and the older I get, the more I find this to be true. When I think back on what I'm proudest of and when I feel most aligned, the underlying theme is that I took a risk, told my fears to shut the hell up, bet on my inner guidance, and embraced the unknown. Putting out music I truly believe in, diving headfirst into a hit Broadway show, jumping out of a plane, sitting in the depths of grief, choosing to believe in love, humbling myself in daily practices, and writing this book. All of those things exemplify what I want my next chapter and beyond to feel like: growth. I hope to keep evolving in ways I couldn't have anticipated. And I want to be of service to others along their journey and help them make sense of the pain and beauty of being a human in this world. Particularly in the music industry.

After months of typing my fingerprints off on this manuscript and making brand-new music for the first time in almost three years, I booked a quick solo trip for myself to Iceland (on my way to London to record) so I could completely unplug and finish up the first draft strong. This formerly resentful only child had fallen in love with the art of solo-tripping in the US, so why the hell not overseas? I had too many stamps in my passport to not have many nonwork memories. So this time was for exploration. It was storming the whole three days I was there, but I still rented a car and drove through the rain to go see a waterfall after a night of no sleep from being so damn excited the night before. I visited the National Museum of Iceland and geeked out over ancient wood carvings and drinking gourds (low key, we need to bring these back). I tried all kinds of different foods and met some cool people while exploring Reykjavík for hours, just totally enchanted.

But one of the most majestic parts of the trip was getting to visit the famous Blue Lagoon, a geothermal hot spring that's become a super popular spot for travelers. As I dipped my head back into the milky blue waters, I took a deep breath and let the experience really sink into every pore. If everything in my life had unfolded just the way I thought it was supposed to, would I have still ended up here—unfettered and alive, free as fuck—in this moment, somehow?

The fuzzy mist grazed over my temples as I closed my eyes, surrendering to the warmth, letting the water lick me clean.

Don't get me wrong; I'm sure there's more healing to do. I look down at the Serenity Prayer coiled around my wrist that reminds me to accept what I can't change, find the courage to change what I can, and have the wisdom to know the difference.

The wisdom.

As much as I've made peace with the past, I still have traces of anger, resentment, and grief that linger in my body. And learning to accept this duality, and all that comes with it, is part of the healing, too. I have great tools in my belt that I've picked up over the years. And I can forgive myself and others for decisions that have been made, while also rejecting a corrupt system that's designed to profit off talented kids and then send them down the river when they are no longer down to play pretend.

Now, what any adults did or didn't do in my childhood simply doesn't matter. It's 100 percent up to me to stop selling myself short and start trusting my own instincts. Period. Obviously, there will still be times when I question what I'm doing or when things don't work out like I'd hoped. Silly example, but the (recent) time I went from bright red to bleached blonde hair in a day and wound up with all these alfalfa sprouts of broken-ass hair. But you know what? We make choices—we can choose to laugh and not take it all too seriously—and move on. We live and hopefully we learn.

In some ways, I'm still trying to figure out where "JoJo" stops and "Joanna" begins. As much as I've come to appreciate the nickname, it's inextricably linked to someone else's vision of what my career should look like. I want to reclaim a sense of ownership over my name. Try not to vomit as I refer to myself in the third person, but for Joanna to be okay, it's clear I have to find a whole new way to be "JoJo."

As I take the last few sips of my sauvignon blanc, I look around the vineyard and wonder what everyone else's stories are like. Because I've thought about my own more than enough now. I'm interested in what connects us. What lens do they see the world through? Have they forgiven the people or systems they once resented? Are they the "good guy" to anyone? Maybe even the toxic "bad guy"? Inevitably, there's at least one other person in this room who feels they're less than. Too much. Not enough. "Other." And I'm willing to bet that in battling their own hungry ghosts, they've learned a few lessons the hard way, too.

As for what's next? I'm actively dreaming about what that will look like and surrendering to the fact that it's going to be different than I imagined.

But one thing's for sure.

No more counting myself out.

Matter of fact, for the foreseeable future—

Count me the fuck in.

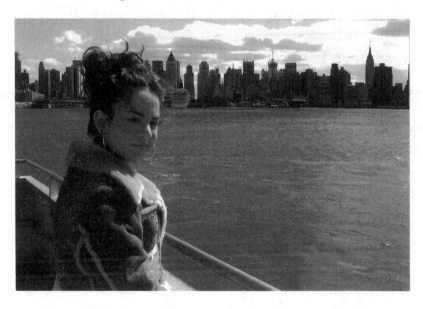

ACKNOWLEDGMENTS

God. Thank you for covering and keeping a sinner like me and guiding me through the darkness when I couldn't see myself or you or anything at all.

Mom. Thank you for letting me share parts of your/our story that I know are hard to revisit. Thank you for encouraging me to be myself and to be courageous in life and art. Thank you for always believing in me as a writer, first and foremost. I hope I did us justice. Thank you for compiling photos and walking down memory lane during this process. And most of all, thank you for showing me, through your actions, that people can change.

Carrie Napolitano. My fearless editor, I would have truly been lost in the wilderness without you. Thank you for caring so damn much. For believing in the importance of me telling my own story and for holding my hand as I tried to cross the bridge from writing three-minute songs to 120,000+ words. For fighting for me like the literary warrior you are.

Scott Blagden. I'm so lucky that one of my favorite writers in the world is also my uncle. Thank you for making yourself available to me through this journey and graciously sharing all your writing resources and expertise with me. Thanks for reminding me that my only obligation is to tell the truth. To just show up and write everyday. To write the first draft like no one's gonna read it and worry about the other shit later.

Katie Gallagher. I am the luckiest girl ever to have you in my corner for all these years. Thank you for being the best manager/friend/God-warrior ever. Thank you for tolerating my moody emotional ass and sticking by my side. Thanks for reading every single draft, giving your thoughts, and lending me your memory. You are one of the best humans I know.

Randy Jackson. Your wisdom and guidance are so appreciated.

Sian-Ashleigh Edwards and Hayley Heidemann at WME. Thank you for fighting for my vision and for your incredibly helpful notes.

Abby Walters at CAA. For believing in my story and making sure it found the right home.

My insanely beautiful, fucking amazing, incomparable family and friends. Everyone along this life journey who has helped, encouraged, challenged, been a mirror.

The people who hurt me and those I've hurt. You have been my biggest teachers. I'm sorry. Please forgive me. Thank you. I love you.

SELECT DISCOGRAPHY

"Breezy"
(K. Holland, B. Muhammad, S. Jordan, Jr., T. Bell, R. Chambers, K. Gamble) Bros. Grimmm (ASCAP), Jahqae Joints/ UMPG (SESAC), Almo Music (ASCAP), Warner-Tamerlane Publishing Corp. (BMI)

"Leave (Get Out)"
(Soulshock, K. Karlin, A. Cantrell, P. "Silky" White) Full of Soul Music/EMI Blackwood (BMI), Soulvang Music/EMI Blackwood (BMI), Godfly Music/Songs of Dreamworks (BMI), Sun White Music (BMI)

"(I Only Know Him) In the Dark"
(Joanna Levesque, Jordan Orvosh) Love You Madly (BMI), JordanXL (ASCAP)

"Disaster"
(M. Marchetti, G. Barletta, M. Himmel, J. Levesque) Marchetti Music (BMI) admin by The Bicycle Music Company, Gino Barletta Music (BMI) admin by The Bicycle Music Company, Himco Music (ASCAP), Flying Dinosaur/Reach Music Songs (BMI)

"Music"

(Joanna Levesque, Jussi Karvinen, Justin Tranter, Hayley Warner) Love You Madly/WB Music Corp. O/B/O Itself (ASCAP), Karvinen Music/Warner-Tamerlane Publishing Corp. (BMI), Justin's School For Girls/Warner-Tamerlane Publishing Corp. (BMI), Hayley Warner Publishing Designee (NS)/Admin. By Warner-Tamerlane Publishing Corp.

"Fuck Apologies"

(Joanna Levesque, Oscar Holter, Matt Friedman, Taylor Parks, Jason Dean, Joseph Kirkland, Cameron Thomaz) Love You Madly/WB Music Corp. O/B/O Itself (ASCAP), Wolf Cousins (STIM)/Warner Chappell Music Scandanavia AB (STIM)/All Rights O/B/O Wolf Cousins and Warner Chappell Music Scandanavia AB Administered by WB Music Corp./WB Music Corp. (ASCAP) O/B/O Itself/Teldar Paper Publishing (ASCAP) Publishing Designee and Mischka Beast/Warner-Tamerlane Publishing Corp. (BMI) and Taylor Monet Music/ All Rights Admin. by Warner-Tamerlane Publishing Corp. (BMI) O/B/O Itself/Noise of Fear More Music and Jason Dean BMI Publishing Designee/WB Music Corp. O/B/P Itself (ASCAP), Fear More Music/Artist Vs. Poet Publishing/WB Corp. (ASCAP) and PGH Sound.

"Orange Skies"

(Samuel "Sam Hook" Jean) Sam Hook Music/Sony ATV (ASCAP)

"The High Road"

(J. Rotem, M. Gerrard, B. Benenate) Jonathan Rotem Music (BMI)/Southside Independent Music Publishing (BMI), Seve Peaks Music o/b/o Itself and Sixteenth Street Songs (ASCAP), Music Of Windswept o/b/o Itself and Dashee Doo Jetty Too Music Publishing (ASCAP) and Blotter Music (ASCAP)

"Think About You"

(Joanna Levesque, Andrew Jackson, Peder Losnegard) Love You Madly (ASCAP), TMP London/These Are Songs of Pulse (ASCAP). All rights administered by These Are Songs of Pulse, Complete Flames Songs/American Songs Beta/These Are Pulse Songs (BMI)

"Joanna"

(Joanna Levesque, Natalie Dunn, Rebekah Muhammad, Jeff Gitelman) Love You Madly (ASCAP), Young & Vicious/Mushroom Music (APRA), Digital Gold (ASCAP) admin. by Songs of Peer, Ltd., Jeff Gitty Music (BMI).

"Don't Talk Me Down"

(Joanna Levesque, Natalie Dunn, Peder Losnegard) Love You Madly (ASCAP), Young & Vicious/Mushroom Music (APRA), Complete Flames Songs/American Songs Beta/These Are Pulse Songs (BMI)

"Bad Habits"

(Joanna Levesque, Coleridge Tillman, Jason Gilbert, Jordan Orvosh) Love You Madly (ASCAP), Coleridge Tillman Music/UMPG (BMI), Jason C. Gilbert/J Eagle Music LLC (ASCAP), Keys To The Guesthouse (BMI)

"Anxiety (Burlinda's Theme)"
(Joanna Levesque, Kennedi Lykken, Robert McCurdy,
Christopher Petrosino) Love You Madly (ASCAP) - Kennedi
Lykken Publishing Designee (BMI) and Marquise Cat
Publishing (BMI) and Warner Tamerlane Publishing Corp.
(BMI), Club Noise and Warner-Tamerlane Publishing Corp.
All rights on behalf of itself and Club Noise administered by
Warner-Tamerlane Publishing Corp. / Noise Club Songs and
Warner-Tamerlane Publishing Corp.

"Porcelain"
(Joanna Levesque, Edwin Serrano, David Williams II, Theron
Feemster) Love You Madly (ASCAP), Lileddiemusic (BMI), Ahh
Haa, LLC (ASCAP), admin. By Universal Music - Z Tunes,
Feemstro admin. by Universal Music - Z Tunes LLC (ASCAP)